Cheryl

MY STORY

Cheryl

MY STORY

HarperCollins*Publishers*

HarperCollins*Publishers*
77–85 Fulham Palace Road,
Hammersmith, London W6 8JB

www.harpercollins.co.uk

First published by HarperCollins*Publishers* 2012

3 5 7 9 10 8 6 4 2

A catalogue record of this book is
available from the British Library

HB ISBN 978-0-00-750015-4
TPB ISBN 978-0-00-750016-1
EB ISBN 978-0-00-750017-8

Printed and bound in Great Britain by
Clays Ltd, St Ives plc

MIX
Paper from
responsible sources
FSC
www.fsc.org   FSC™ C007454

FSC™ is a non-profit international organisation established to promote
the responsible management of the world's forests. Products carrying the
FSC label are independently certified to assure consumers that they come
from forests that are managed to meet the social, economic and
ecological needs of present and future generations,
and other controlled sources.

Find out more about HarperCollins and the environment at
www.harpercollins.co.uk/green

Keep Calm and Soldier On.

Contents

Acknowledgements

Rachel Murphy – thank you for helping me write this. We've had laughter and tears, and I'm THRILLED with the result! Ha ha.

Carole Tonkinson, Victoria McGeown, Anna Gibson, Georgina Atsiaris, Steve Boggs and everyone at HarperCollins – thank you all so much for making this such an easy and enjoyable process.

Solomon Parker, Eugenie Furniss and Claudia Webb at WMA – thank you for giving me this opportunity and starting me off on the right path.

Richard Bray and Ailish McKenna at Bray & Krais.

Rankin.

Seth, Sundraj, Lily and Garry – thank you!

Thank you to my team, my loved ones and all the amazing people I have in my life – and lastly to all the arseholes who have crossed my path and made it so colourful!!!

Prologue

'Can I have your autograph and a picture?'

I was totally stunned. Was this person really here, asking me to sign my name and pose for a photo?

'Well … can I?'

The woman was staring at me hopefully, holding a camera up and pushing a bit of paper towards me.

'No, absolutely not,' I stuttered. I was flabbergasted. Disgusted, actually.

This wasn't a fan at a Girls Aloud concert or someone waiting outside the *X Factor* studios. The woman was a cleaner at the London Clinic where I was being treated for malaria.

I'd literally nearly died just days before, and now I was lying in bed looking and feeling so weak and ill, and trying to get my head around what the hell had happened to me. The cleaner stuffed the camera in her apron pocket and looked quite put out, as if I'd turned down a perfectly reasonable request.

Derek was horrified, and he leapt up and showed her the door. He's one of the most kind and sensitive and gentlemanly men I have ever met, but I swear from the look in his eyes he wanted to kill that woman.

I stared at Derek in disbelief. How had my personal life got so tangled up with my job and my fame that other people no longer treated me like a human being?

'Am I going to die?' I'd asked a nurse on my first day in intensive care. There was a pause before she told me plainly: 'There's a possibility.'

Her words didn't shock me. I was so exhausted that I actually felt relieved. 'If I am dying, just hurry up and make it happen,' I thought. 'I'm too tired. For God's sake, make this end.'

I spent four days in intensive care at the Hospital for Tropical Diseases and was now out of danger, but I was still very ill. My body felt incredibly weak and I'd been drifting in and out of sleep and consciousness for days. My head was heavy and foggy and it was so uncomfortable even just to lie down.

'I've survived,' I thought in the moments after the cleaner was shown out of the room.

'But what's happened to me? Who *am* I?'

Being in hospital is hell. All you can do is lie there and think. I couldn't walk. I was stuck in bed with machines bleeping all around me, trying to make sense of how and why I was here, and what my life had become.

My life was crazy, and it had been that way for a long time. The way the cleaner treated me was just the latest proof of how mad it was. She didn't stop to think that I was a living, breathing woman who had been at death's door. I'd been asked for pictures at inappropriate moments many times before, but this one topped the lot in terms of cheek and weirdness.

I shut my eyes and thought back to earlier that day, when I'd been taken for a lung scan. I was dressed in a hospital gown and I had filthy hair that was so greasy it looked like I was wearing a cap with long pieces of hair sticking out from under it. I hadn't showered or been out of bed for a week and my face was yellow with jaundice, but in that moment I didn't care. It was just amazing to be on the move instead of lying in bed, attached to tubes and machines. As I was wheeled down the corridor I could feel the air blowing through all the hair that wasn't stuck to my head. I honestly felt like a girl in a shampoo advert, wafting my hair about in the breeze.

All of a sudden a little girl pointed at me excitedly.

'I swear that's Cheryl Cole!'

Her words changed my mood in a heartbeat. As soon as she spoke I didn't feel free any more. I felt exposed and extremely uncomfortable.

'Take me back to me room, *please*,' I immediately said to the nurse.

I was so taken aback that I'd been recognised, in here. The hospital should have been a haven for me, but it wasn't. I didn't even *look* like me, yet the girl still recognised me and she must have been poorly too. I felt mortified. I had no privacy, absolutely nowhere to hide. That's how I felt.

In hindsight I can see the funny side of that story and I don't blame the young girl for reacting the way she did. I was in a very dark place then, though, and I just couldn't see any light at all. When the cleaner asked for my autograph and a picture not long afterwards, it was like a light going on.

I had grown up wanting to be a pop star, but I had never anticipated this level of fame. Nobody could have prepared me for this. I'd followed my childhood dream and I'd achieved it, and so much more. I should have been happy, but I felt like my life was not my own at all, on any level, not even when I was recovering from a serious illness. It was out of my control, and as I lay in my hospital bed I could see that I had to make changes, or I would end up going completely crazy.

It's more than two years since I had malaria, and now I feel sure I had it for a reason. It's almost as if it was God's way of forcing me to stop and get off the rollercoaster ride my life had become. It made me take a good look at myself, and that is what I have done.

It's only very recently that I've felt strong enough to talk about what's gone on in my life, and to start to put things in perspective.

I actually feel grateful for everything that's happened, the good and the bad, because my life has been amazingly colourful and eventful. Incredible, in fact. Now I finally feel ready, and strong enough, to open up my heart and tell you all about it.

1

'Follow your dreams, Cheryl'

If anyone had asked me to describe my life when I was a little girl growing up in Newcastle, this is what I would have told them:

I'm seven. We live in a massive house in Byker. Little Garry sleeps in with me mam and dad, I share a room with our Gillian and Andrew, and we all have bunks. Joe, who's our big brother, has a room all to himself. He's a big teenager, seven years older than me, and so I hardly ever see him. One Christmas, me and Gillian definitely seen Santa though, and at Halloween we definitely seen a witch. I like magical things, and the *Chronicles of Narnia* is one of me favourite TV programmes. Me dad plays the keyboard and is always sayin' to me: 'Go on, Cheryl, I'll play something and you make up the words.' Me Nana made a tape of me when I was three. She wrote on it: 'Little Cheryl Singing' – and I was so proud. *Top of the Pops* is always on the TV and I tell me dad: 'I'm gonna be on there when I'm bigger!'

'Cheryl, sweetheart,' he says. 'You'll need to get a proper job when you get big!' He works really hard as a painter and decorator and me mam stays home and looks after all us kids. She tells me, 'Follow your dreams, Cheryl. Do what your heart tells you.' Me mam's very soft and gentle but *she* tells *me* I'm too soft!

'That guy's just punched him senseless!' I heard me dad say one night when he was watching a boxing match on the telly. I cried all night long, thinking to meself, 'When's that poor man gonna get his sense back?' 'Honest to God, Cheryl, you need to toughen up,' me mam said.

Gillian's four years older and Andrew is three years older than me. Everyone says they're like two peas in a pod, so close in age they're like twins. I was four when our Garry was born and he's the baby of the family. Me, Gillian and Andrew like playing fish and chip shops in the back garden. We use big dock leaves for the fish, me dad's white paint is the batter and the long grass is the chips. Andrew's always telling us daft stories that can't be true and making us laugh. Me and Gillian make up dance routines and pretend we're in *Grease* or *Dirty Dancing*, but Gillian's a proper tomboy. She went to disco dancing classes once but didn't like them at all. I absolutely *love* dancing. I do it all; ballet, modern, jazz and ballroom after school, and on the weekend. I've done it since I was three and I've been in shows and pantos and all that. 'Show us your dancing, Cheryl,' everyone always says, and so I do, all the time. I love it.

When I look back on my childhood through adult eyes I feel very grateful to my mam and dad for giving me such happy memories, especially as I know now that it wasn't easy for them.

The 'massive' house I remember was in fact a really tiny, box-like council house that must have been really cramped with seven of us under the one roof. There wasn't a lot of money, but as a little girl I never remember feeling poor. I always had Barbie dolls to play with and didn't care that they were second-hand and out of fashion, and I always got presents I treasured at Christmas, like the one year when I got a sweet shop with little jars you could fill up. I absolutely loved it.

For our tea we ate food like beans on toast, corned beef hash or grilled Spam. A Chinese takeaway was a treat because we couldn't afford it, but we were no different from anybody else on our estate. Mam would buy us things from catalogues and save up to pay the bill at the end of the month. I remember the end of August was always a nightmare because my mother had to get everyone kitted out with new uniforms and pencil cases, all at the same time. I could feel the tension in the house, but we always got through it. Sometimes we wore hand-me-down clothes, but that was completely normal. Neighbours and relatives passed things on; that's what everybody did. Pride is a massive thing for Geordies and Mam made sure that, one way or another, we always looked presentable and we never went without.

I've had to ask my mam to fill me in on some of the details about my really early years, especially with all my dancing, as I was too young to remember a lot of it. I also thought it might be nice to give my mam, Joan, the chance to tell this part of the story herself, and this is what she told me when I started writing my book.

What Mam remembers …

One of me friends told me there was a local bonny baby competition and that I should enter you because you were such a pretty baby. You really were a pretty baby, with very dark hair and lots of it.

I happened to walk past Boots one day in the local shopping centre and saw the competition advertised. I thought, 'why not?', took you in for a picture and then forgot all about it … until I found out you'd won it. Family and friends encouraged me to enter you into other similar things. You won every time and eventually, through winning competitions, a model agency approached us and asked if they could take you on. 'Why not?' I thought again.

When you were about three years old one of me friends said, 'Let's take the kids to disco dancin'.' She told me there was a class on opposite the Walker Gate metro station, run by a lady called Noreen Campbell. 'Why not?' I found meself saying yet again. You loved dancin' at home. The boys did things like karate and trampolining but I tried to give you all a chance to do things I thought you'd enjoy, and I knew this was more your thing. When we got there Noreen told us we'd been mistaken.

She didn't teach disco – this was a ballet, tap and ballroom class. You had a go and loved it, and from that very first day Noreen started telling me you were really good at all types of dancing. 'She's got real talent, something special,' she told me. You couldn't get enough of it, and as soon as you were old enough Noreen entered you for dancing competitions, which you always won.

After that she put you up for auditions for pantomimes, theatre shows – everything. You were Molly in a production of *Annie* when you were about six, at the Tyne Theatre, and at the same time the model agency was putting you up for all sorts of fashion shows in shopping centres, or for catalogue work and adverts. I was asked if Garry could go on the books of the model agency too as he was always with us, and the pair of you appeared in a British Gas TV advert together. You did one for the local electricity board and a big furniture store, too. As long as you were happy I took you along and let you do whatever was on offer, and you always loved it, posing very naturally and even suggesting different poses for the camera, which made us all laugh.

Stage school was another thing you did for a time. I've always been of the opinion that in life you have to give anything a go and whenever another new thing was suggested I'd always let you try it to see if you liked it. You won a 'Star of the Future' competition and a 'Little Miss and Mister' contest run by the *Evening Chronicle*, and you were always very proud of yourself when you appeared in the paper. Any prize money you got from winning competitions, or fees from modelling, all went back into costumes or whatever else you needed, so you kept yourself going. Your brothers and sister didn't mind me taking you places all the time. They loved what you did and were forever asking you to show them and their friends your latest dance routine or pictures.

When you were about eight or nine we were encouraged to try out another ballet school run by a lady called Margaret Waite, who had a really good reputation. It was Margaret who suggested you should try out for the Royal Ballet's summer school, and I know you remember all about that. All I'll say is that I was happy for you to do it, and I was happy for you to give up the ballet. 'What do you want, Cheryl?' I would always ask, because you knew your own mind from a very young age. You had a lot of confidence as well whenever you were performing. I don't know where it came from, especially because at home you were very soft and terribly sensitive. Our first house at Cresswell Street in Byker was always like an RSPCA rescue centre because you'd bring home pigeons with broken wings or stray cats that usually turned out to not be strays at all. Sometimes they just rubbed up against your leg in the street and you brought them home, feeling sorry for them and trying to adopt them. You worried yourself far too much about everything and everybody else, all the time. I remember telling you, right from when you were a very small girl: 'Life is tough, Cheryl. You need to toughen up.'

My mam is right. Of all my dancing experiences I do remember the whole Royal Ballet episode clearly. Margaret Waite was a really amazing dancer who'd had a brilliant career with the Royal Ballet herself before she set up her school in Whitley Bay. It was about fifteen miles from where we lived and twenty-odd stops away on the metro, but it was *the* place to go if you were really into ballet. Margot Fonteyn was my heroine and I couldn't get enough of my ballet classes. I did every competition going and always managed to win.

'You're excelling,' Margaret told me one day. 'At nine you're a bit too young, but I want you to apply to the Royal Ballet summer school. It's extremely hard to get in but I think you're good enough.'

I told my mam, who took me along for the audition somewhere in Newcastle. Mam didn't ask any questions, and I don't think I fully understood what I was applying for. I just put on my favourite tutu, did my best on the day, then went home to play.

One of my favourite games at that time was to pretend I was running a beauty salon. I'd convince Gillian I was really good at doing make-up and then I'd put mascara and blusher on her. Sometimes I'd even persuade my little cousins – the boys included – to let me put eye shadow on them, or lipstick. I'd also tell them all kinds of tales, like the time I convinced one of my really young cousins that the Incredible Hulk lived round the corner. When my mother found out what I was up to she went mad.

Dad was always much stricter than my mam, and I knew I had to behave myself much better when he was in the house. One day I remember my dad looking very serious, and I wondered if I was in trouble about something, but I didn't know what.

'Me and your mam need to talk to you,' he said. 'Sit yourself down, Cheryl.'

He took a deep breath and said: 'You've been offered a place at the Royal Ballet …'

My heart leaped in my chest, but before I could jump up and cheer Mam interrupted. 'We're really proud of you, Cheryl. You've done really well and we know you'd love to go. But the thing is …'

Dad finished the sentence, and my heart sank like a stone. 'We can't afford to send you. I'm sorry, sweetheart. It's such a lot of money and we just haven't got it …'

I ran up to my room and cried, hugging my pillow. It had no cover on it and a jagged line of red stitching down one side where I'd sewn it back together really badly, probably after whacking Gillian or Andrew with it in a fight. I always held onto that old pillow whenever I got upset about something, and this felt like the worst thing ever.

Mam appeared at the door. 'Cheryl, we'll see what we can do. Things are never as bad as they seem. You've got *Gimme 5* again next week. Put your chin up.'

Gimme 5 was a Tyne Tees kids TV programme I'd appeared on a couple of times with a bunch of kids from the dance school. I tap-danced with Jenny Powell once and hit her in the face by accident, and another time I showed off my ballroom dancing skills, doing the rumba.

'Get her back on!' I heard one of the television people say. 'She's hilarious!'

I think this was because when I was ballroom dancing I really got into it and pulled all these crazy faces. I can see now how funny I must have looked because I was only nine years old yet I was trying to look all sensual and sexy, like I thought ballroom dancers should. I didn't even realise I was doing it at the time. I just really felt the music like that, and being on the TV felt normal to me, so I just let myself go.

I can remember going round some of the local old peoples' homes with the dance school too, and the pensioners would howl laughing when I pulled those faces. I loved it. It encouraged me, because I felt like I was really entertaining them.

'You'll never guess what, Cheryl,' my mam said one day, ages after my dad had delivered the bad news. 'We've managed to find all the money after all. You can go to the Royal Ballet!'

I screamed in excitement and gave our dog Monty a big hug. Monty was a long-haired Dachshund who hated every one of us kids but was obsessed with my mother. He wriggled away from me as fast as he could, as usual, but for once I didn't care. I grinned at my mam and said thank you over and over again. This meant I'd be going down to London for a whole week in the summer holidays, to be taught by some of the best ballet teachers in the world.

I knew my mam and dad had been pulling out all the stops but I hadn't wanted to get my hopes up. I found out later they'd done a newspaper story to help raise the money they needed. I think the whole thing cost about £500 but they'd been at least £200 short. The paper sponsored me, and I ended up doing a photoshoot and a story to say thanks to everyone who'd helped.

It was August 1993 by now and I'd turned ten in the June. I'd never been to London before. In fact, I had not set foot out of the North East. We never had a holiday and all my life had taken place in Newcastle. I thought the whole of the country must be the same as it was on our estate, and I assumed everyone spoke like me because I didn't know any different.

'Gals, I will teach you all how to cut an orange into neat segments so you can eat it *nicely*,' one of the prim and proper ladies at the ballet school told us on the first day.

She had a very tight bun in her hair and didn't look like she'd ever cracked a proper smile in her life.

That's my first memory of being there. Mam had dropped me off with a tiny little suitcase and I was staying for a week all by myself, at this posh place called White Lodge, in Richmond Park.

We'd been given salad and fruit for lunch on the first day, which put me off right away. 'I want chips and beans,' I thought when I saw the lettuce leaves and oranges. I wasn't even used to the word 'lunch'. As far as I was concerned you ate your dinner in the middle of the day and had your tea at night. What's more, when you ate an orange you peeled it with your fingers and the peel would magically disappear when you left it on the table or dropped it on the floor.

I caught other girls giving me sideways glances whenever I spoke. Nobody sounded like me, and I felt out of place. They were all very well put together too, in clothes that were actual makes, while mine were from C&A or the Littlewoods catalogue.

'Cheryl Tweedy, please step forward.' We were in a grand hall, and I was being asked to show off a little routine.

I could sense the other girls giving me funny looks and it put me right off because I was used to being super comfortable and completely fitting in, whatever I did.

'What?' I said when the teacher said something I didn't quite hear. 'Pardon,' she corrected snootily. 'We always say "pardon" not "what", don't we, gals?'

I thought to myself, 'That's funny, none of me teachers at school ever tell me that.'

We slept in a big dormitory and I hated it. I just wanted to go home and climb into my bunk bed. Even if Andrew was there fighting with me or trying to dangle me off the top bunk like he sometimes did for a laugh, I would have felt much happier than I did here.

I wrote a letter home and said, 'Tell Monty I miss him.' Really, I missed everything and everyone back home but I didn't want anyone worrying about me. I missed the noise and the chaos in our house, I missed bumping into my aunties and uncles and cousins who all lived two minutes away from our house, and on Sunday I really, really missed having a roast dinner at my Nana's, knowing everyone else would be there as usual. Sometimes it was bedlam, but I still would have swapped places in a flash.

One time Andrew and Gillian got caught smoking behind my Nana's settee. They'd taken her ashtray and lit the old cigarette ends. My dad saw the smoke coming from behind the settee and went crazy. Gillian and Andrew were only small at the time so it must have been quite a few years before, but memories like that came back to me as I lay in my bed in the dormitory, feeling a million miles away from home.

I thought about my school as well. I went to St Lawrence's Roman Catholic Primary, even though we weren't Catholics. It was just down the road from our house and had a very good reputation; that's why Mam and Dad sent us there. I loved it, and I'd even asked Mam if I could take my Holy Communion like the other girls because I wanted to wear the white dress and gloves. 'You can decide your own religion when you're old enough,' Mam told me. Our head teacher was a nun and I felt peaceful in that school, and like I belonged. I had a go at playing the cello, the clarinet and the flute. It was fun and easy and not strict.

Mam would walk us to school every morning and I remember one day she suddenly made us stop in the street.

'Look! There's a hedgehog stuck down there!'

I peered down and saw this huge hedgehog completely wedged at the bottom of an open manhole. Mam made us run home and fetch a bucket and spade and rubber gloves, which we used to rescue it. We then took the hedgehog to the park to set it free. We were late for school but my mam explained what had happened and we didn't get into trouble.

Joe was the one who usually got into trouble, not the rest of us. There'd often be a knock on the door and a neighbour would be standing there fuming and telling my mam: 'Your son's bashed my son.'

He was just like many of the other teenagers in the neighbourhood and Mam would wallop Joe when he misbehaved, even though she is only four-foot ten. I couldn't remember a time when my big brother wasn't taller than her, in fact. Mam was pretty strong for her size and we all got smacked by my mother when we were naughty, usually on the back of the legs. It always stung like mad and I remember we'd threaten to phone ChildLine whenever that happened, though we were never serious.

My dad would be more likely to shout when things went wrong, like the time when Joe broke his leg after getting drunk and falling down an open drain. Dad exploded and shouted really loudly, and I had to put my hands over my ears.

It was chaos a lot of the time, but it was home, and it was all I knew. Lying in this neat and quiet dormitory, surrounded by girls who wore Alice bands and spoke like the Queen, made it seem like Newcastle was in another world, or even another universe.

On my last day at the Royal Ballet my mam came to watch the farewell presentation. I was that happy to see her sitting there amongst all the other mothers that I couldn't help waving and grinning at her. All the rest of the girls stood like little statues, as we'd been told to do, but I was so excited I just couldn't help myself. Even when Mam tried shaking her head and mouthing at me nervously to stop, I carried on.

'How could they all stand there like that?' I asked her later that day, when we were finally heading home.

I'd skipped out of the gates as fast as I could, absolutely delighted to be getting out of that stuffy place.

'It's called etiquette,' Mam said.

'Pardon?' I replied, not for the first time that day. I could see that word was annoying my mam but I couldn't help using it, because it had been drummed into me all week.

'Cheryl, if you pardon me once more I swear I'll knock your block off,' Mam replied. She wasn't joking, either, but I was so happy to be back with my mam. It had felt like I'd been away forever, and I just wanted to get back to everything I knew and loved.

'I want to give up ballet,' I announced just a few days later, when I was eating a packet of crisps at home in front of the telly. 'It's not fun any more.'

'That's fine, Cheryl,' Mam said. 'If you don't like it you don't have to do it. That's the end of it.'

I didn't give up dancing altogether. I still did some other classes, but not as regularly, and definitely not as passionately.

I was in my last year of primary school by now, and so it was inevitable that my life was changing in other ways too. I was about to leave St Lawrence's and go to Walker School. I was growing up, and it was a little bit daunting, but exciting too.

There was also another big change about to happen in my life, although this was one I definitely didn't see coming. I was eleven years old; I can remember the day it happened like it was yesterday.

'Tell me the truth! What the hell is happening? What's going on?'

It was Andrew, and he'd burst in the front door in a terrible rage. I'd never, ever seen him in such a state and he started ranting and raving at my mam and dad. They both looked really worried and my heart started beating super fast in my chest.

'I'll explain it,' Mam said. Her eyes looked sad and she had deep frown lines in her forehead. Dad had gone all quiet, which panicked me, as normally he'd have gone mad at Andrew for shouting and screaming like that.

The atmosphere felt much more chaotic than I'd ever known. It was like a big bomb had gone off. I didn't know how or why, but it felt like another bomb was going to explode any moment.

'Is Dad my real dad?' Andrew screamed in my mam's face. I swear the clock stopped for a second when he said that.

'I want to know the truth – all of it!'

Andrew was shaking now, and shouting that someone had told him in the street that my dad wasn't his real dad. He'd asked my aunty if it was true.

'How do you know?' my aunty had said. 'You'd better ask your mam!'

Andrew was going so berserk that he looked like a crazy person, but however mad he looked, this was sounding horribly realistic.

I was listening to every word, trying to make some sense of it all, but I wasn't sure what the truth was, or why this was happening. Gillian was in the room, and she was going mental now too.

'Sit down, everyone,' my mam said eventually. 'Will everyone calm down and sit down, please!'

We all sat round the kitchen table: me, Mam, Dad, Gillian and Andrew. My dad looked absolutely shell-shocked, I was sitting there panicking so much I wanted to be sick and Gillian and Andrew were still shouting and just going into meltdown.

'Be quiet and let me tell you,' Mam said, shushing Gillian and Andrew. At last there was silence, total silence, and Mam spoke softly.

'I was 21 when we met, me and your dad.' Mam nodded towards my dad, to make it clear she was talking about him. 'I already had Joe, and you two.' She looked at Gillian and Andrew now, but not at me. My brother's and sister's eyes were on stalks, bulging out of their heads.

'I was married to your dad, to your real dad,' she told them. 'But we broke up not long after we had you both. Andrew was only a baby. Your dad, Garry, was very young when I met him. He was 17. And he took me on, with three kids. Then we had Cheryl and Garry together.'

Mam took a deep breath and we all just stared at her.

I think it took us all a few minutes to take in what she had said. What she was telling us was that Joe, Gillian and Andrew were only my half siblings.

'Is that what you mean?' I asked her once I finally felt able to speak. 'Gillian and Andrew aren't my real brother and sister? They have a different dad to me and Garry?'

Gillian and Andrew were asking loads of questions too, shouting and stomping around the room. I don't know where Garry was, but he was only seven at the time so was too young to hear all this anyway.

'Our Cheryl and our Garry are only our half brother and half sister?' Gillian screeched. 'Is that what you're telling us, after all these years?'

'Yes,' Mam said, in a quiet but firm voice.

My dad had lost all the colour from his face. 'When did you and Mam get married?' I asked him.

'Actually,' he replied, looking anxiously at my mam. 'We're not married.'

I think it was the first time he had spoken. I was stunned into silence again, but Andrew was shouting and getting more and more angry.

'How come we're all called Tweedy then?'

'Well, your mam just uses my name, so we're all the same.'

'The *same*?' Gillian screamed. 'I don't think so!'

I can remember a lot of sadness, falling right down on us like it came out of the ceiling and just surrounded the whole family. Andrew and Gillian's faces were filled with confusion; devastation, in fact. They were asking more and more questions and shouting and screaming a lot, at each other and at my mam and dad. I was just staring at my dad and thinking, 'How could you know all these years and say nothing? How can this possibly be?'

I don't think anyone got an explanation as to why this secret had been kept for so long; at least I certainly don't remember hearing one.

Garry doesn't remember any of this chaos at all, and Joe wasn't there either. When I thought about it later, I wondered if Joe already knew, or had at least suspected something. I mean, I eventually worked out that my dad would have been about 13 when Joe was born, as my dad was four years younger than my mam. Maybe Joe had worked things out for himself already.

At this point Joe was 18 and my dad was 32. Maybe that's why I don't remember Joe being a part of that day. Maybe he just didn't need to hear this.

'I'm going and I'm never coming back,' Gillian yelled. She slammed the front door so hard I was afraid the glass in the windows would break, and I started to cry.

Gillian had gone from being my sister to my half sister to not being there at all in the space of about 30 minutes. The police came knocking on the door later that day and I remember seeing nothing but anxiety etched on my mam and dad's faces for a very long time. Gillian didn't come home that night or the night after that and soon the days became weeks. I felt sick with worry every day, from the minute I opened my eyes in the morning until I eventually fell asleep, exhausted, hours and hours after getting into bed and staring at Gillian's empty bunk bed each night.

Joe was out looking for her every day and night, going crazy. He used to fight with Gillian a lot and they had some terrible arguments in their time, but if anyone or anything outside the family threatened her he was on it, straight away. He was combing the streets, doing all he could to track her down. He always had that same super-protective attitude towards all of us.

Joe eventually found Gillian after six weeks of sheer hell at home. She'd been staying with a friend and I heard she had taken drugs, trying to block out what had happened. Joe literally barged into the friend's house, got hold of Gillian like his arms were a straitjacket and carried her home, kicking and screaming.

'I've met my real dad,' I heard Gillian tell my mam. 'I'm gonna keep in touch with him.'

He was called Tony and lived not far from us in Newcastle but Mam had not kept in touch with him after they got divorced, which was about 13 or 14 years earlier. I don't know how she found him, but Gillian had marched right up to his front door and hammered on it until a woman answered.

'Is Tony there?'

'Who's asking?'

'His daughter. Who are you?'

'His wife. You'd better come in.'

Gillian was 15 years old when she did that – maybe the worst age possible for something like this to have happened. It must have been a terrible ordeal for her, but she waited for Tony to get home from work and met him that same day. It turned out he was a tattoo artist, which fascinated us all when we found that out, because Joe had always been very artistic and amazing at drawing cartoons. We'd often said: 'I wonder where he gets that from?' and now we knew.

'You'll have to meet my dad,' Gillian told me. 'You won't believe it. He looks exactly like our Andrew.'

'So … do you like him?'

'I think I will.'

I didn't know what to say or how to react. It was a hell of a lot to take in. I'd suffered major anxiety when Gillian was missing and now I began to worry constantly about everything, every day.

Andrew started running away a lot too, and whenever the police knocked on the door I'd panic, imagining all kinds. I was aware that Andrew had started sniffing glue, though I couldn't tell you exactly when his habit started, or whether it was already a problem before the bomb went off in the family. All I know is that I'd lie in bed waiting for him to come home, not being able to sleep until I knew he was safely back in the house. I'd look out of the window, watching for him coming up the street, sometimes right through until five or six o'clock in the morning. When it was time for school I could never get up.

'Are you awake, Cheryl?' Mam would shout. 'Yes, but I'm just resting my eyes,' I always replied. I was late and tired all the time.

One night, Andrew had been out with no key and so he smashed a window to get back in. I nearly jumped out of my skin, and I listened as a huge row kicked off between him and my dad.

I didn't care about the shouting; I was just glad Andrew was home, even though the whole house started to stink of glue once he was inside. The fumes rose up the stairs and hung in the air, and to this day I still feel sick at the smell of glue.

'Get to bed, go on with you!' Mam would shout, and I'd lie there wide awake and on red alert for a long time after the house fell quiet.

This wasn't the first time Andrew had been in trouble. He was done for thieving when he was 13, which was a year or so before all this kicked off with my mam and dad, but to be honest I don't really remember that being a big hoo-hah. The bizzies, as we usually called the police, were always knocking on doors all over our estate. If someone got arrested or even sent to prison the neighbours were more inclined to sympathise and ask if there was anything they could do to help the family, rather than to judge or look down their noses at you. It was practically an everyday occurrence, which must be why Andrew's early problems with the police really didn't stick in my mind.

'Who's that now?' I remember my mam snapping whenever the police hammered on the door.

'Can't you tell?' I always thought, because to my ears the 'bizzie knock' was instantly recognisable. It always made my nerves tense and my stomach sink as I wondered what would happen next.

Andrew became more and more volatile and unpredictable after he found out about his real dad, and before long he was completely unrecognisable as my funny brother who used to tell silly, exaggerated stories and make us all laugh.

'I got struck by lightning,' he told us once, when he came home soaking wet in a rainstorm at the age of about 10. '*Really*, Andrew?'

we all asked. '*Really*,' he replied with wide, serious eyes. I remember we all laughed our heads off because he actually thought we would believe him, but *that* Andrew just seemed to vanish from our family, almost overnight.

My mam and dad split up not long after the family history had been laid bare. My dad had an affair and my mam tried to take him back, but they couldn't make it work any more. I was still only 11 years old and that's about all I knew. Mam went absolutely crazy for what felt like a long, long time, understandably so with all the trauma she had gone through. She was still only in her mid-thirties but the stress of bringing up five kids on her own, with the police banging at the door all the time, must have been very hard to cope with.

It was around this time when I first noticed my mam starting to become what you might call 'spiritual'. She was always floating round the house being unbelievably calm when all hell was breaking loose, saying stuff like: 'things happen for a reason' and 'live one day at a time, that's all anyone can do'. Even if there was absolute hell going on in the house, with Andrew off his head on glue, ranting and raving, she'd stay incredibly calm.

Mam's got lots of sisters and sometimes I'd hear her saying to one of my aunties, 'Eee, there's no good telling the kids what to do or they just want to do it more, don't they? What can you do but hope they'll grow out of it?'

When Andrew was 15 he stabbed someone in a fight. This guy had punched Gillian in the face in a pub and so he stabbed him. That's what Gillian told me when she eventually came home, crying and in a terrible state, and without my brand-spanking-new trainers she'd borrowed from me that night.

'Sorry about your trainers, Cheryl,' she sobbed.

'When will I get them back?' I moaned, telling her I wished I hadn't lent them to her because I wanted to wear them that weekend.

'The police took them away for forensics. They got splattered with blood. Could be six months.'

'*What?* They'll be out of fashion by then. Anyway, as if I'd want them, after they've had blood on them.'

I was 12 years old and by now I was well used to Andrew being arrested regularly for thieving and stealing cars. That meant the seriousness of what he had done this time round didn't hit me at all until I saw the rest of the family just crumbling in front of me. Everyone was in pieces and it was so painful to see. Mam cried a lot. People were talking about sentences and prison, and I was lying awake yet again, worrying myself sick.

'We'll go and visit him as much as we can,' my mam said after the court case. 'He'll not serve the full sentence years, I'm sure.'

I hoped not. My brother had been sentenced to six years and was being locked up in a young offenders' institution to start with as he was too young for an adult prison. I'd be 18 by the time he was released, so I felt like part of my childhood was taken away that day too.

By now Joe had left home and me, my mam, Gillian and Garry had moved into a three-storey house in Langhorn Close, Heaton, which was not far from our old family home in Byker.

Once a week I'd pop over and see my dad. I'd either get a bus over to his new house, which wasn't far away, or I'd see him at my Nana's. There was never any formal arrangement in place or anything like that; I was old enough to see him whenever I wanted to. Whatever my mam thought of my dad after their split, she never tried to poison our minds against him and I don't really remember my relationship with my dad changing that much; he just didn't live with us like he used to. 'Want to listen to some Level 42?' he'd ask, just as he used to when he lived with us.

It was my relationship with my mam that changed more, probably because she altered so much in herself. Without Dad there, I think me and Mam started to become closer, like friends as well as mother and daughter, and it's more or less stayed that way ever since.

* * *

Throughout all this upheaval I carried on dancing every week. Whatever was going on in the rest of my life I always smiled when I was performing. It wasn't my way of escaping the bad things that happened at home or anything as deep as that; dancing was just a part of my life I really enjoyed, while the family problems were something I accepted and got on with, because I had no choice and that was the way it was.

'There's a panto coming up, I'm gonna audition,' I said to my mam one day.

'That's nice. We'll go and see Andrew after.'

I'd go on my own to shows and auditions now, taking buses or getting lifts from other parents, because Mam couldn't drive and we never had a car. Sometimes I'd still be in a sparkly costume when we visited Andrew in the young offenders' institution. It was like a kind of foster home, with a lounge and a place you could play pool, but I knew Andrew was locked in his bedroom at night, which was a horrible thought.

'Tell Andrew about your next show,' Mam would say. She never seemed to get upset, blame Andrew or ask him why he had committed crimes, and we'd just talk about normal stuff, as if we were sitting in the kitchen at home like we used to.

'It's a panto but I haven't got the part yet. I've made up my own dance routine, though, and I've done a tape of the music for the audition.'

'What have you picked, Cheryl?' Andrew asked.

'"No Limit", from 2 Unlimited. I got it off one of them "Best of" tapes my dad got me for Christmas. You know the one: "No, no, no, no, no, no, there's no limit!"'

I sang the words a bit too loudly, which made everyone smile. Then we said our goodbyes and went home to have chips and egg for our tea. With Andrew inside, life seemed a lot more simple, and once I got used to the idea of him being away, I was glad I didn't have to worry about what he was getting up to or what time he would come home.

'Good luck, Cheryl,' Andrew said, and I told him I didn't need luck. 'Thanks,' I shrugged. 'If I don't get this one I'll get another one.' My belief that I was going to succeed as a performer was the one constant in my life. It was not a question of 'if' I was going to make it, just 'when'.

2

'You need to get your head out of the clouds'

'Cheryl Tweedy,' the teacher called out at afternoon registration. 'Yes, Sir. Here, Sir,' I replied. 'Oh, and by the way I was late this morning. Sorry, Sir.'

The teacher rolled his eyes as if to say 'not again' before giving me a late mark for the morning, even though I had not even been there, and then marking me in for the afternoon. After registration I walked straight out the back doors of Walker School at the first opportunity, as cool as you like, wagging off for the afternoon with my best friend Kelly, who'd pulled the same trick.

'Can you believe he fell for that *again*!' we both cackled before pegging it down the road.

Kelly was as feisty as hell and I loved being with her. Usually we went back to her house because her mam and dad both worked, but if we heard someone come in the house we'd run out the back door and go and sit on the train tracks at the bottom of her street, or hang around Walker graveyard. God knows why we went to the cemetery; it seemed quite cool at the time and nobody would ever see us there.

I had no interest in being educated. *My* life took place outside the school gates, not inside them. I was always more focused on getting the next dancing part than wasting time working out why x equalled a plus b or whatever my teacher was on about.

'Cheryl Tweedy, you will amount to nothing!' the maths teacher exploded one day. I was chewing gum and rehearsing my dance moves in my head. The audition for the Christmas panto I'd made my 'No Limit' music tape for was tonight, and all I wanted to do was get out of school and practise.

'Amount to nothing?' I thought cheekily. 'Just you wait and see. I'll show you!'

I couldn't have cared less what any of my teachers thought of me, because I knew for a fact I was going to make my living by performing. Nothing and nobody was going to stand in my way.

It's just as well I had that attitude, because at break time I went to find the music tape I'd left in my locker and found it had been stolen. I was really annoyed because I'd gone to all the trouble of making the cassette myself, and there was no time to make another one.

'What will you do?' the man at my audition asked later that day, looking worried for me.

His name was Drew Falconer and he'd come into the dance school to watch a few of us.

'Don't worry, I'm gonna sing the song meself,' I said. Then I just started singing and dancing in front of him, giving it my all.

'The poor guy must have thought I was mental,' I laughed to our Gillian that night.

'He sat there lookin' at me gobsmacked while I was bustin' these moves and singin'!'

I was offered a part in the panto the very next day, but my excitement was short-lived because it turned out they couldn't fill the other places and the show had to be cancelled.

'There'll be another one, Cheryl,' Mam said.

'I know,' I replied. I was disappointed but I wasn't too bothered. I didn't ever feel I had to chase my dream, because I firmly believed I'd make it happen one day, when the time was right. It wasn't about being famous or rich, I just wanted to dance and sing and entertain people, because it's what I loved to do. It was that simple, that clear.

I remember explaining all this to Dolly one day, who was an old lady who lived across the road from us. Dolly had six kids and lots of grandkids and I'd known her and her family all my life. After I started at Walker School I'd begun to spend a lot of time with her, partly because she didn't care if I wagged off school and her flat was another place to go to during the day, if I wasn't with Kelly.

'Eee, Cheryl, it's lovely to see you,' Dolly would say every time I knocked on her door, even if it was clearly during school hours and I was in my uniform. 'Come in, and stay with us for a bit of company.'

Being with Dolly was far more interesting than being at school. She told me stories about the war and I was absolutely fascinated by her. She didn't have a tooth in her head and her language was shocking, but also very funny to listen to because she couldn't pronounce an 'f' through her gums.

'Who's that knocking on the buckin' door!' she'd shout whenever someone came to her flat.

I soon learned why she reacted like that, as it was often the police asking questions about one of the colourful characters in Dolly's large family.

'You haven't got a warrant!' she'd shout, knowing all the spiel. 'You can't come in here!'

Whenever a woman came in from social services or the home help service, Dolly always made a point of telling them proudly that I was her granddaughter.

'Hi darlin',' she always greeted each helper warmly. 'Do you want to put the kettle on an' we'll 'ave a nice cup of tea? This is me lovely granddaughter, Cheryl. She's going to be a pop star, you know.'

Whenever the visitor was out of earshot Dolly's smile would fall from her face and she'd whisper to me behind her hand: 'Watch that one, she'll be all nice to me face but she'll be dippin' in me purse when me back's turned.'

I found out many years later that when *my* back was turned Dolly would often say, 'Cheryl? She'll never be a buckin' pop star!' That was typical Dolly, and I don't mind at all, not now.

I'd push Dolly in her wheelchair to the shops along the Shields Road, which was the big main road separating our estate from

Walker, or I'd go out and pay her rent or get her some teabags and milk if she needed me to.

Dolly would forget all about cups of tea when the helpers weren't around, mind you. She liked vodka and Irn-Bru, and even when I was just 12 or 13 years old she'd be trying to give me tumblers of the stuff. I'd take a swig just to keep her happy even though I didn't like the taste at all, but sometimes I'd go home feeling drunk and dizzy at 5pm.

Her daughter lived in the flat upstairs and if there was any noise Dolly would take a broom and bash the ceiling like a mad woman, making dents in the paintwork and shouting, 'Keep the buckin' noise down!' I'd often stay the night at Dolly's, and my mam was quite happy with that. She knew Dolly well and she always knew where I was, so she didn't mind. It wasn't out of the ordinary where we lived to be in and out of each others' homes like that. Besides, Mam had her hands full being a single mother, especially with Garry still at primary school, and she was always happy to let me come and go as I pleased.

One afternoon Mam told me there was a little festival on, just two minutes down the road. 'Let's take our Garry,' she said. 'There's hook a duck, toffee apples and all that. Shall we go and have a look?'

As soon as we got there I saw someone I recognised. 'Mother,' I hissed. 'That's that guy that auditioned me for the panto.'

'Never!' Mam said.

The man started walking towards us, smiling. 'It's Cheryl, isn't it?' he said.

'I'm Drew Falconer,' he told my mam, shaking her hand enthusiastically.

'We were very impressed by Cheryl's audition. It was a real shame the panto never went ahead. Your daughter is very talented. I reckon she has it in her to be a pop star.'

I couldn't believe it when I heard that because it was absolutely amazing to hear someone as important as him confirming what I already felt in my heart. It turned out that Drew ran a local talent management company and was always looking for young acts to bring on. He put up-and-coming singers on the stage at Metroland, which was like a big indoor theme park within the Metrocentre shopping complex in Gateshead.

'What d'you think?' my mam said when he left us with his card, asking us to get in touch to discuss giving Metroland a try.

'As long as I can still do me dancing as well as singing, I'll do it,' I said. Even though I'd been telling people for ages I was going to be a pop star, dancing was still the biggest thing in my life; the singing just came along with it.

'You're a weirdo,' Kelly said when I told her I was going to meet Drew to listen to music and plan some stage routines the following week. 'What d'you wanna do that for?'

'Why not? It's brilliant,' I told her. 'I love all this.'

I don't think any of my friends really understood how passionate I was about music and dancing, or how I could be so convinced that was where my future lay. My dad was the worst, forever repeating what he'd said to me for years.

'Cheryl, sweetheart, you need to concentrate on getting a proper job. You need to get your head out of the clouds.'

'No, Dad, being a pop star *is* a proper job. I'm going to be on *Top of the Pops* one day and I'll be number one. Watch.'

None of my mates took the mickey or anything like that. I was never bullied or picked on for doing something different, but neither was I ever one of the in-crowd, or the 'it' girls as we called them. I was somewhere in the middle, and I liked it like that. I had just a few close friends, and when I wasn't singing or dancing I spent my time either with Dolly, hanging around with Kelly, or messing around with another good mate of mine, Lindsey, who was a year older than me and lived up the road.

Lindsey was always up for a laugh, and it was around this time that she suggested we should sneak out one night and go camping with some of the boys we knew on the estate. I readily agreed, but I was just 13 and I knew my mam wouldn't let me go out camping at night with boys.

'We need a plan,' I said. 'You tell your mam you're staying at mine, and we'll sneak out when my mam's asleep.'

Why I didn't just say I was staying at Dolly's I don't know, but I suppose Lindsey had to say she was staying at mine so her parents would let her out. When the big night came, Lindsey and I pretended to go to sleep in my bedroom, but underneath our quilts we were fully clothed, waiting to make our escape at 2am.

Meanwhile, the group of boys we'd arranged to meet were in my back garden waiting for us. Lindsey and I peeped out of my bedroom window and saw them mucking about. One of them, Lee Dac, was doing Mr Motivator aerobics routines to keep warm, because it was the middle of winter. The other boys joined in and they were all flexing their muscles and posing. We thought it was hysterical, but we buttoned our lips and scrambled back into bed when we heard footsteps on the landing outside.

'It's me mother!'

Lindsey and I were trying not to snigger under our quilts, but the boys gave the game away because they'd started chucking clumps of mud at my bedroom window to get our attention. My mam must have heard them from her bedroom, and she stormed in and went berserk, pulling back my quilt and smacking me so hard that she nearly took my head off my shoulders. I literally saw stars, and I couldn't believe it because my mam normally flounced around the house like a little fairy, being super gentle and soft. She'd given me a clip round the ear plenty of times before, or a smack on the legs when I was naughty, but nothing as bad as this. I'd never seen her lose it like this, ever. I was so shocked, and really annoyed that our camping adventure was over before it began.

We couldn't sleep and Lindsay and I stayed awake for ages, whispering to each other.

'Have you kissed anybody yet?' she asked me.

'John Courtney,' I confessed.

My first kiss had happened quite recently in fact, in the back alley one afternoon after school.

Me and John just liked each other and so we had a kiss, that was all. I was at that age when I was starting to get interested in boys, but it was all very innocent. I was a typical teenager, giggling like a little girl with my friends one minute and wanting to be all grown up with the boys the next.

All of our family was close with John's and I really liked him because he was very cheeky and always smiling. He was also a really good footballer. People said he had the potential to play for Newcastle one day. He trained hard and was ambitious, which I admired. I know it can't have been true, but at the time it felt like me and him were the only two around our area who knew where we wanted to go. I never said that to any of my friends, of course, but that's how it felt, especially now I was working at Metroland

'I've got you a gig, Cheryl,' Drew told me one day. 'I think you're ready for it.'

I'd done lots of rehearsals with him by now and I'd been on the stage plenty of times at Metroland. I honestly can't remember much about my early performances there, but I think that's because it really didn't feel like a big deal to me. I must have been only 12 the first time I took the microphone, but right from the start I always felt very comfortable on the stage. It felt just like an extension of all my dance shows, except I happened to be singing as well.

I think my experience of ballroom dancing, as well as ballet, helped. When I was younger I'd had a regular ballroom partner for a few years called James Richardson. We won loads of competitions and made the finals of the National Championships in Blackpool. The pair of us also appeared on *Gimme 5* together and on Michael Barrymore's *My Kind of People*, which at the time was a really popular TV show. We went our separate ways when I suddenly got taller than James, but it had all been good experience for me, and it meant Metroland just felt like the next step in my career. The audience would typically be made up of families on a day out, or other kids who'd been dropped off while their mam went shopping. I never felt under pressure because the atmosphere was always friendly and people always clapped and cheered. 'What's the gig?' I asked Drew confidently.

'You're doing the warm up for Damage,' he replied, which made my heart skip a beat.

'Bring it on! Wait till I tell me sister!'

Damage was a really well-known boy band. To me they were proper, famous pop stars, but I wasn't fazed at all. I felt ready, and I was really excited. When my big moment came I wore high-top trainers and baggy trousers with a little crop top, trying to look all cool and R&B like the boys. I remember my heart was pounding when I ran off the stage after completing a few well-rehearsed numbers, but my biggest memory from that time is being invited along to watch Damage perform on the *Smash Hits Poll Winners' Party*, which was a TV show filmed at the Metro Arena.

This was a programme I'd watched for years, dreaming of being on it one day. I remember standing in that arena literally open-mouthed, feeling within touching distance of making my dream come true.

'Wow! This is it!' I thought. 'This is what I want to do.'

From that point on I started performing regular gigs at Metroland. It was on the other side of the River Tyne to where we lived and took me 40 minutes to get there on the bus but I always did it willingly, every time. I just loved being on that stage. I felt alive. It's where I felt like *me*.

By contrast, when I was wearing my school trousers with their little pleats down the front, blue shirt, black blazer and striped Walker School tie I felt completely disinterested and out of place. My tie had a red stripe in it, showing I was in Walker House. 'Red for danger' the teachers probably thought, because I was nothing but trouble.

'Cheryl Tweedy, you have brought shame on this school,' my head teacher told me one day, after hauling me angrily into his office.

I knew what this was about. A boy had spat at me on the bus, and so I'd sworn at him. That's how I was brought up. If someone attacked a Tweedy, we were taught to defend ourselves.

Right from when I was a small girl Joe and Andrew used to say to me: 'Come on, Cheryl, if you don't hit back you'll get chinned.'

'But I'm a ballerina!' I'd say.

'Well, what are you going to do – pirouette them to death?'

My brothers would then hold up a couple of cushions and tell me to punch each one in turn.

'Come on, Cheryl, left, right, left, right!'

I'd reluctantly hit the cushions as my brothers drummed it into me to always stand up for myself.

'It wasn't me that started it,' I complained now to the head teacher, rolling my eyes insolently.

'Take that chewing gum out of your mouth this instant! There was an old lady on that bus who has complained to the school, and she has identified you from a picture line-up.'

I was suspended for two weeks, which was the second time I'd had that punishment. On the previous occasion I'd been caught fighting, again when I was trying to stand up for myself. My dad never found out about the suspensions because he would have gone mental. Mam just said: 'When will you learn, Cheryl?' and sent me to go and tidy my bedroom, which was always a complete tip with crisp packets all over the floor.

I spent the fortnight's suspension mostly with Kelly. She wagged off and we went and stood outside the newsagent until we spotted someone who we thought looked like a 'cool' adult and wouldn't mind buying us some cigarettes.

'Excuse me, can you buy us 10 Lambert & Butler?' we asked if we were feeling flush and had some of our £1.50 weekly pocket money left. Otherwise we asked a likely looking adult to buy us a 'single', which usually meant we got a Regal cigarette.

I smoked from about the age of 13, because everybody did. It was like with the vodka and Irn-Bru Dolly gave me. I didn't really want the booze or the 'tabs', as we called cigarettes, but I knew

that despite the scrapes I got into at school, most people saw me
as a Goody Two-shoes because of my singing and dancing, and I
didn't want to stand out any more.

For the same reason, it wasn't long before I smoked weed too.
Everybody did it and I gave in to peer pressure at a party in someone's house one weekend.

'Go on, Cheryl, it won't kill you,' one of the lads said, and so
I puffed on a joint. I didn't particularly like it, but after that I
started smoking more and more. Loads, in fact. It didn't seem to
affect me that much; it just made me feel a bit more relaxed, like
nicotine did. It did have one big advantage over cigarettes
though: weed was a lot easier to get hold of because you didn't
have to ask an adult to go into the corner shop for you. It was
always readily available on the street and that's why I smoked so
much of it.

Other drugs were a different matter. I knew stuff like speed
and Ecstasy and even cocaine were available on the street, but I
was scared of all those drugs. I'd seen some of the older boys in
local gangs looking completely out of control, off their heads on
God knows what. Andrew's glue-sniffing had freaked me out too,
and I hated to see anyone with that crazed look in their eyes. My
dad was fiercely anti-drugs, and so was Drew. They both
drummed it into me to avoid drugs and I listened. I didn't think
they meant weed because *everyone* smoked weed, and it didn't
worry me because it didn't make people lose control like all the
other stuff did.

Once I was well established at Metroland Drew started to encour-
age me to think about recording music as well as performing, and
he began fixing up some studio sessions, both in Newcastle and
down in London. I just went along with whatever he suggested. I
was keen to learn, and going to London seemed like the right
move if I wanted to make it as big as a band like Damage.

'You hated it down there when you went to the Royal Ballet,'
my mam said.

'I was only 10 years old!' I replied. 'It's different now. I'm 14. I'm ready for it.'

She sent Gillian with me the first time I went to London, and a few times after that. We travelled in a tiny Mini Metro that only did about 60mph. A friend of Drew's drove, and it felt like it took us about 20 hours to get down south.

When I was there I did a 'showcase' for different record labels and met the 'development team' of a 'management company' called Brilliant.

'What the hell does all that mean?' Gillian asked.

'I don't have a clue,' I replied. 'I'll just do me singin' and then we'll go home.'

It was always like that. It probably sounded quite glamorous to my mates back home but to me it wasn't much different to going into the studio in Newcastle. I'd be asked to have a go at different tracks, and I knew I was one of lots of other teenagers who were looking for a break and doing exactly the same as me.

We would usually travel there and back in a day, and I remember once the car got broken into when we stopped on the North Circular to go and get a McDonald's on the way home. Gillian's quilt was stolen along with a few of her bits and pieces, but the worst thing was that the whole back window was smashed out, and we had to drive all the way back to Newcastle with a plastic bag taped over the gap where the window should have been. The rustling noise did our heads in all the way home. It was freezing cold and we clung to each other for the whole journey, trying to keep warm.

'Why is there always some kind of drama with you, Cheryl?' Gillian moaned.

'With *me*?' I replied indignantly. 'It's not *my* fault we get into these types of pickles, is it?'

Not long after that trip I decided to dye my hair blonde. I loved Destiny's Child and I wanted to *be* Beyoncé. 'Blonde hair looks brilliant on her,' I said to Gillian. 'I'm sure it'll work for me too. It'll look good with me dark skin.'

Gillian didn't try to stop me, even though I had form when it came to experimenting with this type of thing. One time I decided to wax my sister's top lip by melting some candle wax, sticking it on her 'tash' and then ripping it off quickly when it hardened. Once that was done I dabbed the red-raw skin with lemon juice. God only knows what I was thinking. Gillian had a massive red rash for ages afterwards and Mam went crazy with me. I did the same to myself and to one of my cousins' eyebrows once too, with the same disastrous results.

Anyhow, I took myself off to a local hairdresser's one day, where they put coconut bleach on my head for about eight hours. I sat there patiently, thinking it would all be so worth it, but I was absolutely mortified when they'd finished. I didn't look anything like Beyoncé. Instead, to use Dolly's phrase, I looked more like a 'buckin' Belisha Beacon'.

I cried and cried, and Dolly's daughter was so angry she took me back to the shop.

'Cheryl, you look ridiculous!' she said. 'You should get a refund!'

Red-faced, I trailed back to the hairdressers with her, only to be sent away with the offer of a free conditioning treatment I didn't even want.

'If they think I'm stepping foot in there again they've got another thing coming,' I sobbed.

Before long Drew introduced me to Ricky, a musician friend of his down in London. Ricky had heard me sing, and he and his wife took quite a shine to me and said I could stay with them whenever I wanted to. Sometimes I did, or sometimes Gillian and I stayed in a £19-a-night hotel with just a bed and a sink, but at least it meant I didn't have to go up and down to Newcastle in one day if I had the opportunity of some studio time at Brilliant.

I began writing songs with Ricky and I just loved it. I'd go down to London during every school holiday and sometimes at the weekends, getting a lift or taking the train to King's Cross. I wasn't being paid and I had never signed anything with Drew; I was just trying to get as much experience under my belt as I could.

Brilliant eventually became the hugely successful 19 Management company, but back then it was only a small outfit, which was perfect for a teenager like me taking my first steps in the music industry.

'You know what, Mam?' I said one day. 'Every time I get past Stevenage when I go down south I get a warm, tingling feeling in me body. It's like I belong in London. It's where I'm gonna be. And the funny thing is, the closer I get to home on the way back, the less I can breathe.'

Mam howled laughing, which was quite irritating seeing as she was supposed to be the spiritual one. I really did feel drawn to London, though. Everything looked twinkly down there. I can clearly remember the first time I saw Piccadilly Circus. 'What *is* this?' I thought, standing there looking at the giant advertising hoardings and flashy neon signs. Everything was sparkling, all around me. I'd been brought up to be streetwise and my dad in particular had always tried to keep my feet on the ground. But in London I couldn't help dreaming big dreams. I *was* going to be a pop star. It was absolutely what I was going to do.

I was 15 now, and my school days were very nearly over, thank God. 'You need to try hard, Cheryl,' my dad would say. 'Get some exams under your belt and then you can get to college.'

'Dad, you don't need GCSEs to have a number one record, and that's how I'm going to make my living.'

While I was in my last couple of terms at school I got myself a job in the local café, JJs on Heaton Road. I wanted to earn money for clothes, as well as for my trips to London. I loved United Colours of Benetton at the time, and to afford clothes like that I'd started taking out loans with the 'Provi' man. He was always on the estate, the 'Man from the Provident', lending money out. I borrowed £200 from him the first time, which I had to pay back in weekly instalments, with interest, of course.

The café was perfect for me. It was only down the road from our house and I could work part-time, which meant I could earn a bit of money but still concentrate on my music. Right from the start I enjoyed chatting to the customers and making teas and coffees and all-day breakfasts. The owner, Nupi, was a lovely old Asian guy who'd led an amazing life. I was always attracted to people who had stories to tell, and we really hit it off.

'Two teas, please, Smiler,' Nupi said to me on the very first day, and the nickname stuck.

I have to be honest here; a lot of the time I was smiling about something else that was going on in my life, rather than at the joy of frying bacon and making tea. I had a boyfriend, who I kept secret from just about everyone. I have never spoken about him before, but he was actually my first proper boyfriend, and he affected my teens in a massive way.

Dave lived locally and I'd seen him around the estate for years before we started dating. I bumped into him in the street one day on the way home and I swear that something literally went 'boom' between us. I hadn't seen him for a while and I had never fancied him before, but I fell for him in a big way, right there and then. I'd never experienced anything like it in my life before. He was absolutely gorgeous looking, and I could tell by the way he looked at me that he fancied me too.

'Are you going to let me take you out for dinner?' he asked after we'd done a bit of flirty catching up.

The question took me completely by surprise. I'd never been taken out to dinner before. I knew Dave was quite a bit older than me and I felt very flattered. I'd kissed a couple of other boys since my very first kiss with John Courtney, and I'd been out with one or two other boys for a week or so here and there, but nothing serious.

I'm sure I blushed, and I excitedly agreed to let Dave take me out.

'How old are you?' I asked on our first date.

'24.'

I gulped.

'Don't worry,' Dave smiled. 'I will take good care of you.'

We were in a fancy restaurant and I felt incredibly grown up.

Dave really knew how to treat a girl, or so I thought. After that he took me out for lots of candlelit dinners and he regularly bought me flowers, CDs, teddy bears – you name it. I fell for him in a huge way, and I mean *huge*.

I didn't tell a soul at first, because I was only 15 and still at school, and I knew my dad and Joe would go absolutely mad about Dave's age. It was easy to meet in secret anyhow. Everyone was used to me going to Metroland on my own for hours on end, or to the local recording studios. It meant I didn't have to lie or even sneak around when really I was going out with Dave.

'Would you like to learn to drive?' he said one night when he picked me up near school in his car.

'I'm too young. How can I?'

'I know where we can go. Hop in.'

He took me to an empty car park in town, and that's where I had my first driving lessons. It was so exciting. I'd still be in my school uniform, but I felt like a proper grown-up woman, madly in love for the very first time. It was a really amazing feeling.

'Go on, have a smoke,' Gillian said one day, passing me a joint. She was 19 and had left home by now and moved into a flat of her own, but she was in the kitchen of our house at Langhorn Close, smoking weed, with my mam standing right beside her.

Mam knew Gillian smoked weed and just let her get on with it, saying: 'You're old enough to make your own decisions.' But I was four years younger, and I would never have dreamed of smoking in front of my mam. I started shaking my head and looking at Gillian as if to say, 'Are you mad?'

'Go on,' my sister said cheekily. 'Don't pretend you don't smoke it, Cheryl. I know you do.'

I was mortified, but Mam just looked at me and said very calmly, 'If you're going to do it, Cheryl, I'd rather know, and I'd rather you did it here.'

Gillian passed me the joint and I had a smoke. I didn't enjoy it and I was furious with Gillian, but at least we all knew where we stood. I think my mam's open-minded reaction that day helped me confide in her about my relationship with Dave, not too long afterwards. I was relieved when she didn't seem too bothered about his age and was only concerned that he was treating me well. 'He's amazing,' I reassured her. 'He can't do enough for me. We're so happy together.'

It wasn't long before Dave and I became intimate, and I wanted to take precautions. I confided in my mam again and she listened patiently and agreed to take me to the GP for the Pill.

'I'm not one of those girls who sleeps around,' I told her. 'I'd *never* have a one-night stand.'

'I know that, Cheryl. I'm glad you're being sensible.'

I was telling the absolute truth. I had always been ridiculously protective and respectful of myself, to the point where I'd been accused of being a prude many times.

'We really love each other, Mam,' I said. 'He's just the best.'

'As long as you're happy and safe, Cheryl, that's what matters.'

Dave and I were together for about 12 months, and he became the centre of my world. I lived and breathed for him, to the point where even my singing and dancing took a back seat. I'd write lyrics in my bedroom and I always had music playing, always. I couldn't imagine a world without music, and R&B and soul were my favourites. I still loved pop music, especially anything by Destiny's Child, but I'd been drifting away from Metroland for months now, and I'd also stopped going down to London.

'What are you doing about your singing?' Joe asked when I left school in the summer of 1999 and turned 16 a few weeks later, at the end of June. 'Don't you give it up! You need to sort your life out.'

I'd tell him not to worry. 'I'm working more days in the café and it'll happen when the time is right.'

'No, you need to *make* it happen,' he'd argue.

'I will … when the time is right.'

Working in the café *did* leave me less time for my singing and dancing, but the real reason I wasn't pursuing my career was Dave.

Thankfully, nobody else questioned me like Joe did. I think other people in the family just assumed things had changed in my life because I'd left school. There was also plenty going on in the family to take the focus away from me. For one thing, we'd just found out that Gillian was pregnant. She had a really strong relationship with her partner and everyone was very excited that there was going to be a new baby in the family. Mam was very pleased. It's always been the done thing where I grew up to have your kids young, and it wasn't unusual to become a grandmother in your late thirties or early forties.

'Eee, I can't wait,' Mam told everyone who would listen. 'A new bairn in the family. What could be better?'

'Will you be with me for the birth?' Gillian asked me the minute her pregnancy was confirmed.

'Of course I will!' I replied, although I didn't have a clue what I was letting myself in for.

We were both staring at the pregnancy test, and we worked out her baby was due in January 2000.

'Oh my God, you might have the first Millennium baby!' I shrieked, promising to hold Gillian's hand every step of the way.

The other big distraction for the family was Andrew. He was in Durham Prison now, having been moved there as soon as he was old enough to leave the young offenders' institution. Garry and I went with Mam for prison visits sometimes. I always found the trips upsetting, even though the routine was soon so familiar it quickly became commonplace.

'I've brought all your favourites from the machine,' Mam would say, passing Andrew some Pot Noodles, fruit jellies and hot chocolate drinks.

You had to put all your belongings in a locker before you went into the visitors' room, but my mam would always make sure she had plenty of change in her purse for the vending machines once we got inside. Nobody talked about what Andrew had done. He would tell us about the canteen food or the latest fight he'd seen in the corridor and Mam would go 'poor you'. It was always like that.

'How's the singing and dancing, Cheryl?' Andrew usually asked me.

'Fine. Just not doing so much now I'm in the café more.'

We'd shuffle out when the bell went, promising we'd be back soon.

'Bye, pet,' Mam would smile. It was the same smile she used when she said goodbye to me at the Royal Ballet all those years ago, or when she waved our Garry off on a school trip. She treated us all exactly the same, no matter what any of us did.

'I've done something really stupid,' one of my friends told me one day. She'd come into the café for a cup of tea and some sympathy.

'It can't be that bad. Tell me what you've done.'

She was in a terrible state and I sat down beside her and held her hand as she struggled to get the words out.

'I had a one-night stand last night with someone ...' she sobbed.

I gave her hand a squeeze. 'Don't cry. Do you want to tell me who with?'

She took a deep breath and said, 'You know that Dave, the one who lives ...'

Nothing could have prepared me for that. It literally took the breath out of me and I felt I was going to suffocate. Never, ever, could I have imagined Dave would have cheated on me, let alone with someone he knew to be my friend. We'd been dating for 12 months and he meant the whole world to me. I was madly in love with him and I thought he loved me too.

I don't remember my friend finishing her sentence but I heard enough to be left in absolutely no doubt she was talking about my boyfriend. My heart sank into my shoes and I started panicking like mad. I just couldn't believe my ears.

Nobody beside my mam knew I was dating Dave. My friend didn't have a clue, and I certainly wasn't going to enlighten her now. It was all far too much to deal with.

'I'm sorry, I've got to get back to work,' I gasped. I felt the colour fall out of my face and I ran into the kitchen, thinking I was going to choke or be physically sick. I don't know how I struggled through to the end of my shift, but I did, smiling at the customers and chatting away as best I could.

Afterwards I ran home, locked myself in my bedroom and cried my eyes out for hours and hours. I was *heartbroken*, absolutely devastated. They say the first cut is the deepest and they're not wrong, or at least that's how it felt at the time. I couldn't imagine feeling a worse pain than this. It was like an actual physical stab to my heart.

I eventually went round to Dave's and went crazy, and I mean *crazy*.

'It's not true. She's making it up,' he said pathetically, but I knew it was him who was the liar. My friend was so ashamed of what she'd done and wished it *wasn't* true. By contrast Dave had good reason to lie, and his deceit was written all over his face. I felt so disgusted and insulted that he had the cheek to deny it to my face after behaving like that behind my back.

'I was so proud of you,' I shouted. 'I was so proud of us! I had a *ridiculous* amount of pride in our relationship. It was so good! You've ripped me heart out!'

The betrayal was just unbearable. I didn't know how I was going to cope with it, and the truth is I didn't. The next morning I got up late, moped around the house and smoked weed before I'd even eaten anything. It sounds so disgusting now, but that's what I did. I literally turned into a depressed teenager overnight. At first I couldn't bear to tell my mam what Dave had done to me because I knew it would have devastated her too. Instead, I bottled everything up, smoking more and more weed every day.

I managed to drag myself into the café on the three or four days a week I worked and I somehow put on a brave face for the customers, but it was never easy. I remember having a row with Nupi once that must have been really bad, because he fired me on the spot even though we were close friends by then. I got another job in a pizza place, but after two weeks I was in a terrible state and Joe demanded to know what was going on.

'I have to clean out this big dough machine,' I cried. 'And the owner is horrible. He keeps making suggestive remarks to me.'

Joe went crazy, threatened the guy and told me I was never stepping foot in the place again. When Nupi found out about the trouble he gave me a job in a new café he'd opened on the Quayside.

'Thank you, Nupi, you're a real friend,' I told him, but inside I was dying, wondering how I was going to hold the job down when I felt so bad.

All of those events are quite blurred in my head because, looking back, I had sunk into a very deep depression. I began having panic attacks, gasping for breath and feeling my heart racing for no reason. I was skinny to begin with but now I had absolutely no appetite, and my weight dipped to less than six stone. I was incredibly anxious all the time, to the point where it felt like my heart was beating so fast it was eating me up inside. I ate crisps and junk food to survive, but stopped having proper meals. I didn't have a clue about healthy eating and couldn't have told you the difference between protein and carbohydrate, so I had no idea how bad this was for my health.

As the weeks went by I also became quite reclusive. If I didn't have to go out to work I'd stay in the house in my pyjamas all day. Then I'd start feeling frightened and paranoid about ever going out again. I think I was a bit agoraphobic, because when I did step out of the house I felt really vulnerable, like something really bad was going to happen to me. Needless to say, my singing career was put completely on the back burner. I didn't even have the will to sing in my bedroom or write the odd lyric, let alone think about getting back up on a stage.

'I'm takin' you to the doctor's,' Mam said one day. 'I've had enough of this.'

I think a few months had gone by, and I didn't argue. The GP took one look at me and said flatly: 'She's depressed.'

I was given a prescription for beta-blockers and was told I was actually suffering from clinical depression. Apparently there was a history of it in the family.

'The pills will slow your heart rate,' I remember the doctor saying.

'Good,' I thought. 'I'm sick of it beating so fast.'

The tablets were bright blue, but were not the magic cure I'd hoped for. From the very first day I hated taking them because they made me feel dizzy and sickly, and at night when the rest of the world got quiet my brain became super noisy and loud.

'What's the point of life?' I'd think to myself. I was too much of a wimp to think about actually ending it all, but for a long time the thought wasn't far away.

'Pick your chin up,' Joe would say to me if he came round and saw me still not dressed in the middle of the day – but some days I was too low to care what anybody thought of me, even my big brother. Sometimes I'd go round to the neighbours' house, still in my pyjamas, and play with their dog, Oscar. I must have looked a total mess but I didn't care about anything, least of all what I looked like. 'You need to snap out of this,' Joe would tell me, but I just didn't know how.

Joe had got himself a good job at the Nissan factory and his life was sorted, but I knew he'd had some problems in the past. He of all people was somebody I should have listened to, but I don't think I was ready or capable of doing anything other than wallowing in my depression.

'I wish I *could* snap out of it but I can't,' I'd think to myself, but I never said that to Joe.

My dad was kept in the dark about a lot of this. 'Cheryl, you're looking a bit thin, sweetheart, are you eating enough?' he would ask, but I never told him the half of it. He'd have gone mad if he'd known I was taking pills, and so I kept it from him.

'It'll pass,' Mam said many times, but I didn't believe her. Other relatives who knew I'd split up with my boyfriend, though they'd never met him, would say things like: 'Never mind, Cheryl, that's puppy love for you,' or, 'You'll be seein' someone else before you know it.' I just couldn't visualise myself with *anybody* else, and those sort of comments made me feel so alone, because it felt like nobody understood what I'd lost and the pain I was going through.

It took at least six months for me to even begin to pick myself up and start seeing my friends again, but even then I was a shell of myself and it took me a few more months before I'd agree to do normal teenage stuff, like going out for a drink or to parties. One night I got talked into going to a house party on the other side of the estate, which I really wasn't sure about.

'I don't want to be here,' I thought as soon as I walked in the door.

There was a guy sitting in the living room called Jason Mack, who was quite a bit older than me and ran a second-hand furniture shop on the corner of the street. I'd seen him around since I was about 10 years old, and I knew there had been a fire at his shop a few months earlier.

'What happened?' I asked him, just for something to say. My confidence was low, and I definitely wasn't in a party mood.

'I split up with my girlfriend and she tried to burn the shop down,' Jason said.

'My God, I'm sorry to hear that. *I've* had a horrible time too. I split up with my boyfriend not that long ago.'

We shared sob stories, smoked some weed and just chilled out together. I felt a connection to Jason, and that night I saw him as an equal for the first time, rather than the much older person I'd always viewed him as. I fancied him, actually. He had blond hair, blue eyes and nice teeth, and he told me he was 27. I was still only 16, but after my experience with Dave I definitely didn't feel like an inexperienced young teenager, far from it.

At the end of the night Jason gave me a kiss and I felt a spark of life inside me for the first time in nine months, which was the length of time I'd been on my own after Dave.

'Do you fancy going out tomorrow, just the two of us?' Jason asked.

'Why not?' I replied. I actually smiled and felt excited, and when I went to bed that night the noises in my brain weren't quite as loud, because I'd cleared a little bit of space in my head to think nice thoughts about Jason. Maybe my life was about to become happier. I felt like it was, and I surprised myself by actually feeling ready to be happy again.

3

'Open up now or we'll take your kneecaps off'

'I want Tweety Pie on me bum with "Warren" underneath,' I told Tony as I lay face down on the couch in his tattoo parlour.

Gillian had had the baby, a gorgeous little boy, and her dad Tony was buzzing, like everybody else in the family.

I went through the whole labour by my sister's side, though I can't have been any use at all. I was still only 16 and didn't have a clue about birth or babies. 'Try this position,' I said at one point, showing Gillian a poster on the wall. 'That's telling us what NOT to do, Cheryl,' she yelled in agony and frustration.

When Warren was born it was the most mind-blowing, beautiful moment ever. It completely and utterly took my breath away and I felt incredibly close to my sister, and my new nephew.

'I'll help you look after him,' I volunteered straight away. I just wanted to squeeze Warren and never let him go, he was that adorable.

We all wanted a tattoo to celebrate the new arrival. Tony had done my first tattoo, the tribal one on my lower back, and I wanted him to have the honour of doing this one too. He was so proud to be a granddad, and by the time it was my turn he'd spent all day inking the word 'Warren' onto the arms and backsides of about half a dozen relatives.

I'd got to know Tony quite well over the past five years or so, since the big bomb went off in the family and we found out about him. Once the initial shock had subsided, I went round to meet him and was absolutely gobsmacked. 'He looks like our Andrew. He even walks like our Andrew!' I said. 'I can't get over it!'

Right from that first day I viewed Tony more like another brother, rather than seeing him as Joe, Gillian and Andrew's real dad.

I showed my new tattoo off proudly to Jason. We'd been seeing each other for a little while, and I was really into him.

'I'm so happy with it,' I told him. 'You look it,' he said, smiling and giving me a kiss.

By now I'd stopped taking the beta-blockers but I wasn't completely better because I was still having panic attacks from time to time. I just couldn't seem to shake them off, but whenever I was with Jason I felt happy. He'd take me for dinner or to the pictures. Other times we'd order takeaway pizzas or buy loads of sweets and crisps from the corner shop and sit in watching *Corrie* together at my mam's. I was really enjoying working at the café on the Quayside, and I'd try out my cooking skills on Jason and make him scrambled eggs with melted cheese on top, or sausage and bacon sandwiches. I liked to spoil him, and on my days off I'd take the food into his shop at lunchtime.

Gillian was working in the café now too, and I looked after Warren for her on my days off. I'd learnt how to feed and change him and I absolutely loved him. 'I want lots of children,' I thought to myself. 'And I want to have my kids young.' Gillian was only 21, but that was seen as the perfect age to start your family, and I definitely wanted to start early too.

'How's the songwriting going?' Jason asked me from time to time. He knew all about the singing and dancing I'd done over the years, and how I'd let everything slip after my last relationship. I'd started writing a few lyrics again but I didn't have a plan about where I was going from there. I was just happy to be back on my feet after Dave, and I'd tell Jason, 'It's good. I love it,' and we'd leave it at that.

Jason's furniture business was thriving. He was doing a lot of house clearances as well as running the second-hand shop, and he had a good reputation in the trade. Locally, he was viewed as someone who was making a success of his life. My family didn't like the fact Jason was 11 years older than me, but if anyone said anything I always reassured them I was fine. 'I've got an old head on me shoulders,' I'd say. 'Jason understands me.' They could see how much better I was, and they left me alone.

Andrew came out of prison around this time, which was another positive thing in my life. He'd served four years and I assumed being locked up would have taught him a lesson and that he would put his criminal past behind him. He'd been inside for most of his teenage years, and I hoped he'd start a great, new life.

My relationship with Jason progressed really quickly, and when I was 17 we moved into a flat together just over the road from my mam's. It was that close, in fact, you could see into the kitchen from her front window. All Jason and I had to begin with was a second-hand kettle from his shop and a tiny black-and-white TV with a piece of wire sticking out the top, which you had to twist around to stop the picture from fuzzing. There was one bedroom and a bathroom you couldn't turn around in, but it was ours.

'What's for tea tonight?' Jason would ask when he went out to work in the morning, because he knew I liked to cook for him and was enjoying being a little homemaker.

'I'm makin' us chops with gravy and veg,' I'd say excitedly. I was feeling stronger all the time, and I was looking a lot better and gaining a bit of weight. 'Can't wait,' he'd wink. A look from him would make my heart jump. I felt alive, like a normal teenager. I was finally through the darkness.

One night I arranged to meet Jason at a friend's flat not far from ours. We were all going to just chill out together, that's what I thought. I took a bit of money in case we wanted to get a takeaway and I was looking forward to a relaxing evening, but when I walked in the flat my heart nearly stopped. Jason was standing there in front of me, but he looked like a total stranger. His jaw was swinging everywhere, he was talking absolute rubbish and his eyes looked black instead of blue, because his pupils were so big.

'What's he taken?' I screamed. Jason was swaying in front of me with a crazed, aggressive look on his face and I started panicking like mad. 'Tell me what he's taken! Jason, what have you taken?'

I knew he hadn't got like this by smoking weed, but I knew nothing about the type of drugs that did this to you.

'Cocaine,' his mate confessed. 'He did cocaine.'

I got Jason home eventually but I didn't sleep a wink all night. When he finally came down and took control of himself again I begged him, 'Please don't ever do this again. It was so horrible to see you in that state.'

'I won't. I'll never touch it again,' he promised. 'I don't know what possessed me.'

I hated drugs with an absolute passion. Anything other than weed frightened me to death, and I couldn't understand why anyone would want to get high like that, or into a state where they were out of control and frightening the people who cared about them.

'I'm so sorry, Cheryl,' Jason said, when I told him exactly how I felt. 'The last thing I would ever want to do is scare you.'

Not very long after that night I bumped into my old friend Lee Dac. He was one of the boys who had been in my back garden doing the Mr Motivator routine the night my mam found Lindsey and I fully clothed in our beds, planning to sneak out and go camping. I saw Lee standing outside the metro station and he told me brightly that he was going to see Andrew at a party in two days' time.

'That's good to hear,' I said, thinking it was just like old times, with my brother back in the neighbourhood. 'Hope you enjoy yourselves.'

'Thanks, Cheryl. You take care of yourself.'

Just four days after that encounter I was talking to another old friend, a girl I'd grown up with, when her sister ran over to us in a panic and said, 'Have you heard about Lee?'

We both looked at her sister blankly and I felt my pulse quicken.

'No, what's happened?' I asked.

'He's been found dead. Suspected overdose.'

The words hit me like bricks and I could feel my legs buckle.

Lee had always been in and out of my life, ever since I was about 10 or 11 years old. He was one of the lads everybody knew and I was just so shocked. I started shaking and feeling sick as my friend's sister went on to say he had taken heroin. 'It just shut his whole system down, just like that,' she said.

My friend collapsed, sobbing hysterically, and that was a shock in itself because she was a super-confident person, the type we called an 'it' girl. I'd never seen her lose her composure before, ever, and I started crying and trembling and thinking about how I'd seen Lee alive and well, just a few days before. It didn't seem possible.

The news spread like wildfire, and Andrew came round to see me in a terrible state.

'I'm gonna kill the drug dealers,' he ranted. 'How can this happen? I saw him two days ago! We had a laugh together. I saw him at a party. It was just like old times and he was absolutely fine. This is just insane! Someone's gonna pay for this!'

Andrew asked me if I'd go with him to the funeral parlour to say goodbye to Lee, and I agreed even though I didn't want to.

As soon as we got there I really wished I hadn't gone. I was totally unprepared for what I was about to see, and the hideous memory of that day has stayed with me ever since.

Lee was lying in his coffin wearing his best shirt and smelling of his favourite aftershave. The smell was so powerful it made him seem alive, and I wanted to speak to him but knew I couldn't. He still had the spots on his face he'd had the few days before when I'd seen him at the metro station.

'What have you done?' Andrew screamed at Lee. 'What have you done?' It was just so painful and heartbreaking. Lee was like a waxwork of himself and I just couldn't take it in that he was not breathing and I would never talk to him or see him again.

I didn't feel strong enough to go to the funeral because I knew Lee's mother was in a terrible state and I couldn't bear to see her grieving so badly, so I stayed at home and cried all day long.

Jason wiped away my tears. He was as shocked and gutted as the rest of us.

'What *is* this drug?' I cried. Heroin seemed to have just come out of nowhere. I'd heard of people taking speed and Ecstasy on our estate and I knew about cocaine because of Jason, but in my mind heroin was some obscure rock-and-roll drug from the Seventies that had no place on our estate at all. What was it doing *here*, killing my friend?

Lee's death sent shockwaves around the whole of Newcastle. It was the first case anybody really knew of, or at least that's how I remember it. You'd have thought such a disturbing death of a teenage boy would have shocked people into running a mile from heroin – that's certainly how it made me feel – but no, it wasn't like that at all.

Unbelievably, my other friend was so cut up about Lee's death she lost it completely and started taking heroin herself. I knew users said it gave you the most amazing feeling, but I'd also learned by now that you could get hooked after taking heroin just once, and then if you didn't carry on smoking or injecting the drug it would make you feel very ill.

'I don't get it,' I said over and over again to Jason. 'I just don't get it. Is this really happening?'

Not long after Lee's death a girl I went to Walker School with also died from a heroin overdose. Then another friend of mine, Kerry, who'd been in the year above me at school, started taking it with her boyfriend. She was killed after going round to her drug dealer's flat armed with a knife. A fight broke out and Kerry was stabbed in the main artery in her neck and bled to death. Other friends of mine went to see her in the funeral parlour and told me she had a patch on her neck, and I couldn't get that image out of my head for the longest time either.

'It's like an epidemic,' I cried to Jason. 'Like this evil presence has just landed here and started killing all my friends.'

It felt like heroin divided the estate overnight after Lee's death. You were either on it or you weren't, but most people went to it.

According to the papers a lot of them were trying to escape from the pressures of unemployment and living in what was, at the time, one of the most deprived areas in the country. That was the explanation, but I didn't understand it at all. Heroin was cheap compared to cocaine, yet people were thieving to pay for their habit and ending up in prison. It was a hideous vicious circle of self-destruction.

'Why?' I kept saying, each time I heard of another neighbour or old friend using it. 'Can't people see it's ruining lives?'

I just didn't get it at all, but it seemed that people who kept away from it like me were a rarity. My world was shrinking, because I was outside the dark circle, and the dark circle was growing bigger all the time.

My friend who I was with when I found out about Lee went into total meltdown and became a full-blown junkie. I remember walking into her flat one day unannounced, and she jumped up and shoved something under the settee. It was silver foil and I just screamed at her: 'You're smoking heroin. I think you're an absolute disgrace!' She told me it made her feel good, gave her an escape. I just couldn't comprehend it. She was someone I'd known since the age of seven. She'd always been the one who was popular and had nice clothes. I'd looked up to her for years, and now she was crumbling in front of me.

I thanked God I had Jason, because the rest of my world was disappearing so fast.

'I'll bring you some dinner into the shop,' I said to him one day.

'You don't have to,' he said. 'I can just grab something.'

'I know, but I want to.'

I was on a day off and I didn't have anything else to do. So many of my friends were now on drugs I hardly saw anybody else outside of my family, and Dolly. I didn't even look after Warren any more because Gillian had decided she was missing out on seeing him grow up and had given up working at the café.

At lunchtime I walked into Jason's shop with a bacon sandwich, expecting his face to light up when he saw me. He didn't notice me come in because he was searching through the Yellow Pages, but my heart stopped when I looked at him. Jason had a roll of silver foil behind his ear, wedged there like a cigarette. It was the same silver foil I'd seen my friend trying to hide in her flat, and I knew exactly what it was used for. To complete the picture there was a known heroin addict sitting in the corner of the shop.

'What the hell are you *doing*!' I screamed, charging over to Jason and slapping him across the face as hard as I could.

I must have knocked him into the middle of next week I hit him that hard, and then I pegged it down the street with tears streaming down my cheeks.

'Come back! I can explain everything! It's not what you think!

Jason chased after me, screaming and shouting and swearing blind he wasn't on heroin.

'Look at me,' he said when he caught up with me outside my mam's house. 'Do I look like I'm on heroin? You've got it all wrong, Cheryl.'

He certainly didn't look out of control, not like he had done when he took cocaine. His pupils weren't huge and he wasn't being aggressive or talking rubbish.

'What about the silver foil and that smackhead in the shop?'

'The foil belongs to *him*, and you're right, I shouldn't have him in the shop. But honest to God, I'm not on it, Cheryl. What do you take me for? I swear to you, I'm *not* taking heroin.'

'Look me in the eye and say that again,' I said to him, and he did, over and over again.

'I swear I'm not on heroin. You have to believe me. I'm not like that. I'm not stupid. I've seen what it does to people. I only smoke weed. Come on, Cheryl, don't do this.'

I was too young and naïve to realise it at the time, but Jason was an extremely good liar. In the months to come he would pull every trick in the book to disappear and take drugs, always coming up with a more elaborate excuse.

Sometimes he'd pick a fight with me about absolutely nothing, and then go missing for four days because of what *I'd* said or done.

Whenever he did one of his disappearing acts I'd be beside myself with worry, not knowing where the hell he was or even if he was alive or dead. We didn't have mobile phones, and I literally had to sit tight and wait for him to come back. I'd get so worried I could barely sleep or eat, and I'd survive on cups of tea and the odd McDonald's.

'Have you calmed down now?' he'd ask when he finally came home, pretending he'd had to get away from me because we'd had a row.

'Where have you been?' I'd cry.

'For God's sake, Cheryl! Why are you starting on me *again*?'

It was like that all the time. I should have just walked away, but I'd already had one bad relationship and I wanted to believe this one was different. I was determined not to let it fail, however much Jason pushed me. It seems ridiculous now, but at the time it was almost like the worse it got, the more I fought to make it work.

For instance, one night Jason and I stayed the night at my mam's house and when we got into bed he suddenly started kicking the blankets off, really violently. Then I noticed his nipples were unnaturally hard, like plastic, and he had these absolutely massive goosebumps over his whole body.

I didn't know what was happening but I was sure his behaviour had to be linked to hard drugs. I should have just kicked him out and ended the relationship there and then, but instead we had another massive fight that ended up with my mam phoning Jason's brother to come to the house to help.

'I'm sure he's using heroin,' I told his brother.

'She's crazy,' Jason replied, though he was shivering and sweating and twitching now. 'I only smoke weed. She's been depressed. She's a nutcase. She's been on pills. Don't listen to her. I'm going home.'

He messed with my head so much I didn't know what to believe, even though I look back now and think it was so obvious he was cold turkeying that night, as he hadn't had his fix of heroin and was experiencing withdrawal symptoms.

Another time, I got back to the flat to find I was locked out and Jason wouldn't let me in. I took off my shoe and put the window through, because I was desperate to get inside and stop him taking drugs. Jason picked up a shard of the broken glass, and when I ran back to my mam's screaming he followed me with it. I was terrified. My mam was in the bath, and she got out when she heard my screams.

'I was bringing this to show you what she's done,' Jason said to my mam, waving the glass in front of her. 'I don't know why she's behaving like this. She's crackers.'

Even when I walked into our flat in broad daylight one time and found two guys sitting on *our* bed, trying to hide a big roll of foil under their feet, Jason denied he was on heroin. I went crazy, clonking all three of them over the head with the foil roll before hitting out at Jason with my fists.

We'd had plenty of fights before but, although I'd slapped him in the shop, that was the first time I'd actually punched him. I shocked myself. I didn't even know who I was any more. I just didn't recognise myself.

'You've got users in my flat,' I screamed. 'You've told me lie after lie after lie and now you're rubbin' me face in it!'

Jason threw me out of the flat. This relationship was killing me, but still something inside made me determined to keep fighting for him. I'd seen so many people turn their backs on addicts, and I just believed I had it in me to be able to get us both out of this dark, dingy hole we'd sunk into.

'Cheryl! What just happened?'

It was Dolly's daughter, and she couldn't believe she'd just seen Jason behaving aggressively towards me, or that I was even in a situation like this.

'Cheryl, what's going on?' she said.

Dolly's daughter knew me as a skinny little thing who wouldn't say boo to a goose, not someone who would be fighting with her boyfriend in the street. 'It's fine,' I said. 'Don't worry about me. It's nothing serious.'

I was too proud to tell any of my friends what was really going on, and nobody knew how bad things really were or how aggressive and unpredictable Jason's behaviour could be.

Not long after that incident, Jason's drug-taking took me to a whole new level of terror.

'Open up now or we'll take your kneecaps off!'

It was the middle of the night when I woke up to hear that threat being growled through the walls. I thought I was having a nightmare at first because it sounded like something out of a scary film, but when I sat bolt upright in bed I knew it was very real. There were two men hammering on the door of our flat, and I started shaking from head to foot and asking Jason what the hell was happening.

'Keep quiet,' Jason hissed. 'They'll think we're not in.'

The banging and shouting went on for ages and the walls of the flat were so thin I could feel our whole bedroom shaking. I was so scared I could hardly breathe, and I wanted to throw up.

'How come we've got crazy men knockin' on the door, threatening to hurt you, if you're not involved in drugs?' I said when I eventually got my breath back, after the men gave up and went away.

'How the hell do I know? They must have got the wrong address.'

The lies were pathetic, but Jason was very clever. By now I had seen him many times with his head hanging and no pupils in his eyes, which is what heroin does, but I had still never caught him actually smoking it. Whenever he'd been wasted like that he'd always tell me I was crazy to think he was on heroin. 'I've had a few joints,' he'd say. 'Just chill out. What's wrong with you?'

I'd stopped smoking weed myself by now because I didn't know if it was making me paranoid or not, and I knew I had to be normal so I could work out what the hell the truth was with Jason.

One morning, not long after the crazy men had been to the door, I woke up with a very clear head and had an incredibly powerful feeling that I was about to find the proof I needed, to show Jason I was not mad, and that *he* was the one who had the problem.

'Check his pockets.' That's what I thought as soon as I opened my eyes.

I'm not like that and I have never snooped on anybody in my life, but I felt such a strong instinct that I just had to do it. Jason had gone to work and his jacket was right there in front of me. The coast was clear but I was still shaking with nerves, because I almost knew what I was going to find before I looked.

Inside Jason's pocket I found a yellow plastic capsule from the inside of a chocolate Kinder egg, and in the middle of it were loads of wraps of heroin. Seeing the drugs with my own two eyes changed everything, in a heartbeat. I wasn't going to give Jason the opportunity to lie his way out of this. That would have been just too insulting, even by his standards.

I wanted to flush the heroin down the toilet but I didn't want to be responsible for Jason getting kneecapped by the dealers, so I opened the wraps and sprinkled the drugs all over our bed. Then I wrote Jason a Dear John, spilling my heart out onto two sides of A4 paper: 'It's over. I've lost sight of my dreams. I have to get out of this dark hole. I'm killing myself with worry.' That's what it was like. I left it there and went to my mam's in floods of tears.

Jason flipped when he got back. He came round to my mam's like a mad person, fighting with me and screaming, telling me I was crackers and paranoid, but I said to my mam, 'This is it, it's over.'

She came with me to the flat to help me get my stuff. One of the only things I owned besides my clothes was a set of jars for the tea, coffee and sugar. I'd loved buying them, enjoying setting up my first flat, but now I started emptying the contents all over the kitchen worktop. I thought I had to empty the jars before I could take them away; that's how distraught and disturbed I was.

Jason appeared at the door as I was tipping the sugar out, and he charged straight over to me, looking exactly like he was going to kiss me. I had no time to react before his lips were on mine, but he didn't kiss me – he bit my mouth, hard. I had a scar on my lip from an old dog bite, and I felt it rip open.

'Mam!' I cried out as soon as I managed to pull away from him and draw breath.

'He just bit me face!'

'She's cracked in the head,' Jason said, looking my mam straight in the eye. 'Don't believe her. She's mad.'

Jason didn't realise it, but my mam had been on her way into the kitchen just as he bit me, and she'd seen everything.

She was looking at me in absolute horror. Blood was seeping out of my lip now and there was no denying what had gone on, yet Jason carried on looking at my mam very calmly and continued to repeat his defence. 'She's mad. She's making it up.'

It was the first time anybody had fully witnessed just how badly Jason treated me, twisting the truth and trying to make me question myself like that.

'I'm getting you out of here right now, Cheryl,' Mam said, bundling me and my belongings out of the flat as quickly as she could. She was so shocked by what she'd seen, and she couldn't get me out of there fast enough.

When I got back to my mam's the sense of relief was overwhelming and immediate. Without realising it, I'd been very alone for a long time when I was living with Jason.

Mam cuddled me and told me things would get better. It was the best feeling ever and as I cried in her arms I realised that I felt relieved to be rid of Jason – not just for myself, but for my whole family too. He'd driven a wedge between me and my family and had been a burden to everyone, although I couldn't see that until he was finally out of my life.

It had been my eighteenth birthday about six months earlier, and I thought about how a big group of us had gone out to a local Chinese restaurant. I really wanted it to be a special evening. I pretended it was, but I knew that Jason was out of his head the whole time. None of the family said anything but, as I looked back now with my eyes wide open, I could see their faces in a whole new light. They were all looking at Jason as if to say: 'Are you for real?' A weight had been lifted from all of our shoulders now. That's how it felt, very powerfully.

Joe was on my case straight away. He'd met his wife by this time and his life was all mapped out, which made him act the big brother even more forcefully than usual.

'What are you gonna do with your life?' he'd ask me every time I saw him. 'You're not doin' anything with your singin'. Why not? You need to sort yourself out, Cheryl, because nobody else is gonna do it for you.'

I knew he was right, but I also knew I had to get myself strong again first, both physically and mentally. My heart ached for ages, and I just needed some time for the pain to heal.

'I'm gonna do it, Joe, don't worry. I'm gonna make it.'

I firmly believed this, even though I'd slipped so much further away from my dream than I ever had before.

'I'll get my dream back on track,' I promised.

4

'I'm so proud of you
I could pop'

'I've seen this advert on TV for a show called *Popstars: The Rivals*,' I said to our Garry one day. 'I'm thinkin' of applyin'.'

'I thought you *hated* all that,' he said, looking at me as if I'd gone crazy.

Garry had a point. When the shows *Popstars* and *Pop Idol* had been on in recent years I'd always said I'd never go down that route.

'I'd rather do it by meself,' I remember saying cockily, several times.

This was a new show, though, and the idea really appealed to me. *Popstars: The Rivals* was going to create one girl band and one boy band which would compete against each other in the race for the Christmas number one.

'How cool would that be?' I said to Garry. 'Imagine being in a girl band and hanging out with a group of girls all the time. I'd love it. If that ad comes on again, write the number down for me ...'

Spookily, at that very second the advert flashed up on the telly. Garry and I looked at each other and screamed in surprise as we scrabbled for a pen and he wrote the number down. I phoned up straight away and asked for an application form, hardly able to believe this had all happened in the space of a few minutes.

'How *weird* was that?' I said to my mam afterwards.

'It must have been meant to be, Cheryl. Good luck.'

'Thanks, Mam. Don't tell anyone else I'm applyin', will ya?'

It was about four or five months since my split from Jason and I was in a much better place. Even so, if this didn't work out, I'd rather keep it to myself. I didn't want anybody worrying about me all over again.

A few weeks after leaving Jason I had started contacting old friends I'd slowly cut myself off from when I was with him. One friend, a girl from Liverpool, had asked if I fancied a waitressing job on the Tuxedo Princess, which was a floating nightclub on the Tyne. It was only about six weeks after the split when she asked me and I was still a shell of my former self, totally lacking in confidence and all skinny and washed out. I didn't even have my job in the café any more, because Jason had got me in such a state towards the end of our relationship that I couldn't even cope with that.

'Surely you don't want to give *me* a job?' was my reaction.

'I'm proud of you for getting out of that relationship,' my Scouse friend said. 'I believe in you.'

She needed someone to serve shots of cocktails like 'sex on the beach' on the boat two nights a week, and after a bit of persuasion I agreed to give it a go. Right from the first night I could feel that it was doing me good to have to do my hair and put on a dress, and it was amazing how easy I found it to socialise again.

Meeting people who were normal and pleasant and out to have fun on the boat was just so refreshing, and each time I went to work I smiled and enjoyed myself. 'I can see the future again,' I thought.

That's exactly how I was feeling in August 2002, when I received a letter inviting me to the London auditions of *Popstars: The Rivals*. In my application form I'd explained all about my performances at Metroland and my recording experience, and I'd attached a little passport-sized picture I'd had done in a photo booth in the shopping centre. I was quietly optimistic when I sent it off because even though I'd done nothing with my singing for a good couple of years, I had a very strong gut feeling that the audition would go well. The feeling I had was so powerful I swear it was almost spiritual, but I was determined to be very level-headed about it too, and not let my intuition rule my head. 'I'll just do me best,' I told myself as I prepared to travel down to London a week or so later. 'That's all I can do. There's nothing to lose.'

I got a loan from the Provi man for £100 and took myself off to River Island, where I bought some little shoes with heels, a pair of brown trousers with a pleat down the front, a flowery top and a choker with a cross on it. As I packed I practised the song I'd chosen to sing. I was heavily into R&B and soul music, but I knew because of the title of the show I needed to sing a pure pop song, and so I chose S Club 7's 'Have You Ever', because it was the poppiest thing I knew.

'If you don't get in, you can just come home.' That's what I was thinking to myself as I got on the train to London.

I was 19 years old. I was all by myself and my heart and head were full of nervous excitement the whole journey.

When I arrived at King's Cross I felt the old familiar tingle in my bones that I first experienced four or five years earlier on my trips to London. It was that exciting feeling that I was in this twinkly, sparkly place, where I felt sure my future lay. It was like a sixth sense; I can't explain it any other way.

This was exhilarating and terrifying all at the same time. That's how I felt as I made my way to a little hotel near Wembley Stadium, close to where the auditions were being held. I was on my own, and my future was completely in my hands. Nobody was there to help me, but then again nobody was there to drag me down, either. This was all up to me, and on top of all my other emotions I felt proud of myself for being there, for pursuing what I loved. I could so easily have curled up into a ball in Newcastle, but I hadn't, and I felt good about myself.

I can barely remember singing my song to the producers, which was the first hurdle I had to face, because I was that nervous. I will never forget coming face to face with the three judges though: Louis Walsh, Pete Waterman and Geri Halliwell.

I knew Louis managed Westlife and Boyzone and had been a judge on the Irish version of *Popstars* the year before, but that was about it. I also knew that Pete Waterman was one of the famous Stock Aitken Waterman music producers and had also been a *Pop Idol* judge. The person I was most daunted by, though, was Geri Halliwell, because she was *so* famous. I'd listened to the Spice Girls when I was growing up and had really liked them, and to be stood in front of Ginger Spice herself was really intimidating.

'Breathe,' I told myself as I took centre stage, wearing a badge with my identification number: L786. 'And don't forget to smile.'

I think I only sang for about half a minute before the judges stopped me, and Louis said, 'I wanna put her through.'

'You have the most beautiful eyes and skin I think I've ever seen in my life,' Pete Waterman said, which took me completely by surprise. I couldn't remember the last time I had a compliment like that and it gave me a real boost.

Then all three judges started saying things to me at once, asking if I was sure I wanted to be a pop star, and if I realised how much hard work it would be. Geri told me it wasn't glamorous, and Louis said: 'It's early mornings, late nights and lots of bullshit.'

I told them I wouldn't be happy doing anything else, which was the honest truth.

As I walked out of the room shaking, smiling and thanking them all, it felt surreal. I'd got through to the next round, and it had all happened in one crazy minute! My head was spinning and spinning. It was just so exciting. I phoned my mam straight away to tell her the good news.

'That's nice,' she said. 'I'll tell our Garry. I'm just cooking his tea.'

There was no hoo-hah, but I think that was a good thing. I needed to keep my feet on the ground and focus on the next stage of the competition. There was a whole week of singing and dancing auditions to get through next, with the aim of selecting 10 girls and 10 boys who would battle it out for a place in the boy band and the girl band.

Looking back, that entire week is quite a blur in my head as I was a complete emotional wreck.

I spent the whole time either on my own in my hotel room thinking about what I had to do next, or giving it my all in front of the judges. There was nothing else in my life, because nothing else mattered.

When Louis told me I'd made the last 15 I couldn't stop crying, but it was Geri who delivered the really big news, travelling up to Newcastle to tell me I'd got into the final 10 and would be competing in the finals, live on TV. Geri didn't tell me quite as plainly as that, of course. As I would have to learn myself in years to come, it makes better television if you string out the moment when the big decision is revealed. It's something I hated then and I still hate now, but Geri played the game brilliantly.

I remember sitting in my mam's front room listening to Geri rambling on and on for what felt like an age. I really couldn't make head nor tail of what she was on about, and I felt absolutely terrified.

'You're in!' she said eventually, to which I replied, 'You shouldn't do that. That was really horrible. You shouldn't be allowed to do things like that to people.'

I was so excited and wanted to tell everybody, but the news had to be kept secret until all the auditions and heats we'd gone through so far had been shown on television.

In the meantime, I had to move down to London to share a house with the other girl finalists and prepare for the live shows. Just as I was packing my bags, the phone rang and I ran downstairs to answer it.

It was Dolly's daughter, and my immediate thought was that I wished I could tell her and her mam my good news before I left Newcastle.

'I'm sorry Cheryl, it's not good news.'

'What do you mean?'

'Me mam's died. It was the emphysema. I'm sorry to be the one to tell you.'

I think I just stood there, gasping for air. Dolly had been like a grandmother to me, and her death devastated me all the more as I hadn't been able to share my news with her before she passed away. I immediately wondered if I should still go down to London.

'When's the funeral?' I whispered, although straight away I knew that I wouldn't want to go. Funerals made me think of Lee Dac lying in his coffin, and I absolutely hated them with a passion. I also thought of the deaths of two of my own grandparents. My mam's dad had died of drink when I was 14, and I never met my other grandfather. He died of a heart attack after playing a game of football, and actually collapsed in my father's arms, when my dad was only 17. The first time I heard that story I sobbed my heart out, thinking how terrible that must have been for my dad, coping with that at such a young age. I imagined him crying, and ever since that day I've never been able to bear seeing grown men cry.

I definitely didn't want to go to this funeral, but I desperately didn't want to let Dolly down either.

'Next week, not sure which day yet,' came the reply.

I felt panicky. I had no idea what my schedule was the following week. I cried my eyes out when I came off the phone, but when I eventually dried my tears I had a very clear thought in my head.

'What would Dolly want me to do?'

'Get on the buckin' train, Cheryl,' I heard Dolly's voice say, and so that is what I did.

I was told later that I was named as one of Dolly's granddaughters at her funeral, which was very moving. Looking back, I think Dolly's passing made me more determined than ever to succeed, not just for myself, but to make the people who loved me proud.

In what felt like the blink of an eye, I now found myself living in a huge mansion worth millions of pounds in Weybridge, Surrey, along with nine other girls, including Nadine Coyle and Sarah Harding and, eventually, Nicola Roberts and Kimberley Walsh. The house absolutely amazed me. I'd never even stayed in a nice hotel before, let alone a place like this. Everything was shiny and luxurious and there was even a swimming pool, which made it seem even more grand.

'This is just mad!' Nicola said when she moved in a little while after me.

I clicked with Nicola straight away. I've always liked Scousers because they tend to have the same mentality and sense of humour as Geordies, and I soon found out that Nicola was from a similar background to me too. We laughed our heads off about how different this house was to what we were used to back home in Newcastle and Liverpool.

Nicola was very striking and I thought her long red hair was absolutely stunning, but she was painfully shy and right from the start I felt very protective towards her. She was only 16 and I wanted to take care of her, like she was my little sister. Nicola had actually been sent home from the competition earlier on but was given a second chance after another girl decided to pull out at the last minute.

I would have found that very stressful, but despite the set-back and her shyness, Nicola actually had an amazing amount of self-confidence, because she knew she was a good singer.

'I know I'll get through,' she'd say every week.

Deep down, I also had plenty of self-belief, but that didn't stop me suffering badly with nerves.

'Whatever you do, don't let the nerves ruin your chances, not now you've come this far,' I told myself over and over. I also had the attitude: 'If I don't make it this time, I'll still get there,' which was a great leveller for me.

I was enjoying myself like I never had before, which helped a lot too. It was summertime, the sun was shining and I was spending my days practising my singing, making friends with girls who were all chasing the same dream, and all in such amazing surroundings. Even if I didn't make the band, I knew I would never regret this time.

'What will you do if you don't get through?' Nicola asked.

'Learn from the experience,' I said confidently.

That's honestly what I thought, and when those words came out of my mouth I knew that just getting this far in the process had done wonders for my self-esteem.

'Your skin's amazing,' was the very first thing I'd ever said to Kimberley, when we'd met in the earlier stages of the competition. I had walked up to her, completely out of the blue, and said that to her because I was just so fascinated by how beautiful she looked. Kimberley had looked at me deadpan, muttered 'thanks', and said something about using a certain foundation cream. At the time the only make-up I wore was eyeliner and a bit of mascara and lip-liner, and I felt embarrassed and wondered if Kimberley thought I was a weirdo.

She had been given a second chance too, after another girl who'd originally made the final 10 left because she was pregnant. I was absolutely delighted when I heard Kimberley was returning, because once we started to get to know each other at the auditions we really hit it off and had promised to keep in touch, come what may.

When she was initially voted off I'd felt devastated. 'Look, Kimberley,' I said very seriously. 'If I don't make it either, you and me will make a group together.'

She'd agreed, and so when she was brought back into the competition we already had a bond, and I loved having her in the house.

I liked the fact that Kimberley was a very down-to-earth person – a typical Yorkshire lass – and I noticed we'd both go 'wow!' at the same things. We did that quite a lot whenever Sarah was around, actually, because Sarah stood out. She has such a big personality and I'd never met anyone quite like her. She was very loud and you couldn't miss her, but despite that I felt I hadn't got to know her through the auditions at all. Sarah was another Northerner, having grown up in Stockport, but it felt like we were from completely different worlds.

In the house she was the one who was always doing crazy things like wrapping her whole body in clingfilm before she went to bed, saying it was a good way to detoxify. She'd done a beauty course and was always giving us tips, but to me all this stuff was new and really unusual.

I knew more about Nadine than any of the other girls to begin with because I'd actually seen her on TV. Nadine had won a place in Irish *Popstars* the year before, but was disqualified when she was found to be too young. It had been a bit of a scandal because she had said she was 18 when she wasn't, but Nadine was really quiet and sweet and it was hard to believe she was the same person who'd caused such a drama.

'Hi Nadine, it's nice to meet you,' I said when I first met her at the auditions. 'I remember you from Irish *Popstars*.' She seemed quite shy but right from the start, I don't think anybody doubted that Nadine would make it through to the band, because her voice was just *so* good.

'Who wants me to make some chicken and rice?' one of the other contestants in the house asked one night. This was Javine Hylton, and she loved to cook.

'Yes please!' the rest of us chorused. I didn't have a clue how to cook anything fancy like that and nor did Nicola or our roommate Aimee, so we were always grateful for Javine's chicken and rice. It was really good, and I ate so much of it I noticeably started to put on weight for the first time in years.

We had several weeks in the house together before the live shows started, during which time we were encouraged to have singing lessons.

'Use your chest voice, Cheryl,' the teacher said to me one day.

'What's me "chest voice"?' I replied. I'd never had a singing lesson in my life and I didn't know what she was on about.

'Well, how do you breathe when you are singing?'

'I just do, with me lungs.'

Nicola and I retreated to our room afterwards and collapsed in a fit of giggles. Nicola painted my nails and I taught her how to put on eyeliner. Day by day our bedroom got messier and messier, until eventually you could barely see the carpet for all the clothes and shoes, hairbrushes and towels strewn all over the floor.

One morning a really awful pair of trainers arrived at the house. I don't know where they came from or who they were for, as I don't remember us having stylists or anything like that in those days, but I was full of mischief and I saw the opportunity for a joke.

I took the trainers to each girl's room in turn and told them very seriously, 'These have been sent for you. Davina McCall says you have to try them on now and then wear them for your first performance.'

Their faces fell but they dutifully tried on the trainers, not wanting to go against the wishes of Davina, who was the host of the show. When they eventually found out it was a wind up each girl had a fit and then cracked up laughing. That's what it was like all the time in the house. It was full of fun, like being on a daft girls' holiday.

I phoned my mam most days and she would always tell me if there had been a mention of anything to do with *Popstars* in the papers. There were bits of tittle-tattle all the time, with stories of the girls sneaking out of the house to party with the boys and silly things like that. I never took much notice because I wasn't involved, but one day my mam phoned me up to warn me there was going to be a story all about me, and it didn't sound good.

'Cheryl, I think someone's done one of them kiss-and-tells on ya.'

My mind went into overdrive. Only the day before I'd spoken to my dad, and he'd told me, 'I'm so proud of you I could pop.' Now my mind was going crazy. I was wondering what had been written about me, and what my family was about to read. Mam didn't know what was in the story yet, explaining that she'd just taken a phone call at home from a reporter trying to get her to make a comment, and she thought she'd better let me know.

I panicked and worried about every single boy I'd ever kissed, until I actually got to read the article the next day.

I was totally stunned to discover it was a completely fabricated kiss-and-tell from a guy who used to come in Nupi's café, who I didn't even remember talking to.

This was my first experience of being the focus of a made-up tabloid story and I just couldn't believe a newspaper could print such rubbish and get away with it, but they did. It was so weird and frustrating to find myself in that situation. I felt incredibly uncomfortable; the feeling was like nothing I'd ever experienced in my life before. I had to phone my dad and tell him the guy had made it all up, and warn him not to read the paper, which was just horrible, especially so soon after he had told me how proud he was of me.

Not surprisingly, my heart stopped when my mam phoned me again a few weeks later to tell me there was going to be another story on me in the papers.

'Oh my God, what next?' I asked. I was still rattled by the last one, and I wasn't sure I could take another.

The live shows were in full swing now and even though I wasn't afraid of being kicked off, I was suffering badly with anxiety each time I had to step up to the mic. My nerves used to completely consume my body, in fact. Even if I sang perfectly it felt to me like they were trying to take the breath out of my body on every note.

'Just tell me, mother. Nothing can be as bad as the last story.'

'It's not like that, Cheryl,' my mam said. 'Some of your friends have hung a banner over the Tyne Bridge. It's huge and it says "Vote For Cheryl Tweedy". They had to get special permission from the council.'

I burst out laughing, as much with relief as pleasure. That was pretty special. Geordies are so proud of their own, and it gave me a real boost.

I was doing really well in the competition and getting voted through each time. I can't remember any of the comments now, but I know the girls competed against each other every fortnight, alternating weekly with the boys. Each time I'd think, 'Am I really still here?' Being on the television didn't faze me, but the whole idea that I was being judged was horrible, because I wasn't used to being in that position when I was singing.

I found it very hard when some of the friends I'd made started to be voted off, and it was absolutely terrible when my roommate Aimee went. I genuinely wished I could go in her place, because I was older and felt I could cope with the rejection better.

My mam and sister came to the final show and were cheering like mad in the audience, but practically the only thing I can remember in amongst all the tension and excitement is Davina standing up to announce which five of us, out of the six remaining girls, had made it into the band.

'The first member of the band is ...' I could almost hear my heart beating.

'Cheryl!'

I jumped out of my seat, looking more like a Newcastle fan when the team had just scored than a pop singer, and the memory of it still makes me cringe.

Davina had to make me sit down and I perched on a stool in disbelief, shaking and trembling as first Nicola, then Kimberley and finally Nadine and Sarah took their seats next to me. Javine was the sixth girl who hadn't made it, and I was absolutely gutted for her.

The rest of us just started screaming at each other, and we kept on screaming for what felt like the whole night. I remember going up to the bar and being pulled from pillar to post by so many people wanting to congratulate us. Then it was straight to a London hotel, because we still had the competition with the boys to go through, and the record label wanted us to start work the very next morning. I lay in bed staring at the ceiling for literally the whole night. I couldn't sleep a wink. I had adrenalin pumping through my veins so fast I thought I was going to go bang. I was absolutely *euphoric*. My life was changed. I felt it, very strongly, as I lay there in the dark. My life was going to be different now. I was a member of Girls Aloud, as the band had been named. And I just knew that we were going to absolutely smash the boys when it came to the battle for the Christmas number one, which was our next challenge.

Looking back, I was completely naïve about the world I had entered. I desperately wanted to be on the *Smash Hits Poll Winners' Party* show on TV because I'd always watched it as a kid, and in my head I would be able to do that now. Going on that show, and on *Top of the Pops*, was the be-all and end-all for me.

It never occurred to me that there was a lot more to the music industry than making records and singing on a stage. I should have known better, especially after the whole kiss-and-tell hoo-hah, but it still took me totally by surprise the first time Girls Aloud were criticised in the press.

The headline was incredibly rude. 'Porkstars: The Rivals' it said, or something like that. It was true that we'd gained a few pounds between us. Javine's chicken and rice had seen to it that *my* weight had gone up to more than nine stone, which was the heaviest I'd ever been. At just five-foot three the extra weight did make me look on the chubby side, but I was still shocked that the whole band was under scrutiny for something that seemed so un-newsworthy and had nothing whatsoever to do with our music.

I'd never looked at food as a problem, ever. Food was never an issue in my life, and growing up I never knew anybody who was on a diet. You just ate what was put out for you, and that's what I'd done in the *Popstars* house. Now, it seemed, I was paying a price.

To make matters worse, as the boys-versus-girls chart battle got under way, we were working every hour God sent in the recording studio, as well as making our first video, promoting Girls Aloud on radio and TV shows and generally doing our best to put the boy band, One True Voice, down at every opportunity.

For two weeks we just got in a car with our newly appointed tour manager, a lovely guy called John McMahon, and went all over the country, appearing on *GMTV* and *CD:UK* and giving interviews to radio stations and magazines. We ate McDonald's for breakfast, dinner and tea some days, or we'd fill up on pizzas and rubbish we picked up at service stations. We never ate one bit of green for a whole fortnight, and at the end of it we got a phone call from Louis Walsh, who had been appointed manager of Girls Aloud.

'Lose weight,' he told us bluntly, and we were all so shocked we actually listened. That was the only good bit of advice Louis ever provided actually, and it gave us a big reality check. It made us realise that we weren't just being picked on by the press with their 'Porkstars' headline because they didn't have another angle for a story. We really were eating an unhealthy amount of junk food, and it had to stop. We had new jobs, and looking our best was part of the job description.

Looking back, it says a hell of a lot about the music industry that this is my abiding memory of those first two weeks. Here I was, doing what I'd dreamed of for years, yet only a tiny percentage of our energy was going into the actual singing and we were all starting to moan every day, about the early starts and long hours and the bad press we got.

'Good moaning,' became our make-up guy's regular early-morning joke when we got up and prepared for promos, as we all complained so much at having to get up at the crack of dawn. The battle with the boys got quite nasty, too. It was a *real* competition, and the media had the boys down to win. Everyone was saying that our single, 'The Sound of the Underground', was too 'out there', and that girls bought more records than boys and would back the boy band, and so One True Voice would beat us on sales.

'Do you wanna bet? Don't underestimate girl power,' I said time and time again.

I was back home in Newcastle, visiting my family, when I finally got the call I'd been dreaming of, telling me that Girls Aloud had annihilated the boys, and we actually had the Christmas number one. What's more, we were the first girl band *ever* to debut at number one.

It was simply amazing news, and I will never, ever forget my dad standing up in the local pub, where we had a party, and saying: 'I have to eat the biggest piece of humble pie ever, because Cheryl told me as a child she was gonna have a number one and be on *Top of the Pops*, and I told her to take her head out of the clouds.'

I imagined 2003 was going to be the best year of my life so far. The girls and I had all started to bond really well as a group, and we were all really excited about recording our first album together.

I was living the dream, and nothing was going to burst my bubble.

5

'You're arresting *me*?'

'I'm really sorry to be the one to tell you this, Cheryl, but John has died in a car accident.'

It was Sundraj Sreenivasan on the phone, head of publicity for Polydor, Girls Aloud's record label. I could scarcely believe it, but he was talking about John McMahon, the guy who'd driven us all over the country when we were frantically promoting ourselves as a newly formed band. All of us girls had spent more time with John in the past month than with anybody else but each other. He was 43 and had children, and we all thought he was such a great person. He'd been so much more than a tour manager; he'd been like a dad to us really, looking after us and making sure we had everything we needed. It just didn't seem real at all.

'What happened?' I cried, unable to stop the tears rolling down my cheeks.

John had been drinking, and he'd crashed into a telephone pole near his home in Stafford on Christmas Day. He was actually in the car we'd toured in, which had Girls Aloud painted on the side, and he had died at the scene. All of us girls went to his funeral just after the New Year, which made us bond even more, but in a way none of us could ever have anticipated.

The record was still number one, but the moment had passed, and we all just huddled together saying to one another, 'Are you alright?' We were lost for words, and none of us could believe our eyes when photographers turned up at the funeral and took pictures of us crying.

'That's disgusting,' I said to Nicola. 'His family has got to grieve in peace.'

'I know, it's sick,' Nicola replied, and she sobbed her little heart out.

I felt super protective towards Nicola. Not only was she the youngest in the band, but she had also received the worst press so far. She had been branded the 'ugly one' of the group, and one magazine even published a picture of her with a brown paper bag over her head. I didn't understand how anyone could be so cruel towards such a young girl. To me, Nicola was the funny one, like the sweet little sister I never had. It was downright nasty. We were all fat and she was ugly. It wasn't even as if we were super famous or were parading around like divas, asking to be taken down a peg or two. We were just a bunch of young girls who'd been in the band for a matter of weeks, and all we wanted was to make a success of it.

'Do you fancy coming out to a club?' a group of guys asked. It was the week after John's funeral, we were still at number one in the charts and we'd also started to record our first album. Nicola and I were having a drink together in the bar of a hotel we were staying at near Guildford, as it was close to the recording studio.

'Shall we?' Nicola said.

'Why not?' I said. It was the first time we'd had a chance to really let our hair down after all the stress of the funeral, and we'd been working hard in the studio all day.

I was in the mood to party and had been in high spirits in the bar, but when we set off with the guys I had the strongest gut feeling ever, telling me not to go out. It was overwhelming but I ignored it, which is something I have learned never to do again.

We went to The Drink nightclub in Guildford. As soon as we arrived, Nicola and I were recognised by the management, who welcomed us into the VIP area and sent us champagne. This was all new territory to us and we were having great fun. I'm not a good drinker, though, and I get drunk really easily. We lost the guys almost straight away and decided it was boring on our own in the VIP area. We wanted to be with all the other young girls having fun in the club. Nicola and I hit the dance floor crazily for about an hour, making friends with a group of girls who also recognised us, before I decided I needed to go to the toilet. Nicola came with me, and I was surprised to see there was a female attendant in the Ladies, selling sweets and perfume. I'd never seen that in a club before, and after I'd been to the loo I asked her if we could buy some lollipops.

I was used to buying sweets in shops like Cloughs, which was an old-fashioned sweet shop on Heaton Road, legendary in my area back home. There, you helped yourself to whichever sweets you wanted and paid the old lady, Mrs Clough, when your paper bag was full.

I wanted five lollipops; one each for Nicola and me, and one each for the three girls we'd met on the dance floor.

After I picked up the lollipops I started fishing in my purse for the 50 pence I owed the toilet attendant, with Nicola standing right beside me, reapplying her make-up. Then, completely out of nowhere, I was hit in the face. I swear on my mother's life that's what happened. I remember very clearly hearing Nicola screaming in her thick Scouse accent: 'Oh my God, warra ya doin'?'

'Go and get security!' I screamed.

It was the toilet attendant who had hit me and, in confusion and self-defence, I hit her back instinctively.

Everything happened so fast. Before I knew it, I was being bear-hugged by the security guy, who was carrying me out of the toilet and taking me back to the VIP area. The club was extremely apologetic, and Nicola and I accepted the apologies from the management and asked if the three girls we'd met could come into the VIP area with us, where we sat and talked about what had just happened.

About 45 minutes later we were still in the VIP area when I spotted some police officers in high vis jackets come into the club.

I was still drunk, and in my drunken state I said to Nicola and the girls: 'Do you think I should go and tell them what happened in the toilet?'

I don't think they even had a chance to answer me before a policeman came over and told me they were there to arrest me.

'You're arresting *me*? You're joking!' I said. I was absolutely stunned. 'The toilet attendant started it. I'm the one who got hit in the face first. I only hit her back.'

It was no good protesting. In total disbelief I was driven away in a police car, crying and shaking, and was locked up in a cell in Guildford police station. Nicola was completely distraught, and she had to go back to the hotel on her own and tell the other girls what had happened.

'Just tell the truth, Cheryl, and you can't go wrong.' That's what my mam had always taught me, and I really believed that if I just told the police the whole truth they would let me go.

I sobered up pretty quickly in the cell, and I sat there quietly, feeling self-conscious in the little black top and burgundy trousers I had on. They took away my high heels and gave me some little flat shoes with smiley faces on, which seemed like a complete joke. I just wanted to get this over with and get out of there.

'You're being accused of assault,' a police officer told me eventually, after 11 hours in the cell.

My heart stopped.

'But she hit me first and I just retaliated!'

I started to cry.

'Where is she?' I asked. 'Why isn't the toilet attendant in here, why isn't she being accused of assault too?'

I just couldn't believe it. I'd only been in the group for three weeks. I was number one in the charts, and I was locked in a police cell with the threat of an assault charge hanging over me.

What was it Gillian had said to me that time, when our car window got smashed in during one of our trips to London? '*Why is there always some kind of drama with you, Cheryl?*'

I was beginning to ask myself the same question, because it did always seem to be me at the centre of a drama. I gave the police a full statement and was released on bail in the morning, which was just as well as I was due to record something for *Ant & Dec's Saturday Night Takeaway* show that day with the girls.

The news hadn't been in the press yet and so I just asked make-up to cover up the bruise that had appeared on my face, and got on with the recording. I couldn't tell you what I said or did on the show; my head was just filled with worry and confusion.

All the time I was just telling myself: 'Tell the truth, and it'll all be OK,' but I didn't bank on what was about to happen next.

A newspaper story appeared showing the toilet attendant with a big black eye. She'd been wearing glasses, and the bruise was really bad. It was horrible to look at and I couldn't believe it was me who had done that. That was shocking enough to take in, but I was absolutely flabbergasted by what she was saying about me.

'She punched me in the eye and screamed, "You f***ing black bitch ..."' was what the woman told the newspaper. I was also meant to have called her a 'Caribbean jigaboo', although I'd never even heard that phrase before. It wasn't the sort of language we used in Newcastle and I didn't even know what it meant.

'We're re-arresting you,' the police said when I went to the station to answer bail.

'No way! Is this some kind of a sick joke?'

Unfortunately it wasn't, even though the woman had not made any allegations of racism against me in her initial statement to the police. That had only come out in the newspaper, and I later discovered that she subsequently changed her police statement, four days later, to match what she had told the newspaper.

'The journalists must have put words in her mouth,' I protested. 'I would never say anything like that. I'm not a racist – ask anyone who knows me. *Anyone.*'

It was no good. I had fingerprints and a mug shot taken and in the March, two months after the incident, I was charged with racially aggravated actual bodily harm.

'I'll leave the group,' I told the girls, and I meant it, wholeheartedly.

'I'm not spoiling things for the four of you. This was my mistake and I'll take the rap.'

I'd been through hell every day. I had literally worried myself sick for two months, and once I was charged I felt much worse. This was a very serious allegation, and to be accused of being a racist was utterly devastating. I had black friends, and literally *anybody* who knew me could have vouched for the fact I was most definitely not a racist.

'You don't have to leave the band. Absolutely not,' the girls all said to me, even though I knew they'd all been suffering too.

'But I don't want to ruin your careers. I'm strong enough to bounce back. I'll just go, it's best for everyone.'

'No way!' they each told me. 'You're staying with us.'

We'd got to know each other really well by now. Nicola and I had become very close, and I'd gelled really easily with Kimberley and Nadine. Sarah was trickier. She'd been brought up practically as an only child as her brother was 16 years older than her, and she didn't know how to be with other girls initially. We all accepted her the way she was though, and there was never any problem with that.

Despite having the court case hanging over me I did my best to focus on the band, and the girls and I worked very well together in the studio, putting together our first album. The bosses at Polydor told me they were standing by me, and the support really kept me going in the months leading up to the trial, in October 2003.

In every single interview I was asked relentlessly about 'the incident'. I couldn't say anything until the case had gone to court, which was just so annoying. I felt like everywhere I went people were judging me or feeling wary of me and it broke my heart to think that some people must actually have believed I attacked the woman because she was black.

'It's just ridiculous. Why are you even bothered?' my mam said when I poured out my heart to her about how upset I was by the racist allegations.

'*You* know it's ridiculous but other people don't,' I said. 'It's hell. I've gone from the happiest I've ever been to being dragged so low, practically overnight.'

'The truth will come out in court,' my mam said. 'Don't worry about it.'

I'm sure I would have sunk into depression again if I hadn't been so busy with the group. The girls and I had something on every day all day, whether it was doing photoshoots, radio and TV shows or fittings and rehearsals. I should have been living my dream, but the truth was the court case hung over me like a dark cloud, taking the shine off everything.

'Spill,' Nicola would say when we got home at the end of the day and she could see I was upset. The record label had found us all one-bedroom flats in Westminster because the location was handy, but we all hated it because the building looked like an old folks' home. Nicola's flat was right next to mine, and having her to confide in was a godsend.

'I feel like people are wary of me, even in the studio,' I'd tell her. 'It's either that or they're crackin' stupid jokes, and it's just not funny.'

'Get lost! People aren't scared of you,' Nicola would say. 'And nobody thinks it's funny. They're just trying to cheer you up.'

Nicola was a little rock, and it helped so much that she had actually been there that night and knew exactly what had gone on in the nightclub.

I must admit, when the incident first took place my immediate reaction had been to think I had done nothing wrong whatsoever. In my mind, because of the way I'd been brought up, I thought that acting in self-defence was a reasonable excuse for hitting the woman. As the months went on and I prepared for the trial, I started to see that it was not acceptable to have hit her under any circumstances, even in self-defence. I was prepared to say that in court, and I was actually looking forward to taking the stand because I wanted the whole truth to come out, and I had absolutely nothing to hide.

'Wear the same outfit every day,' Sundraj advised, because we knew the case would go on for several days. 'Then the media hasn't got a new picture of you to use.'

If I'd needed any more proof of how this case had become as much about my newfound fame as my behaviour in the nightclub, that was it. Throughout the trial there were journalists camped outside Kingston Crown Court, and I hated having to walk past them each day.

As soon as I sat in the dock I was flanked by two big security men.

'Like I'm gonna run anywhere,' I thought. 'I wouldn't get very far with the media following me.'

When it was the toilet attendant's turn to take the stand she appeared to be flapping and stuttering, which didn't surprise me at all. The court heard that she went straight from the hospital, where she had her black eye treated, and back to the club, where it was alleged that staff were already putting their heads together to come up with a good story to sell to the press.

The court also heard that the racism allegation only emerged after the *Sunday Mirror* became involved in the story, and on top of that, two girls came forward independently to say they had been the victim of unprovoked attacks by the same toilet attendant in completely separate incidents.

I knew it had gone well, but waiting for the verdict to be delivered felt like an absolute eternity.

'Guilty or not guilty?' I heard the judge say. It was a horrible moment.

I was cleared of racially aggravated assault but convicted of assault occasioning actual bodily harm. It was a bitter-sweet victory because the toilet attendant had wrongly accused me of being a racist *and* she had hit me, yet she walked away scot-free.

I had to pay her £500 compensation and £3,000 prosecution costs, and I was ordered to do 120 hours of unpaid community service.

Afterwards it felt like I'd been subjected to two trials – one in court and one in the media. The tabloid 'verdict' on me was summed up in one very memorable headline that appeared the next day: 'The Girl's a Lout but she's not a Racist'.

'How do you feel?' Sundraj asked me.

'Shocked at how newspapers can print lies and get away with it. It's terrifying, actually.'

'You must be relieved, though?'

'"Relieved" is not a word I would use. I've still got to do the community service and it feels unjust – I just wish this whole thing would go away.'

I asked if I could do the community service in Newcastle, because I wanted to go home and get it over and done with, away from the press in London. When I look back through old diaries, I can see that in between the trial and completing my community service I was working flat out with the group, promoting our new single, 'Jump', every day. We performed it on *Top of the Pops* and went on stage at the National Music Awards, and when 'Jump' was chosen as part of the soundtrack for the movie *Love Actually*, all five of us walked the red carpet together at the film premiere in Leicester Square. Earlier the same night, Kimberley and I appeared on *The Frank Skinner Show* too. I would never have remembered any of those things if I hadn't been reminded, and that says a lot about how the trial had affected me.

I'd suffered very badly with stress throughout the whole ordeal, and I was still suffering for a long time afterwards. I was traumatised, basically, and I'd lost weight because it made me feel physically sick to put something in my mouth.

'I can't stomach it,' I said all the time, because that's actually how it felt. I was so full of worry that I felt that I couldn't fit anything else inside me. The stress took over everything. It should have been so memorable to walk the red carpet for the very first time, especially when we had the honour of being involved in the film in a small way, but it's a blank in my mind.

Similarly, I have no recollection of being on *Frank Skinner*, although apparently all he wanted to talk about was the trial. I've always felt I had a bad memory attached to him, but I couldn't have told you what it was without reminding myself of that interview.

I really couldn't get over how ironic it was that I'd gone through my whole life with trouble *around* me, yet had never been involved with the police myself until I was at the happiest point in my life, celebrating having a record-breaking number one.

It was only once the trial was over that I began to think like that as I tried to make some kind of sense of it all, but it was really confusing. I found it impossible to take in how my life could go so far forwards and then backwards so quickly.

The community service actually wasn't half as bad as I expected it to be. In fact, it probably did me good to get away from all the madness in London and just be normal and feel more like myself again in Newcastle for a while.

I started off sanding down benches at a little football club, which wasn't difficult, just boring. I'd seen my dad sand things down and paint them my whole life, and I just got on with it like he always did. I also worked in a Salvation Army charity shop in the city centre, making cups of tea and sorting out old bags of clothes in the back.

I was there for a month or so; certainly long enough to bond with the staff, because they cried when I left.

One day, when I was sanding down the benches, I got caught by a press photographer, while I was yawning.

'Why would anyone want a picture of me yawning?' I said to my mam.

We were in her kitchen, eating a Chinese from my favourite takeaway, the Kwok Pao, which was the one we'd used for as long as I could remember.

'Well, I wouldn't know, Cheryl. Seems odd to me,' Mam said, and that was the end of the conversation. There was no

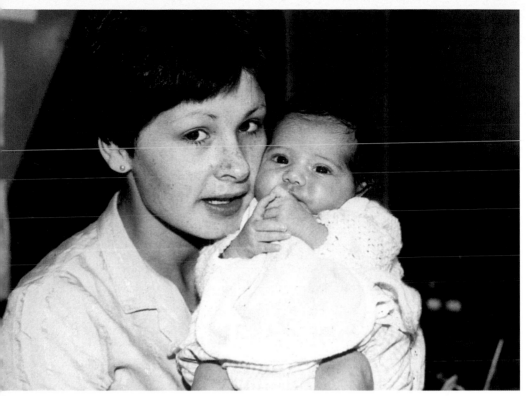

This is me aged six weeks with my mam, Joan. She was twenty-four when I was born, making her a mam of four.

Here I am in 1986, coming up for three, posing with my siblings. Joe, ten, is at the back, Andrew is six and my sister Gillian is seven.

I'm three here, posing for the camera in Boots. Mam entered me for loads of 'bonny baby'-type competitions.

Mam took me into a passport photo booth while I was still in the pink dress I'd worn in Boots. She wanted a photo for her purse.

Here I am sitting on my dad's knee aged four. This is in our old family home on Cresswell Street in Byker, where my dad, Garry, always had music playing.

This is me aged seven and my little brother Garry, aged three, posing for my dad. He was a painter and decorator but wanted to be a photographer at the time.

This is me at home in June 1993, just before I went to the Royal Ballet's summer school. I nearly didn't go because Mam and Dad couldn't afford it.

Here I'm showing off my ballet skills on a photoshoot for *Gimme 5*, a popular Tyne Tees children's television programme when I was growing up.

I loved ballroom dancing as much as ballet for a few years. Here I'm with a girl called Amy from my dance school, smiling after we won a competition.

This one was taken at home (check out the background sheet!) to be sent off to various modelling agencies I was on the books of.

This is me aged eight with James Richardson, my ballroom dancing partner, after winning the Northern Counties Championship.

I took part in lots of fashion shows throughout my childhood, and this is me after winning first prize in one.

▶ Big break for 13-year-old with spot on same bill as teen favourites

ST★R G★ZER

Picture: BILL LAWSON

The local press always supported me. This is an article about me performing on the same bill as Ultimate Kaos, a popular boy band back then. I was thirteen.

● BIG TIME – teenager Cheryl Tweedy who will sing for 9,000 youngsters on the same bill as some top teeny acts

By PETE LEYDON

SINGING sensation Cheryl Tweedy is to perform in front of 9,000 fans at just 13.

The Tyneside teenager will share the stage at the Hull Arena next Friday with hit bands like Let Loose, Bizarre Inc and Ultimate Kaos.

It's the break solo artist Cheryl, from Byker, Newcastle, has been dreaming of since her singing career was launched a year ago - by mistake.

That's when schoolgirl Cheryl turned up for dancing auditions at her school, Walker Comprehensive, Newcastle.

The tape she was supposed to dance along to was lost, so she had to sing through her routine. Her voice impressed watching promoters so much they signed her up.

This year she has already performed at Newcastle's Tyne Theatre and City Hall, and has completed a summer season singing at Metroland, Gateshead.

Her manager, Andrew Falconer, of Newcastle's Bucket and Spade promotions, said: "Because she's only 13 most people wouldn't take her seri-

ously and we were having trouble getting her into the big time.

"But London agency Dance Crazy, who monitor a few North East bands, have given her the chance at this show in Hull Arena.

Perform

"She'll be dashing straight out of school at 3.30pm on Friday and into a car to get there on time."

During her 15-minute slot, Cheryl will perform three of her own songs, Girl's Life, Can You Hear Me Knocking, and I've Gonna Get You.

Cheryl, who lives with mum Joan and her three brothers, said: "I was so excited when we got the call to say

● STAR BAND – Let Loose, one of the bands on the same bill at Hull Arena as Cheryl Tweedy, 13

I would be performing. I'm really looking forward to it.

"I wanted to be a dancer originally and went to audition for a pause. Two months later I had a contract as a singer. It's my ambition to make it to the top."

Cheryl will be in London the following week to perform for record producers at show venue The Black Cat Club. The trip has been paid for by one record company, and two others have shown interest in offering Cheryl big-time deals.

Andrew said: "When people hear how old she is they can't believe it. She has a very mature voice and a wise head on her shoulders."

This is me backstage with Haydon from Ultimate Kaos.

Here I am at the Royal Ballet summer school, held at White Lodge in Richmond. I'm ten, and not really enjoying myself.

Once I was well established as a performer at Metroland I started going to London to record music. Here I'm fifteen, at the home of Ricky, a musician friend.

I was a big fan of Destiny's Child, and I wanted to be like Beyoncé. This was my attempt to try to look like her by having my hair bleached blonde.

My nephew Warren was born in 2000, when I was sixteen. I was with my sister Gillian when she gave birth, and here I am with Warren aged two.

This is one of my first 'artist' cards I had made for me when I was trying to make it as a singer.

AIM MUSIC
CLARA VALE COMPLEX
CLARA VALE, RYTON,
TYNE & WEAR, NE40 3SU

CHERYL

Me and Dad. He could not have been prouder when I won a place on the TV show *Popstars: The Rivals*.

analysis or soul searching about how my life or career was going. My mam just cleared away the dirty dishes and we watched *EastEnders* together.

'How are all the girls?' she asked. That was about the most probing question she put to me.

'Fine,' I said. 'They've all been great, actually.'

This was true, and my relationship with the rest of the girls was just about the best thing in my life at that time. We were all very different, and during our first year together we'd started to fall into particular roles.

Kimberley was the sensible one who was very good at business figures. She knew where every penny was going and she'd sign stuff off with the accountants for us and always knew if someone was being overpaid. On the advice of the label, we'd moved out of Westminster and into new two-bedroom apartments in a posh complex called Princess Park Manor in Friern Barnet, North London. I shared with Nicola, while Kimberley shared with Nadine and Sarah chose to live alone.

I've no idea how much the weekly rent was because Kimberley arranged for it to be paid before we got our wages, which was a smart move. During the first year we weren't earning a fortune, but it was enough pocket money for a teenage girl to have. In the early months I actually used some of it to pay off the Provi man back home, as I owed him several hundred pounds. Once I'd cleared my debts I saved up and splashed out on a diamond cluster ring for myself. It cost £900 and was my absolute pride and joy.

In total contrast to Kimberley, Sarah was always the party girl, enjoying the lifestyle of a pop star and having fun being in the group. Sarah also liked being in the studio, and she was so enthusiastic about singing. Her character definitely added to the group, without a doubt. She sometimes told us she felt a bit left out, but whenever we said 'Come and live with us then!' she always refused. In fact she was the first one to move away from us, out of Princess Park.

Nicola is a very observant person and a very good listener, and even if she doesn't agree with something she just takes it all in. It's a special quality to have, but when it comes to music she's very opinionated. I always sat up and listened whenever Nicola had something to say about the music, because it was always really useful and interesting, and it's still like that to this day.

Nadine was the lead singer and would go into the studio before the rest of us and record the demos. We'd then all choose from the tracks she had recorded and work out who was singing what around her vocals.

Standing up for us as a band and fronting up to the label was usually my job. I was forever asking what the next single was going to be, and if I didn't agree with the choice I told the bosses in no uncertain terms, 'This is a load of crap. We're not doing it!'

I said that of 'Love Machine', actually, which looking back is quite embarrassing as it became one of our best-selling singles. It's hardly surprising I became known as the 'gobby one' of the group, but I wasn't outspoken for the sake of it, I just did it when I thought I needed to fight our corner.

We'd never had any media training and Louis Walsh was nowhere to be seen in terms of managing us, so if anybody said anything bad about us I just used to say exactly what was on my mind. I remember a few years down the line Lily Allen said something bitchy about Nicola and Sarah, and I wasn't having it. Stuff like that bugged the shit out of me and I had a massive go at her, publicly. It was the same with Ulrika Jonsson and Charlotte Church, who both criticised me in years to come. I didn't ask for their opinion and I would never have wanted to start a public spat, but I retaliated because it's in my character to protect myself and the people I care about.

Within the group, though, we honestly never had any bust ups, apart from one morning when Nadine was literally three hours late getting in the car and we all completely lost it.

'You're taking the p***!' we all shouted at her. 'You've been getting later and later every day and we can't be sitting around waiting for you like this!' I think she had just overslept, and she was very apologetic and never did it again.

It was a miracle we didn't fall out more often. In the first couple of years the five of us were practically only apart to sleep because the workload was that intense. We'd eat together and chill out together, often watching *Friends* on TV in each others' flats or going out. We loved to go to clubs in London and we'd drink disgusting bubble-gum shots that were sky blue. I was always the worst drinker, never able to keep up with the others.

'How come you can all drink for fun and I can't?' I'd complain the next day when I had a banging headache and the rest of the girls were all completely fine. I'd get horribly drunk after just a couple of glasses of wine or vodkas and Red Bull, while the other girls would just be buzzing and having a good time. Even Sarah, being the party animal of the group, never got into some of the states I did. Once I actually got refused *into* a club because I was so drunk. 'I'm mortified,' I said to Nicola the next morning. I even had to get her to tell me exactly what had happened, because I couldn't remember half of it.

All the other girls had boyfriends, some more serious than others, but I was never in a relationship in those early years. I had my share of dates, but nothing serious. I think I was just too scared to let anybody in after what I'd gone through before, and the pain both Dave and Jason had caused me in my teens had not been forgotten, not yet.

'You can use the main bathroom and I'll have the bedroom with the en-suite,' I said to Nicola on the day we moved in to Princess Park Manor. She used to put on so much fake tan and it was always absolutely everywhere, and I just couldn't be doing with sharing a bathroom with her.

The apartment was very swanky and it was hard to believe we actually lived there. It was all newly painted with wood flooring and clean lines. There was a balcony off the living room and an absolutely massive TV. The first time we saw it we laughed our heads off. 'Look at the state of us!' we giggled.

The complex had been built around an old Victorian mental hospital that had been converted into loads of luxury apartments, set in acres of parkland. Security guards manned the gates and inside there were tennis courts, a pool and a gym that had been built in an old converted church.

Despite all the luxury, Nicola and I hadn't learned much since our days in the *Popstars* house and we still managed to live like students. 'Shall I make us a bacon butty?' was about the extent of Nicola's cooking skills, and she'd put the rashers in the micro-wave. We left sweet wrappers on the floor, pizza boxes all over the kitchen worktops and our bedrooms were always a complete tip with clothes, shoes, make-up and cans of hairspray strewn everywhere.

We turned it into a flea-pit at first, to be honest. We were still so young and, with working such long hours all the time, we found it almost impossible to take care of ourselves *and* an apartment properly.

'Have you worked out how to use the washing machine yet?' my mam asked a few weeks after we moved in.

'Er, funny you should say that, Mam. I was going to ask you to show us when you came down.' Sometimes we would literally have no clean clothes to put on unless my mother came down and did the washing for us.

The only improvement I made to my lifestyle was that I did start to exercise and think about my diet a bit more, and one day I read an article in a magazine about Jennifer Aniston doing the Atkins Diet.

'That sounds good,' I said to Nicola, who didn't pay much attention, as she never had to worry about dieting.

'She looks amazing on *Friends*. I'm going to get the book.'

For the first time in my life I began to educate myself about the different food groups, and I started to eat meat, eggs, bacon and cheese and avoid fruit, veg and carbohydrates. The weight started to fall off, and over the next few months I actually lost 16 pounds.

At the same time I was working out on the treadmill in the gym because I didn't have a clue how to use any of the other equipment. Kimberley would come with me and we'd just run for as long as we could, watching how many calories we burned.

The label had obviously noticed that a bit of exercise wouldn't do us any harm, and they got us a personal trainer, who ran a boot camp for us in a gym near our recording studios in Kent. It was down in a little village called Westerham, and the studios were in the home of our music producer, Brian Higgins, who ran the record production company Xenomania and was responsible for all of Girls Aloud's music.

Louis was out of the picture completely by now, although on paper he was still our manager. I think in those first two years we probably had two phone calls from him, so we were on a huge learning curve, trying to be across every nook and cranny of the business and do the best we could with absolutely no experience whatsoever and very little help.

'We're putting you in a cage,' I remember being told when we made our very first video, for 'Sound of the Underground'.

'Wow!' I said. 'Sounds amazing!'

I was so grateful to have got into the band and to be doing what I'd always wanted to do that if they'd said, 'Go out and do it for free', I'd have done so willingly.

That first videoshoot was a total eye-opener. It was done on a limited budget, nothing seemed to go smoothly and the styling was awful. It felt like we shot it and re-shot it for 24 solid hours, stuck in a freezing cold warehouse, and afterwards we were all half-dead.

On photoshoots I had one technique, and that was to smile.

'What are we meant to be doing?' we'd say to each other constantly.

'Just smile!' we'd say, because we didn't have a clue what else to do.

We never complained about anything though really, because we loved being busy and we were all young and fresh and raring to go. Nothing was a problem.

We would often bump into other bands like Busted and Big Brovaz, who were 'on promo' at the same time as us, which meant we'd be crossing paths with them at various TV and radio studios. It was always exciting because we felt so un-famous compared to them, but it was amazing how quickly it all became so normal to see people I'd been in awe of not very long before. I'd say 'hi' to the boys exactly like I would with my friends back in Newcastle, and we all started giving each other familiar, knowing looks, as if to say, 'Good luck with your umpteenth interview of the day, we know exactly what it's like …'

There were always a few stories doing the rounds about boys I was meant to be dating or having relationships with. One of them was supposedly Duncan from Blue, which is hilarious, as he later came out as gay. I was forever on the phone telling my dad, 'Don't read that. It's a load of crap.'

'OK, sweetheart,' he'd say. 'As long as you're alright. You are alright, aren't ya?'

'Yes, Dad, I'm more than alright. I'm living me dream,' I'd say, because finally it was true. The court case was behind me, Girls Aloud were doing well, and I had a very strong feeling that my life could only get better.

6

'Ashley treats me like a princess'

'Can Ashley have your number?'

It was the footballer Jermaine Pennant, and I knew he was talking about his friend Ashley Cole.

'No,' I said straight away. It was a gut reaction. I knew what footballers were like and I wasn't interested, even though I did think Ashley was very cute-looking. 'Absolutely not.'

Of the two or three guys I had dated in the last year or so, one had been a footballer, and he'd messed with my head a bit. It wasn't anything serious, but he was the sort of guy who said he'd phone and then left it for weeks. I couldn't be bothered with it all, and I'd said to Kimberley just days before that I was more than happy being single. We were in a busy phase with the band in any case, with a new single and album to get out, and we were even thinking about planning our first ever tour, which I was really excited about.

I'd said 'hi' to Ashley a few times when we'd seen each other around Princess Park Manor. He had an apartment on the other side to where Nicola and I lived and I'd see him out on the tennis courts. One time, after he'd played for England in Euro 2004, I'd said 'congratulations' because I knew the team had done well.

Ashley was very bashful and I think he even blushed, which I found quite sweet.

'There's Ashley again,' Kimberley said to me one afternoon in July 2004. We were on our way to the shops to buy electric fans because the weather was so warm, and Ashley was standing beside the tennis courts fiddling with something on his Aston Martin. We pulled over in Kimberley's car to see what the problem was.

'Have you got a jump lead?' Ashley asked shyly. 'We've run the battery down.' It turned out he'd been listening to loud music from his car's sound system while he and Jermaine played tennis.

'I think I have,' Kimberley said, which made me laugh. It was typical of Kimberley to be prepared for every eventuality. We gave the boys the jump lead and left them to it, and a few days later Ashley came over to me when he saw me around the complex.

'I wanted to say thank you,' he said. 'And can I have your number please?' I think he'd had a drink and he didn't look as shy as before, but I gave him the same answer.

'I'm sorry, I'm not interested.'

'Sure?'

'Yes, I'm sure.'

I was on my way to the gym, and I walked off thinking to myself, 'He's gorgeous, actually.'

The next time I bumped into Ashley, not long afterwards, I was secretly pleased when he asked me yet again for my number.

'OK then,' I said, and I don't think Ashley was prepared for that answer.

'I'll, er, text you,' he said, blushing and smiling.

The first text I received from him a few days later said: 'Wot u up 2?' to which I replied: 'Not much, wot u up 2?'

We started texting each other loads after that, and we were both beginning to wonder where we could go from there.

'We can't go out, can we?' I said to Nicola.

'No!' she said. 'Not unless you want the press out with you. What are you gonna do then?'

Ashley's friends were all saying the same thing, and he texted me one day and invited me over to his flat for a drink. I was cool with that. I didn't know what to expect and I just went round in my jeans and a jumper and thought 'whatever'.

He had a friend there when I arrived, who stayed for a few hours, which looking back is funny and typical of Ashley, and then he and I had a glass of wine together. He'd eaten a takeaway with his friend, and he put out a few nibbles but didn't cook for me. I can say that with absolute certainty, because Ashley never once cooked for me, in our whole relationship.

I wasn't bothered at all. We chatted about our families and our backgrounds and it felt very comfortable, right from the start. Ashley came from a council estate like me, and his mother, Sue, sounded quite similar to my mam, always having told Ashley and his brother Matthew to stand up for themselves and follow their dreams.

'Can I kiss you?' Ashley asked at the end of the night, and I found that really sweet. He was handsome and nice and shy. I'd only ever been out with people who became ugly once I got to know them. I couldn't ever imagine that happening with Ashley, because he was just so sweet, and I let him kiss me.

'He's gorgeous!' I giggled later, telling Nicola all about him. I was buzzing. I hadn't felt this way for a long time, and I couldn't wait for our second date a few days later.

'Cheryl, get in here!' Nicola screamed. I was due round at Ashley's in an hour and I wondered what on earth was going on. I'd been out shopping and got back to the flat to find the front door wide open and the bedroom doors both shut tight. Nicola's terrified cries were coming from my bedroom, and I ran in, panic-stricken.

'There's a cat in my room!' she shrieked. 'Shut the door! It's *huge*. It's like a lion!'

I started laughing, told Nicola not to panic and went back out and found the cat lounging on the floor of her bedroom. Admittedly, it was the biggest cat I'd ever seen in my life, but I managed to show it the door without too much trouble.

'It's only a cat,' I said to Nicola, but she was having none of it.

'That was *dead* scary!' she wailed. 'I never want to see that creature again! It won't come back, will it?'

An hour later, I arrived at Ashley's flat only to find him trembling on the doorstep.

'I'm not jokin', there's a cat in there the size of a tiger!' he shrieked.

He looked properly freaked out, actually, and was panicking just like Nicola.

'Let me in,' I said, rolling my eyes. 'I think I know the one you mean.'

Sure enough, the same gigantic cat was spread out on Ashley's furniture, purring contentedly, as if it owned the place.

It looked at me as if to say, 'Not you again – party pooper!' and snarled as I heaved it out onto the corridor.

I found it absolutely hilarious, especially as there were hundreds of apartments in the complex and Ashley's was miles away from ours.

'What are the chances of that?' I laughed, but I think Ashley was too shaken up to see the funny side.

I loved the fact he wasn't aggressive or arrogant as I imagined most footballers to be. He was one of Arsenal's biggest stars, he had loads of money and everybody seemed to adore him. In spite of all this he didn't act like the big 'I am' in any way at all. He was soft and gentle, which was just so attractive.

Ashley and I managed to see each other for about three months without the press finding out, which was the best thing ever. I began to spend more and more time in his flat, and we just clicked, in every way.

'Are you sure about this?' Kimberley would say to me. 'He's a footballer, and footballers have girls throwing themselves at them all the time …'

'He's not like that,' I always replied. 'Ashley treats me like a princess. He's the kindest, most reliable person I've ever been out with. If he's gonna to be 10 minutes late, he texts. He never lets me down, and he's so calm and gentle. He balances me personality out nicely.'

This was so true. I still suffered with my nerves. I might have been able to chuck the big cat out, but that had nothing to do with being emotionally strong, just streetwise and practical. Deep down, I was still insecure and anxious about so many things in my life. A knock on the door could scare me, for instance. The Domino's Pizza man would come to Ashley's flat and I'd practically jump out of my skin. The knock would take me right back to my childhood, to the days when the police would hammer on the door and search our house, looking for stuff Andrew had stolen.

One time, I remember Garry sitting in the lounge back home, playing a game on a laptop that his little friend from school had brought round. The police knocked on the door really aggressively, marched in and tried to seize it. Poor Garry told them, 'You can't take that. It belongs to me friend.' He was only about 10, and it must have been so awful for him.

Memories like that were still so vivid it didn't matter that I was sitting in a luxury flat, locked behind security gates. The knock on Ashley's front door could take me straight back to our council house in Heaton, and I would have my heart in my mouth just I had so many times in my childhood. I should never have had that amount of worry growing up. I blamed Andrew, and it was something I could never shake off.

I guess it's hardly surprising that one of the things I loved about Ashley, right from the start, was that I felt safe with him. He didn't invite trouble into our lives in any way at all, and I felt so comfortable in his company. I was happy to open up to him and tell him about my life and my past, because Ashley just listened patiently and didn't judge or even make much comment.

In our first few weeks together I told him about Dave and Jason and I also talked about my brother being in prison, but nothing fazed Ashley. He'd been brought up in a high-rise block of flats in the East End of London, the son of a white mother and black father. They split up when Ashley and his brother were little. His mam Sue raised the boys on her own, and although Ashley never said much about his childhood, I knew those early years weren't easy.

Ashley was first spotted by Arsenal when he was nine and had been incredibly spoilt by the club from then on, but he wasn't a spoilt person. I felt I could tell him absolutely anything about my ups and downs, because his own life had been so unusual, and so incredible. It was like we were meant to be together, and I knew I was falling in love with him.

'Show me your latest dance routine,' Ashley said one night. We were chilling out together in his flat, watching some old film, and this took me by surprise. Ashley was never very impressed by Girls Aloud because he wasn't into that kind of music, and we rarely talked about my job. It was the same with his football. I'd been brought up with my dad and brothers supporting Newcastle and that was my team, but I wasn't big on football and Arsenal didn't excite me at all. Unless it was a really big game I was far more interested in what time Ashley would be home from training than how well he'd played or where they were in the league.

'OK, I'll dance for you,' I giggled. I stood up and did some of the moves from our most recent video and Ashley laughed his head off at me. Admittedly it was a bit cheesy but I thought he was really cheeky to laugh like that.

I starting play-fighting with him, just messing about, and then all of a sudden he pulled me down onto the settee, looked me straight in the eye and said, 'I f***ing love you.'

Now it was my turn to laugh, because this was so unexpected. Ashley had clearly even managed to surprise himself, because when he heard what he'd said he actually went green in the face.

I was really touched, but I didn't say anything back to him that night. I think I knew that once I'd told him I felt the same way there was no going back. In my heart it felt like Ashley was 'the one', but I wasn't sure I was ready to admit that to him, or to myself. It took a good few days for me to crack, and then I sent him a text saying: 'I love u 2'. I felt so happy once I'd done that; the best I'd felt in years and years, in fact.

One night, in October, I went to the National Television Awards at the Royal Albert Hall with the girls, and afterwards we decided to go to the Funky Buddha nightclub in Mayfair. Ashley was there with his friends, and even though I was really pleased to see him, I felt a bit worried about the two of us being spotted in public together for the very first time.

I'd never been in a 'public relationship' with anyone in all the time I'd been in Girls Aloud, and I didn't know how to handle it.

Ashley and I had a dance and a few drinks together, and at the end of the night I said, 'I'll go first – you leave in 10 minutes.' I thought it would be that simple to avoid the press, but of course it wasn't and there was a story in *The Sun* the very next day that said: 'Cheryl is Ashley's Goalfriend'.

'I'm scared,' I told him.

'Don't worry about it, babe,' he told me. 'What does it really matter?'

'You're right, but I can't help it,' I said. 'I'm a born worrier.'

Not long after that we went shopping to Bluewater together. We had a lovely time, strolling round the shops and having some lunch. Ashley was acting so laid back I didn't even worry about us being spotted out together, and there wasn't a photographer in sight. I started to wonder if I'd been too paranoid about keeping our relationship secret, but the next day there were photos in the paper of us holding hands in the shopping centre car park.

'Wow,' I said, trying to take in what had happened and thinking back over the day. 'We were kissing and stuff. Do you think they saw us?'

'Don't worry, they couldn't have done,' Ashley said. 'Or I suppose that would have been in the paper too.'

It was so weird to think we'd been followed to a shopping centre in Kent. 'It's like they were spying on us!' I said to Ashley. 'Can you believe it?'

'Chill out, babe,' he said. 'Forget about it.'

'It's not the same for him,' I found myself saying to Nicola and Kimberley the next day. 'Nobody cares what he does as long as he has a good game. It's all about the football, but it's different for me because the fans want to know everything, and not just about the music.'

There was no answer to that, but the good thing about my relationship with Ashley being out in the open was that we no longer had to ask our friends and families to keep our secret, which we had done up to now.

My mam knew all about Ashley because she still came down regularly from Newcastle to do all my washing, and I introduced them one day in my flat. 'He seems nice,' Mam said, in between loading the washing machine and asking what needed ironing.

'He is,' I said very matter-of-factly, as that's how my mother is, but really I wanted to scream, 'Oh my God, I could not be any more in love with this person!'

Ashley's mam Sue had known about our relationship for a little while too, ever since one really cringe-worthy morning when she unexpectedly let herself into Ashley's flat.

'Hello!' she smiled at me, looking a bit surprised.

'Oh, hiii …' I blushed.

I had just emerged from the bedroom wearing a pair of Ashley's basketball shorts and one of his T-shirts.

Ashley's aunty was there too and they both started looking at me as if to say, '*Really?*'

I was absolutely dying, and I scuttled back into the bedroom as soon as I could. Ashley was still in bed and he just laughed his head off, but I wanted to hide under the covers I was so embarrassed.

By now I would always go straight to Ashley's flat from work, so we were more or less living together even before I eventually moved in a few months later. It was *so* easy to be with him. Nothing was a problem. We didn't argue about anything; he was just calm and nice to be around. We'd usually sit in watching trashy programmes on the telly, eating takeaways, or we'd occasionally go to the pictures or out for dinner.

'I'm paying,' I'd say, and he'd let me because he knew how independent I was like that.

I'd cook for him from time to time too; terrible stuff like ready-made chicken kiev and oven chips, but Ashley never cooked a thing, ever. He didn't even make a cup of tea, but I didn't question it because I got why. He'd had an incredibly cosseted upbringing because he'd been with Arsenal since he was so young. He was used to being pampered and having literally everything done for him, and he just didn't know any different.

I understood, partly because I was starting to experience the VIP treatment more myself as Girls Aloud grew. In our first two years, in fact, we'd gone from doing our own hair and make-up in the car and wearing leggings that had holes in to having stylists fussing over us for hours and designers sending us dresses to wear. We'd built up a good fan base too, and even some of the top music critics were warming to us and giving us great reviews.

November 2004 was quite a turning point for the group. We did 'I'll Stand By You' in aid of Children in Need, and it became our second number one. We also performed at the Royal Variety Show in front of Prince Charles, which was really special, plus we released our second album, *What Will the Neighbours Say?*

We'd all been worried about being dropped by the label after our first few records because nobody expected us to have staying power. We had very nearly been dropped after the first album, actually, because sales weren't as good as Polydor hoped for. Thankfully, Peter Loraine, who was then head of marketing at the label, believed in us and fought our corner. We owe him a huge debt of gratitude, and to have a second album was a blessing.

Now that we had two albums' worth of material we all wanted to do a tour. Performing live on stage was what we all loved most of all, and we were also excited about creating some merchandise, which meant we would need sponsorship deals too. It was obvious we needed a hands-on manager to help us move forward, because these were not things we knew how to organise on our own. So far we'd muddled through, but we'd had quite a few sobering experiences along the way.

I remember once going on a Dutch TV show and having no cue, and we all just stumbled onto the stage looking bewildered when the host shouted '*applows, applows*' to get the audience to clap. It was just so embarrassing. Another time the label had sent the wrong backing track and our choreography didn't fit the music. We ended up bumping into each other on stage, looking like total amateurs.

'We've reached crisis point,' I said to Kimberley at the end of 2004.

'You're right. Everyone's saying the same thing. Let's hold crisis talks.'

Kimberley was as level-headed as ever when we all gathered together.

'We need management, and we need to work out who's best for us,' she said.

As a group we never argued about everyday things like picking outfits, for instance, because whenever the clothes arrived for fittings it was usually very obvious who would suit what, as we were all different shapes and sizes. It was clear that finding one manager to suit all our five very different personalities could be a lot trickier, though. Sarah was flapping, talking at one hundred miles per hour, while Nicola was listening quietly and Nadine was just sitting there taking it all in and making sensible suggestions.

We eventually all agreed to take advice from Peter Loraine because he knew girl bands so well. He was the man who gave the Spice Girls their nicknames, and of course he'd already been a driving force behind Girls Aloud. We knew he would help, but we didn't realise quite how easy he would make it for us.

Straight away, Peter suggested Hillary Shaw, who had managed the hugely successful Eighties' band Bananarama, so she clearly knew how to handle a group of girls. We all liked Hillary as soon as we met her, and we were delighted when she agreed to come on board in the spring of 2005, before our first tour. It was so easy it felt completely meant to be, and I had a great feeling about working with her.

'You know what, I feel like my life is really coming together,' I said to Ashley one night. 'I'm used to everything being a struggle and I can't believe things are running so smoothly.'

I wasn't just talking about Girls Aloud. My relationship with Ashley was going really well too, so much so that I really wanted him to meet my dad.

'I'm taking you up to Newcastle,' I said on the spur of the moment. 'It's important to me that you meet me dad and see where I come from.'

We'd been dating for about six months by now and Ashley agreed, though he admitted he felt a bit nervous at the prospect of meeting my dad.

'At least I know what Newcastle is like, though,' he said. 'I've been there loads of times.'

It was true that Ashley had played plenty of matches in Newcastle and he knew the football ground and the city centre hotels very well, but that wasn't where I was from. I knew he didn't really have clue about what it was like in Heaton, but even so nothing could have prepared me for what happened when he went round to my dad's house for the very first time.

I could see Ashley was feeling shy but he didn't seem to be himself at all, and he barely said a word after I'd made the introductions.

'Shall ah myek weh a cup of tea?' my dad asked, but Ashley just sat there nodding and looking a bit confused.

'What's up?' I whispered.

'I can hardly understand a word he's sayin', babe.'

That was the first surprise, and the next was when one of my dad's neighbours came round to say hello to Ashley. I'd known this young girl for years and she's a real sweetheart, but my heart was in my mouth because she has special needs and tends to say inappropriate things, especially about boys.

'This is Ashley,' my dad said.

'I know,' she replied excitedly, eyeing Ashley up and down.

It was inevitable she was going to pass a remark about his looks and I just hoped she wasn't going to say anything too sexual, which she had a habit of doing. Never in a million years could I have guessed what she was about to say next, though.

'I've seen him in magazines, but I don't fancy him because he's a *darkie*.'

Ashley spat his tea out and I've never seen my dad looking so embarrassed in all his life. Nobody blamed the girl, of course, but my dad steered her out of the house as quickly as he could and apologised to Ashley over and over again.

'Eee, I don't know where she got that from,' my dad said.

'Don't worry about it, I've been called a lot worse,' Ashley said. 'Mind you, it's usually when I'm on the pitch …'

It took a while for us all to see the funny side, but when we did we laughed about it for years afterwards.

My dad told me he liked Ashley, and he teased me many times by saying that the only thing he would have changed about him was the football club he played for. It meant a lot to me to have that seal of approval; and somehow my life down south didn't seem so separated from my home and family in Newcastle once Ashley had been up there.

London had felt like a totally different world when I first moved down south, and it had taken me ages to settle and stop travelling home to Newcastle at every possible opportunity. Nicola had been the same, and when we first got in the group I'd often drop her off in Liverpool and then drive over to Newcastle, even if we only got to spend half a day with our families. Whenever I was at home I used to absolutely love walking to the corner shop near my mam's house in my pyjamas, to get a pint of milk for breakfast, or going to Mrs Clough's for some sweets. It's what I'd always done, and I just felt like me.

'People don't get me down there,' I would say to Gillian. 'I feel like I'm on another planet. They have a totally different sense of humour and I say things for a laugh sometimes and they look at me like I'm a crazy person.'

'I know,' my sister would say. 'I remember that from when we used to go down there together. I don't know how you put up with it, to be honest.'

Sometimes I wondered why I did, I was *that* homesick. It broke my heart to see how much my nieces and nephews had grown up each time I went back home, because it made me realise how much I was missing out on, and I always tried not to leave it too long between visits.

I remember driving up to Newcastle to see everybody in March 2005, because our first tour was about to start and I knew I'd be away for weeks. I popped up on a quick visit on my own.

'Hi Cheryl!' I heard a familiar voice call as I headed to Gillian's dad's house.

As I turned around I got a shock to see my old friend John Courtney, whose mam lived three doors down from Gillian's dad. He looked absolutely nothing like the John I'd grown up with. The cheeky, smiling boy I shared my first kiss with and the talented young footballer who had aspirations to play for Newcastle had completely disappeared. John was all gaunt and scruffy, with terrible skin and a haunted look in his eyes. I'd heard a few months earlier that he'd started taking heroin, which shocked me completely because John had always been one of the cool people who wasn't on it. I'd never imagined he would get sucked in, and now it was devastating to see him like this.

'Can I have your autograph?' he asked.

I knew he had put his family through hell recently and had stolen from them to buy heroin. That's how I found out about his habit, because Gillian had told me about that.

'What do you want my autograph for?'

'It's amazing what you've done. I'm so proud of you, what you've achieved.'

I asked him what happened to his football and he said he was going to get back into it.

'Who's the autograph to?' I said angrily. I knew that John didn't want my autograph for himself and that he was probably hoping to sell it for a few quid.

'Me, of course,' he lied.

I was so upset with him I scribbled on a bit of paper: 'To John, get yourself off this shit. You deserve more than this, Cheryl,' and I shoved it in his hand.

Not only did I want to make absolutely sure he couldn't sell my autograph to buy heroin, I hoped my words might push him in the right direction.

After my visit I thought about John all the way back to London, and about how different our lives had turned out.

'There's always hope,' I told myself, thinking back to when my life was a mess, and how I had managed to turn it around. 'Come on, John, it's not too late.'

Deep down I think I knew I was kidding myself. I had come back from depression and bad relationships, not drug addiction. There was a world of difference, and I had already seen what happened to people who got hooked on heroin.

This was when I first realised how important it was to me that Ashley had been up to Newcastle, and seen where I was from. The press always made a big deal of the fact I might be singing in front of Prince Charles one minute and then drinking tea on a council estate the next. On the face of it I was living two separate lives, but I never felt like that inside. I was always just me, the same Cheryl I'd always been. I guess I felt like you had to know Newcastle to really know me, because being a Geordie is so much a part of my character and is so special to me. Now I felt that Ashley was part of my whole life.

It didn't matter that sometimes *his* reality was so far removed from mine. Sometimes. For example, Ashley would come home with a new earring he'd paid £25,000 for and I'd say, 'You're jokin', aren't you?' I was gradually earning more money, but even if I'd had it sitting in the bank there was no way I would ever have spent that sort of cash on one earring back then. Ashley would roll his eyes as if to say, 'I can afford it, why not?' but he didn't argue with me, because he knew where I was coming from.

I remember seeing a pair of Christian Louboutins for £800 that I'd have loved to have owned, but back then I just couldn't justify paying out that sort of money on a pair of shoes.

'It's just wrong,' I'd say to Ashley.

When I started earning a lot more money I wished I could give my family things, but it wasn't that simple. Geordies have so much pride they would *never* accept anything from me, and I'd have to get round it by giving them gifts for birthdays and at Christmas that they would not be able to refuse. I got my dad a car and my mam a new kitchen when the time felt right. I enjoyed spoiling them but it was never unnecessary or excessive.

Ashley, though, had been paid a huge salary for as long as he could remember, and he just didn't have the same hang ups about spending large amounts of money as I did. One day I got home from work to find my car hoisted up on a lorry, having bigger wheels fitted. I'd treated myself to a Mercedes SLK sportscar when I felt I'd worked hard enough to have earned it, and I loved it.

'What are you doing – pimpin' me out?' I laughed. I was happy with it the way it was, but I didn't argue with him either.

I was touched Ashley had gone to so much trouble for me. I was ridiculously loved up, and in my eyes he could do no wrong.

7

'Will you marry me?'

'I'm exhausted,' I said to Ashley. 'I can't wait to get on that beach.'

We were on the plane, flying to Dubai for our first proper holiday together. It was June 2005 and the past few months had been incredibly busy. For one thing, we'd both been working flat out. Arsenal had just beaten Manchester United in the FA Cup, and Ashley had scored one of the winning penalties. I didn't see the game because I was on tour with the girls, playing at the NEC in Birmingham, but I'd told Ashley over and over again how proud I was of him. In return he told me how much he enjoyed seeing me on stage at the Hammersmith Apollo, which was the one gig he managed to get to.

'I don't know how you get up there and perform like that,' Ashley said.

'I don't know how you step up to the penalty spot when winning the FA Cup depends on it,' I told him.

We were like the mutual appreciation society and were so loved up, it was embarrassing. We could hardly keep our hands off each other either, and we spent the whole flight kissing and cuddling like a couple of over-excited teenagers.

The first Girls Aloud tour had far exceeded expectations. With two albums' worth of material we were all really up for it, but as we'd never toured before we had no idea how we'd go down with the fans. We did our opening night at the Royal Concert Hall in Nottingham and the minute I stepped on the stage I knew the answer.

'This is it,' I thought. 'This is why I wanted to do this job.' I absolutely loved the vibe we felt from the audience; the fans were going crazy. It was amazing to see them singing our songs back to us, and they inspired us to put on the best performances we could, night after night as we toured the country. Demand for tickets was so high we had to put on extra dates, and in the end we played 22 dates throughout May.

We'd always end up crashed out in the tour bus feeling absolutely shattered, but buzzing so much we couldn't sleep. Sarah would go out partying – she'd even go out and sing karaoke in a local pub when she'd just got off stage – but I usually ended up lying on my bed, drinking tea and gossiping with Kimberley. 'The fishwives are out again,' the other girls would laugh, but that's what we were like. Kimberley and I would talk ten to the dozen about anything and everything.

When we played the Hammersmith Apollo I was completely blown away because the audience was so much closer to the stage than at any other venue. You could clearly see the fans' faces and they knew every word to every song, even the album tracks. That was a real buzz.

When Ashley came to see that gig it was the cherry on the cake for me. As much as I loved being on the stage with the girls, that night I also couldn't wait for the show to end so I could be with him and talk to him.

'How do you dance like that?' he said, which cracked me up.

'Hard work,' I laughed. 'We don't just get up on stage and make it up, you know.'

We'd been rehearsing for weeks on end, working really hard on the choreography. Sarah and Nadine hated it and often said, 'It's alright for you, Cheryl, you've got dance experience.'

'I've not danced since I was 11!' I'd tell them, but really I think all the dancing I did when I was growing up helped me a lot, and I always enjoyed that part of the job.

Ashley didn't have much of a clue about all the preparation that went on behind the scenes. He'd been too busy playing football while I'd been living and breathing this tour, but to be fair, I knew very little about what went on behind the gates at Highbury. Practically all I knew was that he trained really hard every morning, and that the club liked girlfriends and wives to be kept well away from the players before matches, because that was the bit that affected me. Ashley always got whisked off to a hotel before an away game, which I didn't enjoy but had to accept as part of his job.

I also knew that Ashley had had a problem at work recently, though I didn't know all the details. He'd got into a lot of trouble for talking to Chelsea about a possible move, which the media was calling the 'tapping-up' scandal. Ashley didn't say much about it to me, but I knew he'd been fined £100,000 for talking to a rival club without Arsenal knowing, and I knew that he'd got very stressed about it.

Perhaps another reason I can't remember much about the case is that I had a far more distressing event to deal with in my own life around that time. At the beginning of April, just one week after I'd seen John Courtney in Newcastle, he died from a heroin overdose. He was found dead in his uncle's flat, curled up on a dirty, stained carpet, the syringe he used to inject the last lethal dose next to his hand.

I know exactly how he looked, because his mam decided to release a picture to the local press, showing him lying there dead. She hoped it would shock others into giving up drugs. When I saw it, I was on the tour bus and I just froze. I'd been talking to him literally the week before, and his death was so disturbing and so unnecessary.

'I'm so sorry,' I cried to his mam on the phone as soon as I heard the news. 'I'm devastated.'

She told me he'd put the note I wrote to him on the wall next to his bed, but he hadn't found the strength to take my advice. I sent flowers, but I couldn't go to the funeral. It was all too much to take in. John was the only boy in a family of six sisters. He was 21 years old, and just as with Lee Dac, I knew that seeing John's grieving mother would be too painful to bear.

I tried to be strong and lent my support to the local paper, the *Evening Chronicle*, when it began a 'War on Drugs' campaign because of John, but inside I felt anything but strong. I couldn't sleep properly for a long time afterwards, and sometimes I'd cry into my pillow whenever I thought about him.

'Will you be alright, babe?' Ashley had asked me, knowing how devastated I was, and that I had the tour to cope with.

'Yes,' I said. 'There are four other girls out there depending on me and the show must go on.'

That's exactly what I did. I put on a show, because that's what we were all there to do.

It's hardly surprising that Ashley and I were desperate to get away on holiday, and it felt so good to be finally flying to Dubai, just the two of us, leaving everything behind. Dubai was quite a new holiday destination at the time, and I was fascinated by it from the moment we landed. We stayed at the Burj Al Arab, one of the most luxurious hotels in the world. It's shaped like a huge, tall sail, which totally amazed me. I'd travelled around a bit with the girls but I was certainly not what you would call cultured, and Ashley was just as daft. He'd been all over the world with Arsenal, but he hadn't actually experienced differ-ent cultures. It was always just airport, hotel, play the match and then fly home.

'Do we have to cover up?' we said to each other in surprise on the first morning. We were walking through the extremely lavish hotel reception, both in shorts. All the other guests had their legs covered, and there were several woman completely shrouded from head to toe. Ashley and I looked at each other as the penny slowly dropped. 'We're in a Muslim country ...' he said. 'Oh, yeh, I guess you're not meant to walk around like this in here ...' I replied. 'We'd better get to the beach, fast.'

Ashley had forgotten his swimming trunks, and so we quickly went and bought him a pair from a local shop before heading to the beach. The best ones we could find were green with white camels all over them. They were absolutely awful but we just laughed. 'At least nobody's gonna see us,' Ashley said.

I had my hair scraped up in a clip and, despite all the dancing on the tour, I wasn't in the best shape.

'Look at the state of us, we're like Wayne and Waynetta,' I joked. To cap it all I got bitten on the big toe by a crab as soon as we got on the sand, which set me off screaming and making a huge spectacle of myself.

Later that day we got a phone call from back home.

'You're in *The Sun* and, er, you look terrible!' a friend told us.

I was dumbfounded.

'The paparazzi must have been in boats in the sea! Can you believe it? We're in Dubai, for God's sake!'

'I think we need to get me some better trunks,' Ashley said.

'I think we need to not go on that beach again,' I replied.

I was properly freaked out, and so the following day we decided to get away from the beach and go to a nearby desert, where you could do lots of activities like archery, or race around the sand dunes in jeeps. That was such a boy thing and Ashley loved it, but I didn't enjoy it at all and just couldn't see the fun in getting flung around like that in the blazing heat.

There was a sandstorm too, and I was only happy when we finally got back to the hotel and put the TV on. Michael Jackson's child-molesting trial was coming to a close, and I remember sitting there crying with relief every time another 'not guilty' verdict came in.

Ashley seemed a bit distracted when I tried to talk to him about it, and at one point in the evening he disappeared into the bathroom for ages, looking twitchy and guarding his rucksack as if his life depended on it.

'Are you OK?' I asked.

'Fine, babe. Do you fancy going on a camel ride? I know you like animals, you'll love it.'

I agreed because I thought Ashley was worried I wasn't having a good time, and a day or two later we headed back into the desert.

I'd never seen a camel in my life before, let alone ridden one, and I was nervous. It didn't help that Ashley looked really tense, but as the guide helped us both up onto the camel's back I really tried to keep my cool, because there were about 10 other people on the same excursion and I didn't want to make a fuss.

'The camel's moaning and screaming!' I whispered to Ashley the second the poor animal tried to get to its feet.

'It's miserable! I feel cruel!'

I felt really uncomfortable, not only because of the camel's moaning but also because of the blistering heat.

'I'm not enjoying this, babe. Aren't *you* worried about the camels? Their nostrils must really hurt. Don't you think it's cruel, them dragging us big lumps around in this heat? I'm telling you, when we climbed on I definitely heard the camel groan in pain ...'

'It's a camel, Cheryl. Camels groan,' Ashley snapped back.

'But what if his feet are hurting, treading through all those prickly bushes ...'

'Babe! Is there any chance you can shut up?'

I was shocked. Ashley had never spoken to me like that before, ever.

'OK. Not a problem. Just don't talk to me, and I'll not speak,' I replied.

When we got off the camel it did the loudest moan of all and I was not happy, not at all. The sun was setting and we were given strawberries and champagne along with all the other tourists, but I was still fuming with Ashley.

He took hold of my hand and pulled me towards him, and I thought for a minute he was going to do something stupid like push me down a sand dune to try and break the ice. Instead, he led me away from the other tourists and got down on one knee, right there in the sand. It took my breath away, because he looked choked with emotion. He then started crying, told me he loved me and asked, 'Will you marry me?'

It was a really amazing, heart-stopping moment. I started crying too, and I told him 'yes' without having to think about it for even a fraction of a second. Ashley then put the most incredible diamond ring on my finger, and the other holidaymakers applauded, having worked out what had just happened.

We kissed, and I felt like the happiest girl in the world. I had no doubts, no worries. We were meant to be together, and right from that moment I couldn't *wait* to get married.

When we got back to the hotel we phoned all our friends and family to break the good news. Ashley told me that a few days earlier, when he'd locked himself in the bathroom, he had in fact been phoning my dad, to ask for my hand in marriage. He'd introduced himself as 'Ashley Cole' as he was so nervous, which threw my dad a bit by the sounds of it, but of course he had given his blessing.

The girls were just screaming with excitement, and from the minute we put the phone down to my friends I wanted to start planning the wedding.

'It'll have to be next summer,' I said, thinking about the World Cup, and the fact that Girls Aloud were planning to go on tour again in the spring.

'That soon?'

'I don't see the point in being engaged for 10 years – do you?'

'No, babe.'

That's how it went. Ashley was happy for me to do all the planning, and I was happy to do it. I wanted a fairytale wedding, something that would be all girly and twinkly and special.

When we got back to the UK we were absolutely devastated to find there was a picture of us in *Heat* magazine. It showed us both crying, just after the proposal. It was such a private, personal moment and we'd been so overwhelmed that we hadn't given it a second thought when one of the guides had taken a photograph of us.

We were naïve, but it was another lesson learned. It meant that when *OK!* magazine got in touch shortly afterwards and asked us if we wanted to do an exclusive deal for the official engagement pictures, plus the wedding, we decided it was best to be in control of the stories that were being put out and do the deal, rather than leave it for journalists and other people to put pictures and false information out there.

'If you give them the story, nobody else is digging for it,' we were advised by one of Ashley's agents. 'Also, you'll get the best security you could wish for at the wedding, not to mention a fabulous set of pictures.' He explained that, because a wedding is a public event, without proper security we would be leaving ourselves open to a repeat of what had happened with the proposal in Dubai, which we didn't want at all.

Ashley and I reluctantly settled on a deal on the understanding that we'd spend every penny on the wedding, as we certainly didn't want to profit from it.

I still had doubts, though and I bitterly regret not listening to my gut feeling. I should have known from experience that instincts like that should not be ignored – look what happened the night I went to The Drink nightclub with Nicola.

Anyhow, before we knew it Ashley and I were posing in the flat for glossy photos.

'What are we doing?' he said to me through gritted teeth as we smiled and embraced for the camera.

'I have no idea,' I said. 'None whatsoever.'

We found ourselves saying the same thing again when we turned up for a photoshoot to promote the National Lottery's Dream Number. This was in the run up to the wedding, and again was on the advice of Ashley's agent.

'What do we have to do?' Ashley said.

'Just put on these white clothes, cross our fingers and hope the pictures turn out well,' I laughed.

We got slated in the press for those photos, and I'm not surprised. We looked ridiculously cheesy, and you can tell just by looking at them that Ashley especially felt really uncomfortable, posing like a medallion man in a white shirt open down to the naval. I can remember him hissing in my ear: 'Get me out of here,' to which I replied: 'It's too late. Just smile.'

'We should have just pegged it,' we joked afterwards, but then we had to get our heads round the fact the press reproduced the pictures time and time again, complete with stories or jibes from national newspaper columnists.

I'd been labelled a WAG practically as soon as I started dating Ashley, and once we were engaged the term was used more and more. It annoyed the shit out of me, because to me it's a derogatory term, meaning a girl who doesn't earn her own money or have a career in her own right. It baffled me that some girls actually aspired to be labelled a WAG. 'Where's their pride?' I always thought. It never occurred to me that there were also plenty of girls who would *claim* to have slept with a famous footballer, even if they hadn't. Or, even more bizarrely, that there were people out there prepared to start a vicious rumour that Ashley was gay. Unbelievably, both of these things happened at the start of 2006 as we prepared for our wedding that summer.

First, a girl claimed she'd slept with Ashley on New Year's Eve while I was away on a shopping trip to New York with my mam. The *News of the World* was prevented from running the story because Ashley's lawyers got CCTV footage proving he was alone in a restaurant at the time the girl claimed he was with her.

It was horrible to have to deal with that when I was enjoying planning my wedding, but I never doubted Ashley for a second. 'What a load of crap,' were my exact words, as soon as I heard the allegation, and before knowing there was proof it was a load of rubbish. To me, this was simply an extension of the press interference we already had to put up with, although of course it was far worse than having a tour guide sell a picture of us, or being slated by a nasty newspaper columnist.

Ashley was very relieved by my level-headed reaction, but I just knew it was some stupid girl trying to make money or get herself in the papers. 'You don't have to be grateful that I haven't gone mad,' I said to Ashley. 'Why should you worry about anything? We've proved you've done nothing wrong.'

Weeks later, disgusting stories started circulating about Ashley being gay and doing something sexual with a mobile phone and one of his male friends. I actually burst out laughing because it was so ridiculous, but Ashley didn't find it funny at all.

'For God's sake, when are they gonna leave us alone?' he said. It was claimed there was a video proving the allegations, and Ashley just kept saying, 'Go on then, play the tape but don't just write bullshit.'

'Don't worry, the truth will come out,' I told him, but nothing I said calmed him down. He was absolutely fuming, and he told me he was convinced that Arsenal fans in high places were out to get him because of the 'tapping-up' scandal he'd been through with Chelsea. 'They want to get me back for trying to leave Arsenal,' he said. 'They think I should stay there for life because that's where I started.'

This went on for weeks, and it was hell to see Ashley suffering like that. In the end he successfully sued for harassment, breach of privacy and libel and was paid damages, but nothing could compensate for the torment he went through.

'Concentrate on the World Cup, that's where your energies need to go,' I told him, because I knew that if his football suffered because of all this stress, he'd be a hell of a lot worse.

For my part, I had plenty on my plate to take my mind off what the press was saying. There was the wedding to plan, and the girls and I were filming a six-part TV series called *Girls Aloud: Off the Record*. Television crews followed us preparing for our *Chemistry* tour in the spring, which was our first UK arena tour, and we were also filmed on promotional tours to Australia and New Zealand. On top of that we travelled to China as London ambassadors with the Mayor of London, Ken Livingstone, we also did gigs in Ibiza and Greece, and we went to Paris to make the 'Whole Lotta History' video.

I look back now and I think I was so unworldly it was ridiculous. For instance, I moaned about everything from the rain to the state of the toilets in Shanghai, and I don't think I appreciated at all what a huge honour it was to be a cultural ambassador. I'd never been to any of those countries before and I should have been saying: 'Wow! How lucky am I?' but it just wasn't like that at the time.

In my head I remember lots of early morning starts, horrible jetlag, feeling totally out of my comfort zone and missing Ashley like crazy.

I was 22 years old, and I couldn't wait to get home and get married. Our wedding was planned for 14 July 2006, just after the World Cup in Germany. Ashley let me make all the decisions about the wedding.

'Are you sure you don't want to get involved?' I asked him many times.

'No, I just want to marry you,' he always said.

The only thing he did was taste the cake, which I thought was quite sweet. 'You're like a big kid,' I teased.

I hired wedding planners and decided I wanted an angel theme, and I took advice about my wedding dress from Victoria Adcock, who did the styling for Girls Aloud. The next thing I knew Victoria was telling me Roberto Cavalli had offered to make it, and I was flying to Florence for fittings. It was insane really, looking back, but I just got on and did it.

There was only one real hiccup in the arrangements, which had thankfully happened very early on in the planning stages, in September 2005. Ashley and I had just put a very large deposit down on Highclere Castle in Berkshire, because it looked perfect for the fairytale theme I had in mind.

'The model Katie Price is to marry Peter Andre at Highclere Castle later this week …' I heard a newsreader say.

I stopped dead in my tracks. I was in a shoe shop in West London, and *Sky News* was on. I looked up at the TV screen and my heart sank. I phoned Ashley immediately, close to tears.

'It's not 'cos it's Jordan, it's that it won't be special to us. This completely takes the shine off the venue for us.'

Ashley agreed, and I phoned the bank and stopped the transaction straight away, before phoning the wedding planners and sobbing down the phone.

'What are we gonna do?' I wailed.

'We'll need to find another venue soon or we're screwed,' the wedding planner told me plainly, and I left the shop feeling gutted. It was pouring with rain and I stood in a dirty big puddle, then I realised that I'd parked on a yellow line, thinking I would only be in the shop for a few minutes, and my car had been towed away.

'Looking back, do you think all that was a bad omen?' someone asked me recently.

'Nah!' I replied. 'I *never* had bad vibes about marrying Ashley. I wish I was still married to him … if only things had turned out differently.'

8

'You've come a long way, Cheryl!'

'How do you cope with the scrutiny?' I asked Victoria Beckham one evening, when we were in Germany together, supporting our men in the World Cup. We were staying in adjacent rooms at the Brenners Park-Hotel in Baden-Baden, and I was blow-drying Victoria's hair before we went out to dinner. I'd met her several times before at different events and we got on well. Victoria is so easy to talk to and has a great sense of humour – totally the opposite of how she is portrayed in the press. We had a lot in common, with Victoria having been in a girl band too, and unlike some of the other 'WAGs', we were both only interested in supporting our men.

'How do I cope? I cope because I have to, because it's just the way my life is,' Victoria told me.

I'd seen that it didn't matter what anybody else around her did, Victoria was always the one who got the worst press. I remember one time she was literally pulled apart from head to toe in a newspaper article that commented on everything from her pout and her collarbones to her boobs and her bunions.

'I'm hardened to it,' Victoria said. 'I know how I'm perceived is not how I am, and that's what matters. When they say I'm too thin, I just think: 'You know what? I'm happy to be thin. I'm into fashion and I like to be able to wear whatever I like. It's my business, and if other people don't like it, that's their business.'

Ashley and I had been described as the 'new Posh and Becks' ever since our engagement, which I thought was a joke, but nevertheless it was so interesting to be able to talk to Victoria about her life, because to me she was admirable. She had such a lovely family, and I told her I hoped that when we had kids, Ashley and I would be able to juggle our careers and family life together as well as she and David managed theirs.

'You'll be fine, because you're just so normal,' she told me.

Despite what Victoria said, and how normal she was too, I couldn't help noticing that when we went out to dinner that night and I made her laugh she held her handbag up over her mouth. I wondered if it was just an insecurity caused by the media, though I was still learning about the huge level of press intrusion Victoria was subjected to.

Around this time there was talk of a possible move for Ashley, to play for Real Madrid. We'd discussed it and I was very honest and said I didn't want him to go, because I couldn't see how I would be able to continue with Girls Aloud if I lived in Spain. We'd only just started to be completely accepted as a band and I couldn't contemplate giving up now, not after working so hard for nearly four years.

'What's it like, living in Madrid?' I asked Victoria casually over dinner.

'Do not, whatever you do, do *not* live there,' she told me, explaining that there wasn't much for her and the kids socially, and she'd found it tough managing her career from there.

I was absolutely gobsmacked when a Sunday newspaper later reported that Victoria had told me how wonderful life in Madrid was, and that she had supposedly offered to help me find a house there. It just seemed so weird that journalists would completely make up a story like that, especially when the World Cup was happening right under our noses and there must have been so many real stories to report on. No wonder Victoria was so cautious, I thought, if that's the sort of nonsense she had to put up with constantly.

Watching England play Portugal in the quarter-finals was painful, as it came down to a penalty shoot-out and Ashley was taking one of them. I just felt sick. I knew that if he missed it he'd be so down and moody, because that's how he got if a game hadn't gone his way. Even if he got a mediocre write-up on the back pages there'd be hell on at home, because he has a champion's mindset and anything short of winning was a disaster.

'It would be boring if you won everything,' I'd said to him in the past.

'Yeah,' he'd reply, 'I hear what you're saying,' but I knew he didn't agree with me, not at all.

When Ashley stepped up to the penalty spot that day I knew there would be nothing at all I could possibly say to console him if he missed. The whole world was watching, and it was like everybody took a breath at the same time as Ashley took the shot.

'Come on!' I shouted when I saw the ball hit the net. 'Get in!'

I was euphoric. Ashley had scored, and the relief was huge. England weren't through yet, but it wasn't going to be Ashley's fault if they lost. That's what I thought in that moment.

In the end England *did* lose, on penalties. Frank Lampard was crying, as were nearly all the players, and I hated seeing that. David Beckham was going to quit the captaincy so Victoria was all in a fluster with herself, and all the players and their partners had to fly home together in a private plane, without a trophy.

'Nobody knows if they'll have another shot at a World Cup,' I'd heard a commentator say, and that was the hard truth. You could almost smell the disappointment in the air, and I couldn't wait to get off that plane and go home.

Our wedding was just a fortnight away, and I tried to get Ashley to think about that instead of the football.

'You've got your stag do to look forward to,' I said, but Ashley was so upset he could barely speak.

He went off to Marbella on his stag do not long afterwards, and my mam came down to help me with the last-minute wedding preparations. Looking back, there was a hell of a lot going on in our lives. Ashley was thinking of moving to Chelsea, although the deal was not yet done, and he'd just written his autobiography, which was coming out very soon.

I was more than ready to let my hair down on my hen night, and when a group of us went to a bar and then a club in Shoreditch I got absolutely paralytic drunk on champagne, cocktails and shots. At the end of the night Nicola was hugging me at the top of a flight of stairs and I lost my footing. All of a sudden I was at the bottom of the stairs and she was on top of me, roaring with laughter. That's the last thing I remember – lying there on my back with my legs in the air and looking up at my shoes.

All the other girls were going mad, saying: 'Nicola, it wouldn't be good if Cheryl had no teeth for her wedding day!' but we just laughed our heads off.

The wedding venue Ashley and I had eventually chosen, Wrotham Park in Hertfordshire, didn't actually have a wedding licence and so we were taking our vows the night before our big day, at a place nearby called Sopwell House. Thankfully it was just the two of us, Ashley's mam, my mam and the registrar, because when I turned up I had the worst hangover ever. I'd been vomiting all day, and my face was green.

'What the hell happened to you?' Ashley said.

I was wearing a fifties-style white strapless dress with blue flowers on, no make-up and I hadn't even blow-dried my hair. Luckily Ashley was only in a pair of shorts and a T-shirt, and I just looked at him and welled up. He smiled back at me and had tears in his eyes too. It didn't matter what we looked like, we were both ridiculously emotional, and when we said our vows everybody in the room burst into tears, including the registrar.

I was really glad we'd done it like this. It was such a private moment and, because we were already married, it really took the pressure off the next day when we had two hundred guests coming.

'How do you feel?' Mam asked me as I put on my wedding dress. 'Calm, not nervous, not worried,' I told her truthfully.

It was crazy, really. I was in this fabulous Roberto Cavalli gown, about to step into this amazing mansion house that was decked out like something from a magical fairytale, but I really did feel completely at ease. Garrard had loaned me a diamond tiara head-piece and I was travelling in a horse-drawn carriage. I felt like a princess, but one with her feet firmly on the ground.

When I'd been with Victoria Beckham in Germany a few weeks earlier she had said to me: 'Make sure you and Ashley spend the day together,' and that's what was on my mind. I wanted to be with him, all day long. Ashley sent me a beautiful bracelet in the morning, and I had a surprise up my sleeve for him for later. I'd booked our favourite singer, John Legend, to sing at the party, and he'd flown in from America especially for us.

We had a blessing in front of all our friends and family, and my dad made everybody laugh in his speech by presenting Ashley with a Newcastle shirt with 'Cole' on the back. 'Come on, Ashley, make my dream come true,' my dad said. 'Come and play for the Toon.'

Ashley was really, really nervous when it was his turn to speak, and I just remember him looking at me afterwards, holding my hand and saying: 'Babe, babe, I done it!'

I was so proud of him because speaking in public is so not his thing, but he did it really well. He was blown away when the walls opened up after dinner, turning the room into a nightclub and revealing John Legend on the stage.

'Did you get a lookalike?' Ashley asked, because he really couldn't believe his hero was actually there, singing as we took to the floor for the first dance.

There was a great atmosphere and it was a fantastic day and night. It wasn't a celebrity bash. Of course the girls were there, as all four of them were my bridesmaids along with my sister, my niece and my cousin, and there were a few other famous faces. We invited the Beckhams but they couldn't make it. Victoria sent a lovely telegram instead, and David's mam came, as she's Sue's friend.

My old school friend Kelly came down from Newcastle, which meant a lot. 'I'm so proud of you,' she told me, and we laughed

about how we used to wag off school together and smoke cigarettes in Walker Cemetery. 'You've come a long way, Cheryl!' she
beamed. It was great to see her.

My brother Andrew could not be at the wedding, because he
was in prison again, and to be honest I didn't care and didn't want
to know the details of his latest offence. I was actually starting to
lose track of all his charges and convictions because there were so
many.

I went to see him in prison before the wedding, believing it
wasn't too late for him to change his ways, despite the fact he's
spent most of his adult life behind bars.

'Why can't you stop?' I begged him. 'Why can't you change
your ways?'

I was dressed in a tracksuit and baseball cap and could feel other
inmates staring at me, but I just stared back at them.

'Don't look at them,' Andrew hissed.

I didn't care what the other criminals thought of me. All I cared
about was my brother, not whether some convict was checking me
out and thinking, 'Isn't she someone from Girls Aloud?'

'How can you live like this?' I said to Andrew.

'I'm used to it.'

'Well, I'm not. I'll never get used to it. Do you know how you
ruined my childhood? It was plagued with fear and worry because
of you. If I hear a bang on the door, even now, I can still see them
– the police kicking the door in, searching the house for weapons
and drugs. You caused me so many sleepless nights, and you're
still devastating the whole family. Why can't you just stop?'

He shrugged and looked me in the face. 'I'm too far gone.'

I left the prison in floods of tears. I had the means to really
help Andrew now if only he wanted to be helped, but he clearly
didn't.

That hurt like hell. He was my brother and I loved him, and
even if I'd been on the bones of my backside, still living on the
council estate, I would have been saying exactly the same things
to him, and offering as much help as I could possibly give.

Not having Andrew at my wedding was very sad, but I was actually relieved in a way too. It was one thing me stepping into his world, but how might he have behaved stepping into this part of mine? I consoled myself with the thought that at least I wouldn't have to worry about him drinking too much or causing trouble on the day.

Ashley and I flew to the Seychelles for our honeymoon the next day, taking a helicopter from the airport to a super-top-security island. I was ridiculously happy and couldn't stop looking at my wedding ring and telling Ashley how proud I was to be his wife. 'I'm the lucky one,' he said, and my heart was literally melting with love for him. This island had just 16 villas on it and we had our own walkway down to a little garden and beach and a private dining table. It was the most idyllic place I'd ever seen.

On the first night we were sat out there, talking about the wedding, when I suddenly felt a weird sensation on my leg.

'Ashley, there's something hot and warm and heavy, breathing on me leg.'

'Piss off!'

'I'm not joking you. Will you please have a look?'

He looked under the table and started screaming like a girl. It took me right back to our second date, when he'd found that huge cat purring in his living room.

'What is it?' I said, starting to panic.

Ashley had actually jumped up on the table now in fright.

'It's eight inches long!'

I screamed too and shook the thing off my leg. It was a huge, scaly lizard – the biggest, fattest lizard I'd ever seen in my life, but thankfully it scuttled straight off into the bushes.

'You can get down now,' I teased Ashley. 'I've dealt with it myself, thanks.'

We laughed for ages afterwards, and we were like that for the whole honeymoon. It was amazing being finally married and we were both on a real high every day. Ashley had bought me the most incredible yellow diamond wedding ring, and every time I saw it on my finger it put a huge smile on my face. Being called 'Mrs Cole' had the same effect. I absolutely loved being called Ashley's wife.

Back home we had all the excitement of moving house, which actually felt like an extension of the wedding. We were building our life together, planning our future and I was already getting broody.

'Have your career first, you can have the babies later,' Ashley said whenever I mentioned kids. I knew he was right but I just couldn't wait to start a family with him. It was the next step after getting married, and I was really looking forward to taking it.

Ashley finally signed for Chelsea after months of negotiations, and we found the perfect place to live in Oxshott, Surrey. It was handy for him to get to Stamford Bridge and it was a huge house, with loads of bedrooms for when we started a family.

My mam stayed with us whenever she came down, which was quite often in our first year of marriage. We had builders in for months, and it was a necessity to have someone there we trusted, who could make the men a cup of tea and keep an eye on things when we were both working. We had Buster and Coco, our two Chihuahuas, by now, and my mam was great with the dogs too. We couldn't have done without her, especially when Ashley and I both found ourselves laid up at exactly the same time.

Ashley had one of his knees strapped up and I'd had three of my toes broken and reset with pins, because they were damaged from ballet dancing on blocks when I was too young to cope with them. It was a problem I'd put off dealing with for years, but I finally had the operation done after I got married, because I'd reached a stage where dancing in stilettos with Girls Aloud was causing me some serious pain. I honestly don't know how we'd have managed without my mam, because neither of us could walk and she literally had to bring food and drinks up to us both in bed, like we were in hospital.

When she wasn't there one day I actually had to shuffle on my bum down the stairs and across the floor to get something from the kitchen.

'What are you doing, babe?' Ashley laughed.

'Well, what else am I supposed to do?'

We both had hysterics. If anyone could have seen the state of me they wouldn't have believed I was the same girl in our glossy wedding pictures, not at all.

I remember feeling very relieved when the Chelsea deal was finally done because there'd been months of uncertainty around this time, although I must admit I had no clue whatsoever how much trouble Ashley's departure from Arsenal would cause. He was branded a traitor for leaving the club he'd been with since his childhood, and he had to put up with a lot of abuse, both on and off the pitch. It completely shocked me. I had totally underestimated how the fans would react. Ashley was absolutely *hated*, and as his wife I found that very hard to deal with.

He never talked to me about his football much, but we spoke about how he was perceived in the media and how gutted he felt. My heart went out to him, because I knew from my court case what it was like to be so publicly criticised and misunderstood.

Ashley's autobiography had caused trouble too, because in it he described his anger at being offered £55,000 a week by Arsenal.

'People might take that the wrong way,' I told him when I read the manuscript several months before the book went to print. I was thinking how my friends back in Newcastle might read this. It was a hell of a lot more than most people earned in a year, let alone a week.

'I'm not saying £55,000 isn't a lot of money, I'm saying it's less than other players get, and that Arsenal still pays me like a junior even though I'm a senior player now. It's not about the amount, it's about the respect.' The passage stayed in the book, and Ashley was then branded an arrogant money-grabber as well as a traitor.

'I'm gutted,' he said all over again.

'Come here, I know you're not like that at all. It'll pass, you'll see. The papers will have something else to write about next week.'

This wasn't quite the fairytale start to married life I'd hoped for, but then again I was experienced enough by now to know that in my life, there were always bumps and crashes after every high.

It wasn't long before it was Ashley's turn to tell me not to worry about what was in the press, when the papers started speculating that Girls Aloud were splitting up. We'd released our greatest hits album, *The Sound of Girls Aloud*, and went on to do our *Greatest Hits* tour and so I guess the rumours were inevitable, especially as Nadine had decided to move to America. The stories weren't true, though. We'd had our third number one with a cover of 'Walk This Way', which we recorded with the Sugababes for Comic Relief in March 2007, and we had no intention of splitting up.

'You know what, that was our fifteenth consecutive top-ten single,' I said to Ashley. 'It's so frustrating! Why would we stop now?'

As a group we'd become more efficient than ever, too. It didn't even matter that Nadine was living in the States, because Hillary Shaw had our diaries so well organised that we slotted everything into far less hours than we ever did in the beginning. As far as I was concerned, being in the group was still my dream job, and it annoyed me intensely to think people were just waiting for the dream to end.

'Chill out, babe,' Ashley said. 'I'm so sick of having the papers making trouble for us. Don't let it get to you, it's not worth it.'

I knew he was right, and I felt closer than ever to Ashley. It was like we knew each other inside out, and we were just so perfect for one another.

'I'm gonna watch the fight tonight with the boys,' Ashley said. It was 8 December 2007, and the boxing match between Floyd Mayweather and Ricky Hatton was taking place in Las Vegas.

Because of the time difference, it wouldn't be on until the early hours of Sunday morning.

'I don't mind if you want to stay over at John's,' I said. 'If you're having a drink there's no point in getting a taxi home at 4am.'

I always treated Ashley like a free spirit. I'd seen a lot of possessive women when I was growing up, and I never wanted to be like that. He rarely went out with his mates because we both liked nothing better than being at home together, but I never told Ashley he couldn't go anywhere or do anything.

Our marriage was very strong. We were best friends and we never, ever argued, even when there was potential for trouble. For our first wedding anniversary, for instance, Ashley bought me a Bentley as a surprise present. I'm not into cars the way he is and I didn't want it, but I didn't want to offend him and so I took it out for a drive. I'd literally only gone round the corner when two things happened that really put me off. First of all, I pulled up at some traffic lights and there was an elderly man next to me in a tiny little Polo. He'd probably fought in the war, and there I was, swanking it up beside him in a Bentley. It just so felt wrong, and I wanted to hide my face. Then, another Bentley drove past me and flashed its lights, as if we were in some select club. 'You *lemon*!' I thought, and drove straight home and told Ashley the car had to go.

'It was a lovely thought, but I've already got a car, and I just don't need another one.'

'OK, if that's what you want,' he said. There was no drama, and the car went back to the showroom without a fuss.

Anyhow, Ashley went out with his mates the evening before the fight, and I told him I'd see him in the morning. John was a mutual friend of ours and I trusted Ashley implicitly. Why would I not? I knew they were going to have a drink and go to a club before the fight, but that didn't bother me in the slightest.

We were used to having nights apart. I'd been away earlier in the year doing our *Greatest Hits* tour, and only recently I'd been to America to film for a TV documentary I was making called *The Passions of Girls Aloud*.

The idea was that each of us would try our hand at something we'd always wanted to do. Nadine decided not to take part, saying singing was her only passion, but Sarah opted to learn how to play polo – God knows why! Nicola wanted to create a make-up range for pale skin, Kimberley auditioned for a role in a West End musical and I chose to learn street dancing.

My goal was to win a part in Will.i.am's video for his new single 'Heartbreaker', and I flew to LA to be taught how to do it.

Ashley was busy playing football, and so I took my mam with me. It was my first time in LA, and I was amazed by it. I felt like I was on a movie set wherever I went, and I didn't understand why strangers kept smiling at me and telling me to have a nice day.

Part of the trip involved going out onto the streets of Compton, a deprived district, to dance with a character called Tommy the Clown. He's a famous reformed drug dealer out there who uses street dance to help inspire kids, and I felt a real connection to him.

It was an emotional experience, bringing back memories of drugs in my old neighbourhood in Heaton, and all the death and pain I associated with drug taking. It was inspiring to me too, though, and I would have really loved Ashley to be there with me. I couldn't wait to tell him all about it, but when I got home it was hard to put it into words. It was one of those 'you had to be there' experiences, but little disappointments like that were just something we had to accept as part of our lifestyle.

We both had great jobs, we were young, we had no kids and no money worries. We were very, very fortunate, and though we didn't like to be apart, we didn't ever complain about it because we knew how lucky we were.

'How was the fight?' I asked brightly when Ashley came home after that boxing match.

'Horrible. I got too drunk and I can't remember it.'

He didn't look at me and seemed very dismissive, walking away from me. I had a bad feeling in my gut, but I thought it was just typical of me, being a worrier. I told myself Ashley must be very hungover and could probably do without me questioning him, so I left it. My marriage was strong and I trusted him to tell me if there was something I needed to know. He never said another word about it, not until he was forced to, more than six weeks later.

9

'Something happened ... but I don't know what'

'D'you want a cup of tea?' Ashley asked.

We were in the bedroom, it was about 11pm on Thursday 24 January 2008 and he'd been acting weird all evening. I said I didn't want a drink but Ashley went downstairs anyway, and I decided to follow him. He hardly ever made a cup of tea, and I sensed something was off. I found him on the phone in the hallway, and he was clearly flapping. I could tell he was talking to his agent, which set my heart beating ten to the dozen. Then *my* phone rang, and it was Sundraj.

'Can you talk, Cheryl? I'm afraid I've got some bad news.'

'What is it?'

I was standing just a few feet away from Ashley now, staring at him, and I could feel my body going into shock. Ashley was looking straight back at me with a worried look on his face, still talking to his agent.

Sundraj had no idea Ashley was right in front of me like this, and he was clearly trying to break it to me as gently as possible that the news involved my husband.

'I'm sorry to be the one to have to tell you ...'

'Will you please just spit it out, Sundraj? What the hell is going on?'

'A girl has come forward and said she's had sex with Ashley.'

I just froze, and I don't know whether I even said another word to Sundraj. I was still staring at Ashley, and I could hear him asking

his agent what was going to be in the story, and telling him that
I was here, on the phone to Sundraj.

At the same time, I was hearing Sundraj tell me the story would
be on the internet at midnight, and in tomorrow's *Sun* newspaper.
The claims the girl was making went back to last December – the
night of the boxing match, and as soon as I heard that, I knew this
wasn't one of those ludicrous made-up stories, invented out of
nothing.

It was completely surreal, hearing two halves of two conversations, knowing that Ashley was being told the same things, at the
same time. I put the phone down and Ashley carried on talking. I
felt the colour fall out of my face as I stood there, rooted to the
spot. It was like on a cartoon, when they wipe all the colour out in
one fell swoop and the character's face goes white. It felt exactly
like that had happened to me, and then I started trembling
uncontrollably.

'What's going on?' I shouted the second Ashley got off the
phone.

I was expecting, wishing, him to say: 'It's a lie', but he didn't.

'Like I told you before, it was a horrible night. I got too drunk
and I can't remember it.'

I was in proper shock now, convulsing and wanting to vomit. To
me that was like he was admitting it. In that moment I didn't
believe a single word he was saying, not a word, and I was so angry
with myself for accepting his pathetic story in the first place. Why
hadn't I asked his friends what had gone on, or made him tell me
what he *did* remember? He must have had some idea what he'd
done.

'I don't believe you can't remember anything at all,' I said. 'It's
just not good enough. You need to start remembering, and fast.'

'I'm telling you, I was so drunk, it was horrible. I wish I could
remember but I can't … Something happened … but I don't know
what.'

'I'm gonna read it online at midnight anyway, but I'd rather
hear it from you.'

I wanted to know every detail but I got nothing. Ashley's exact words to me after that are a blur because I was in such a terrible state. I just know that whatever I asked, all he kept saying, one way or another, was, 'Something happened ... but I don't know what.'

It was like being tortured, waiting for midnight to come and knowing the hell was only going to get worse. I went and switched on the computer, alone, waiting for the story to appear on *The Sun* newspaper's website. Ashley was upstairs now, in the bedroom. He knew what was coming and so he didn't need to read it. That's what I figured. He was lying to me, and he couldn't bear to see me read the truth.

I was shocked on so many different levels when I got the story up online. Seeing the girl in question was the first blow. She was a blonde hairdresser, and she looked horrible to me, but it was what she had told the paper that was really disturbing.

My eyes were everywhere, all over the page, reading the details of her night with Ashley. I was looking for something that just didn't add up, that would make her version of events totally implausible, but that isn't what I got at all.

The girl said Ashley had been so drunk he couldn't walk straight, that he was incoherent and that he was vomiting during the sex. I was absolutely disgusted, but to be honest my very first thought was, 'What a disgrace of a woman. If a man had sex with a woman who was in that state it would be classed as rape.'

My mind was filling up with questions by the second. Had Ashley *really* had sex with *that* woman? I knew what he was like in drink. Physically, how do you even get turned on, let alone have sex when you are that incoherent?

I had never questioned sisterhood before. In my world, girls always stuck together. Now I was asking myself how one woman could do this to another, sleeping with *my* husband just because he's a footballer, and then selling a sleazebag story to a tabloid?

It was sick. Could I believe what *she* was saying if she was capable of admitting this type of disgusting behaviour in a national newspaper?

'You need to read this,' I shouted to Ashley. 'You need to get your arse down here, now.'

He came downstairs quietly but wouldn't read it. 'I'm not,' he said, looking at the floor and shaking his head. He looked appalled and upset with himself.

'You know what she's saying, don't you? You need to tell me if it's true. I *have* to know the truth.'

'I can't remember,' was all he said, and I really lost it when he said that, yet again. I was sick of hearing it. This was so serious, and he was just shaking his head and telling me he couldn't remember? In other words, that he might have had sex with her but he might not?

'It's just not good enough, Ashley!' I screamed. 'Surely to God you remember something?'

My whole body was shaking and now my head was exploding. We had *everything* and now our trust had gone and we'd lost it all. That's how it felt. It was such a waste of absolutely everything good that we ever had together.

'I can't, I just can't remember …'

I totally lost it then, and I mean I totally lost the plot. I felt every emotion possible: confusion, sadness, physical pain, sickness and fury, like I'd never experienced. Before I knew it I was lashing out at Ashley in every way I possibly could.

I hit him in the face. I couldn't help it. I was shaking him, kicking him, scratching his face, pushing and shoving him like I was a lunatic, and he just took it because it was obvious I'd gone crazy.

In fact, the more I pushed and provoked him, the more Ashley clammed up.

'I hope you enjoyed it!' I screamed. 'I hope she was worth it! It's the end of your marriage! You don't understand what you've done. It's f***ed!'

Ashley still said nothing, no matter what I did or said. After literally hours of me ranting and screaming and crying uncontrollably, I was too exhausted to carry on like that.

'OK. Let's be peaceful,' I sobbed eventually, desperately hoping this might make Ashley open up.

'I'll be calm. Just talk to me. If you talk to me maybe we can work something out.'

'Stop crying, babe, please. I don't know what you want me to say. You've read what she said …'

'Ashley, I need *you* to tell me what happened.'

'But what can I say? I don't know what to say.'

I sobbed and pleaded, but I still got nowhere at all. It was daylight by the time I became so completely drained that I eventually went to bed, leaving Ashley downstairs on the sofa.

There was no way I could sleep and I lay there thinking: 'You stupid *bastard*! Even if you were too drunk to have sex and it never happened, how could you put me through *this*? And why didn't you warn me this was all going to blow up? You must have known it was coming!'

The first person I phoned later that day was Hillary.

'I'm calling to let you know I'm leaving Girls Aloud,' I said. 'I want out of this industry. I've had enough.'

It felt like being in the group made this situation a million times worse for me. Other woman who had been cheated on by their husband didn't have to read about it in the newspaper. I did, because I was a pop star, and I just didn't want to be famous any more.

I then called Kimberley and Nicola, and said the same thing.

'I'm out of here,' I said. Nobody knew what to say to me. I don't think they could believe what was happening but they could tell I meant it wholeheartedly, and they were all devastated.

My mam was as shocked as everybody else, but she is so soft-hearted she still managed to think about how Ashley was feeling. She was staying with us at the time, and she told me she gave him a cuddle. Afterwards she said to me, 'Everybody makes mistakes. Don't forget, he's also hurting.'

Ashley just couldn't wait to run away to his football in the morning. He didn't want to stay at home and face it, and when he went out to training I thought, 'It's OK for you, once you're at the ground the paps can't come near. All you have to do is get there, then you're safe. What about me? You've fed me to the lions.'

I let Sundraj put out a statement a day or so later saying I didn't believe Ashley had slept with the girl and that I wanted to save the marriage. Both were gut reactions that I felt once I'd had a bit more time to think. If the girl was willing to tell the nation she slept with a man who got up in the middle of having sex to vomit, what sort of a person was she? I certainly thought that someone selling their story to a newspaper was not the most trustworthy character and was capable of making things up.

The one thing she and Ashley were in agreement on was how drunk he was that night, and I knew that if he was that bad, he would not have been capable of having sex. That's why I made the statement I did. The alternative was to throw my marriage away because of one drunken night that Ashley couldn't even remember. I felt I couldn't justify doing that, although I really wasn't sure how or if I could come back from this. The statement was out there, but privately I was full of doubt and indecision about where to go from here.

I had to get out of the house, and a day or two later I went to Kimberley's in the middle of the night. She was crying her eyes out when she saw me. I was still in shock, and when I say 'in shock' I really mean that I wasn't in control of myself at all, and I needed medical help. I got Valium tablets off the doctor to calm me down, and I lay on Kimberley's sofa but still couldn't sleep a wink.

My memories are all muddled up, but I know that some time that week we had to do the videoshoot for our new single 'Can't Speak French', and how I got through it I just don't know. The doctor gave me a B-vitamin injection in my bum to perk me up, but it didn't work, not at all.

'Are you sure you can do this?' Kimberley asked.

We were filming in a house in London and it was an all-night shoot. I hadn't eaten or slept for two days, but I knew I had to keep going. There were so many other people involved, and this was *my* problem, not theirs.

'Yes,' I told Kimberley. 'I'd rather be here than moping around the house.'

While we were doing the shoot I heard that the girl Ashley was meant to have slept with had responded to my statement and called me 'ridiculous' for believing he couldn't remember what had happened. I didn't read it, but I was told the gist of it. It baffled me why anyone would want to be at the centre of such a sordid story, but here she was again, prolonging my pain and rubbing salt into an already open wound.

'What is wrong with these people?' I thought.

There was a lot worse to come. The next day the girl claimed that she'd feared she was pregnant after her night with Ashley, and that his agent tried to pay for an abortion. I didn't believe her pregnancy claim for one second, but it did seem like the kind of offer Ashley's agent might make. I knew it was exactly how he would have reacted in the circumstances. The agent's job was to look after my husband, and if Ashley genuinely couldn't remember what had happened that night, the agent had no choice but to consider the claims might be true and try to protect his client.

It hurt like hell when I thought about the agent's involvement. I'd known him for years, and not only that, I'd been out to dinner with him and Ashley in the last few weeks, when all this abortion business must have been going on. It was beyond hideous to think I'd sat there, with Ashley, making conversation with a man who knew our marriage was under threat like this.

The pregnancy claim made me distrust the girl's story even more, but I didn't know what to do next. I was so hurt and confused. When I'd said my vows to Ashley on our wedding day I meant them, but how could we possibly recover from this?

After the videoshoot, I festered on Kimberley's settee for days and days, barely moving. Kimberley's boyfriend Justin helped take care of me, and was really supportive. Ashley didn't know where I was but I thought the very least he deserved was the silent treatment.

Over the next few days I heard that two more girls had come forward to say they'd had sex with Ashley. I didn't read the stories, but I knew one was saying it happened when Ashley and I were courting, and another said she slept with him a few months after our wedding.

'Why would they come forward now?' I asked myself. 'They must be making it up, trying to cash in while Ashley's vulnerable.'

I desperately wanted the stories to be lies and I told myself they had to be made up, but the truth was I didn't know what to believe. I just wanted to run away and hide, and I asked Kimberley and Nicola if they'd come away with me, on a holiday somewhere far away.

'Just go,' Justin told Kimberley straight away. 'Don't think twice.' Nicola said, 'I'm coming, wherever you want me to come.' I don't think she even consulted her boyfriend, because she replied to my text in a matter of seconds.

I picked up the phone to Ashley and told him, 'Guess what? Me, Kimberley and Nicola are going away and I'll send you the bill.' He didn't argue; in fact I don't think he even spoke more than two words to me.

I booked us a villa at a private resort in Thailand, and as soon as our flight took off, I had this overwhelming feeling of 'f*** the world'. I could have fallen out of the sky from the plane and I was certain nothing would have been as painful as what I was feeling inside.

It was now about two weeks after the initial allegations had come out and, looking back, I was completely out of my head on tranquilisers. As soon as we got to the villa I crashed out in my room for two full days. I literally closed the blinds and I was gone.

'Is there any coffee?' I asked the girls when I finally emerged into the light.

We laugh our heads off about that now, because Kimberley and Nicola say it was exactly like the scene in the first *Sex and the City* movie, but the funniest thing is that the film hadn't even been made yet.

I hired a boat even though I hate sailing, but my attitude was that nothing was important any more, and I didn't even care if I was eaten by a shark. 'Nothing matters,' I thought. 'My career *certainly* doesn't matter. All I care about is my friends and my family. The rest of it can go to f***. Girls Aloud can go. I don't care about *any* of it.'

Kimberley, Nicola and I drank cocktails, went to dinner and laughed about some of the funny moments we'd had together.

'Remember when we used to do the university gigs in the early days, and the students chucked beer at us?' Kimberley said. 'I can't believe that really happened.'

'What about when Cheryl's costume ripped all up the bum on the "No Good Advice" video?' Nicola laughed. 'Oh my God, that was so funny. The outfit looked like it was made of tin foil and you had silver gaffer tape holding it together!'

'Wardrobe malfunctions must be my thing,' I replied, reminding the girls about a more recent disaster, when I'd gone out to dinner in a pair of lace trousers and ended up getting stuck to the table, as someone had put chewing gum underneath the table top. 'How embarrassing was that? They literally had to get a hair dryer to melt the chewing gum and get me out of my seat without ripping the trousers!'

We'd sit on the harbour with bits of bread between our toes, dangling our feet in the water to feed the fish and waving to the friendly fishermen in their little boats.

I felt like I'd escaped the world for once. One morning, I came out of my room and saw three arses sticking in the air on the balcony of our villa.

'What the f*** are you doing?' I said loudly. For a minute I thought my tranquilisers were making me hallucinate, but then Nicola and Kimberley started hushing me.

'Shhh! It's yoga,' Kimberley whispered. Their instructor calmly continued the class while I cracked up laughing.

It definitely helped to be away with the girls, in the sunshine, surrounded by beautiful beaches. My heart was racing all the

time, though, and I had a constant, physical pain in my chest. I
didn't feel like eating much, and I was smoking more than normal,
to the point where the girls would say: 'Cheryl, you've just put
one out.'

One night I went out onto the balcony and spoke to a friend
back home. I'd had a few drinks and started pouring my heart out,
saying I couldn't care less what was in the tabloids. 'I'm not a
victim,' I said. 'I don't want sympathy.'

As I spoke I heard a rustle in the bushes beneath our balcony,
and when I looked down there were two men standing there,
looking straight at me. I screamed in fright and they ran off. The
next day we heard that someone had checked into the villa next
door and then left without paying. Sundraj was on the phone soon
afterwards.

'I know you're trying to get away from it all and you don't want
to know what's in the tabloids, but I need to warn you there are
journalists out there.'

'How do you know?'

'Because the conversation you had on your balcony last night,
about not being a victim, is splashed all over *The Sun*.'

I couldn't believe how naïve I'd been, again. When was I going
to learn that the press would follow me everywhere, even to
Thailand? It also turned out that some of the 'friendly fishermen'
were paps, so there were pictures of us in our bikinis too, with me
looking all skinny. Unbelievable.

The next day I sat on my own overlooking the beach. I didn't
know who I was anymore, I thought. I was a heartbroken girl, but
who *was* I, now, without Ashley by my side? I knew I loved him
and I didn't want to end my marriage. I still felt that, very strongly.
Despite all this heartache he'd caused, my initial gut feeling
remained, that I couldn't justify leaving my marriage because of
one drunken mistake that wasn't even in Ashley's memory. Now
I'd had a bit more time to think, I definitely didn't believe the
other two girls who'd come forward, because why had they just
done so now? I'd known something was up after the night of the

fight because Ashley acted so weird, but he'd never behaved like that before, and surely I would have known if he'd been hiding secrets from me for years?

Their stories just didn't add up, but the trouble was that nothing made much sense to me any more. Kimberley and Nicola comforted me and listened whenever I wanted to talk, but they didn't probe or offer advice when I said some of these things. I knew they were both angry and upset with Ashley, and that they were there for me if I needed them. That's what was important.

After 10 days in Thailand the three of us flew to LA via Hong Kong, because I was due to audition for my place as a street dancer in Will.i.am's 'Heartbreaker' video, for *The Passions of Girls Aloud* documentary series.

I was so glad the girls were with me, because when we landed in LA there were more than 30 paps waiting at LAX Airport. My bags had been lost in Hong Kong, so I had to fill in loads of forms that kept us at the airport for much longer than we wanted. When we eventually walked out the paps were being really aggressive, calling Ashley names and trying to provoke a reaction.

'Why's your husband a jerk?' one of them called out.

I bit my lip and tried not to cry, and when we finally got to our hotel I put on Mary J. Blige's album, *Growing Pains*, to try to cheer myself up. Her lyrics are inspiring and it really lifted my spirits, so I kept putting the album on repeat.

'Do we have to listen to that *again*?' Nicola moaned.

'Shut up, it's saving me life!' I replied.

'So what? It's doin' me 'ead in! Come on, let's go out.'

The girls took me out clubbing, and in one club, late into the evening, I was introduced to Will.i.am for the first time. I'd had loads of vodka shots, and I just remember someone saying to him, 'This is Cheryl. She's auditioning to be in your video tomorrow.'

He smiled politely and wished me good luck. I remember thinking to myself, 'How the hell is this audition going to go down?'

All the time I'd been shooting *The Passions* I was a happily married, healthy woman. Now I was miserable and messed up in the head, and I didn't even look like the same person because I'd gone from Size 8 to Size Zero.

I didn't realise it at the time, but I was also going to have the hangover from hell the next day. When we got back to our hotel that night I'd lost my key and the receptionist refused to believe I was a guest.

'Honestly, I checked in as Emma Robinson, but I don't have ID in that name because my real name is Cheryl Cole,' I told her.

She looked at me like I was crazy.

There were some British air stewardesses checking in, who overheard the conversation. One of them assured the receptionist that I was Cheryl Cole, but because I'd signed in under a false name, it all got very confusing.

'This is just typical! The one time I wouldn't mind being recognised I'm not! Why do things like this always happen to me?'

I began drunk crying, making a lot of noise but with no tears, and begging the receptionist to get someone to take me to my room, where I promised I'd get my passport to show her my photo and prove who I really was.

'What's a pretty lady like you crying for?' I heard an American guy say to me. I was just about to turn round and tell him to do one when I heard one of his mates explaining to the other girls that they were members of the R&B band Jodeci.

'Wow!' I said, my ears pricking up. 'I listened to you as a teen-ager! I *love* your music!'

In my drunken state I was thinking, 'That was a time when I was happy! This is a good omen!'

A security guard appeared, who took me to my room, and a few minutes later Kimberley, Nicola, our friend Lisa who had joined us and the two Jodeci guys appeared at the door. The boys had a hand-held camera and told us they were making a behind-the-scenes film to promote their comeback.

'Oh my God! You're making a comeback,' I said. 'That's the best news ever!'

We let them come in and we all started being daft, saying 'hi' to the camera and having a drink together. Jodeci was such a huge group I felt they'd understand the whole fame thing, and so I allowed myself to open up and told them a bit about Ashley and why I was so sad. It was all very innocent. Bizarrely, one of the guys said a prayer for me before they left an hour or so later, and when I woke up the next day with a banging headache I just thought, 'Wow! That was *such* a random night.'

I struggled to the video audition that morning and felt absolutely terrible doing the street dance routine I'd worked so hard to learn for months before. The fact the song was called 'Heartbreaker' was so ironic it was ridiculous, and when Will.i.am turned up to see how I'd done I wondered what the hell he would make of this messed-up, hung-over person who was trying to be in his video.

'Of course I want Cheryl in it,' he told his team as soon as he saw me perform, and I felt like crying all over again.

Will came over to me for a chat, and we connected straight away. It turned out my label had warned him about what was going on in my private life, and he talked to me a bit about his old relationship.

I hadn't expected him to be like that at all. He was one of the biggest names in the music industry and was such a huge star that I imagined he might have been a bit distant, or even on a totally different planet to me. Instead he was a very real, charming person in amongst all the madness in my life, and I really appreciated the fact he took the time to speak to me. Will later asked me to record some vocals for 'Heartbreaker' too, which was also very sweet of him. That was the first time I ever recorded without the girls, in fact, though I had no clue then where this experience would eventually lead me.

Once the video was done I felt ready to go home. I wasn't used to LA and I'd been away from Ashley for several weeks. Despite the hell he'd put me through, I felt very strongly now that I just wanted my life to go back to normal. Splitting up was unthinkable to me. I'd been torturing myself for weeks, going over and over events in my mind. I had no real proof Ashley had been unfaithful. All I knew for sure was that he'd gone out and got blind drunk and met that girl, and my gut reaction remained the same.

'I can't justify leaving me marriage because of one drunken mistake,' I told Kimberley and Nicola as we headed home. It was like I had to say it out loud, to make my decision official, and my friends just listened and told me they would always support me, no matter what.

I made a pact with myself on that flight. I had made the choice to go back to Ashley, and I would not throw all this in his face. I couldn't see any point in that because we had to move on, not look back. He'd been texting me ever since I left, asking me to come home, but he was totally in the dark about how I was going to react. I'd ignored most of his messages or told him to leave me alone, and I knew he was panicking about what I was going to do next.

We had never spoken about the allegations from the other two girls, but right from the start I didn't believe their stories, and I decided I didn't even want to go there with confronting Ashley about them. I wasn't going to tell him all this to begin with, of course, because we had to get a few other things straight first, but that's what was going through my mind.

Before I saw Ashley again I actually had to go straight to the BRITs from the airport, though if I hadn't gone through my old diaries I wouldn't have remembered the event, which shows what a mess my head was in. All I recall is that Girls Aloud were nominated for Best Group and didn't win it, and Nadine didn't show up. I think we all expected her to come up with some sort of excuse, like she'd lost her passport and couldn't get over from America, but she actually just admitted to us, 'It's not really my thing.'

I can remember a sort of stunned silence, like we'd all been slapped in the face, but I was so cut up about my marriage this didn't really make the impact it probably should have.

I met Ashley at home after the BRITs. I actually had butterflies in my stomach, but not the ones I was used to feeling when I looked at my husband. I felt sick and nervous at having to deal with this nightmare, and I could see he felt exactly the same.

'I've come to the conclusion you obviously don't care about me as much as I care about you,' I said.

It was painful to say the words, and Ashley looked pained when I said them.

'It's not true,' he said, shaking his head, and he made it clear he didn't want the marriage to end.

He was very quiet and sad, and I told him that I didn't want us to split up either, but that for us to move forward three things had to happen.

'Just tell me,' he nodded. 'I'll do anything.'

'I don't want you drinking. I don't want you socialising with footballers or the people you were with that night. And I don't want you to deal with that agent of yours any more.'

He agreed to all three in a heartbeat.

'There is one other thing,' I said. 'I'm warning you that if anything like this *ever* comes up again I'm divorcing you. You're lucky I've come back this time and if you *ever* disrespect me like this again, it's all over, I'm out of here, and I mean it.'

Ashley looked relieved but was still very quiet and withdrawn, and for days and weeks and months afterwards he was not himself at all, and nor was I. It was like starting all over again, except we didn't have the blank canvas we had when we were courting, we had one with dirty marks on it that we had to keep trying to wipe away.

I was straight back into rehearsals for the next Girls Aloud tour, which was good in one way as it meant I had no time to sit around and dwell on what had happened to my marriage. Hillary had calmed me down after my initial threats to leave the music industry, and had very sensibly told me that I shouldn't make any rash decisions, especially when I was in such an emotional state.

The downside of going to work was that actually just leaving the house each morning had become a total nightmare, because I was being chased ferociously every day by the paparazzi.

'Have you forgiven him, Cheryl?' 'Ashley's a love rat – why have you taken him back?' 'Can you ever trust him again?'

It was relentless, and it was draining. They wanted pictures of me looking miserable because it went with the story, and they certainly got plenty of me looking that way because that's how *they* made me feel, regardless of what mood I was in when I left the house.

I was working really hard with the girls. When we started the *Tangled Up* tour, which was our third arena tour, we wanted it to be bigger and better than anything we'd done before. There had been even more rumours about Girls Aloud splitting up after Nadine failed to show at the BRITs, but it wasn't true and this was our chance to show we were not just together, but we were at our peak. Millions were spent on the set and the outfits, and we had 24 dates booked, performing to 300,000 fans.

My phone rang during a sound check one day. 'Hi Cheryl, it's Sundraj.'

'What's the problem this time? Has the rest of the tour been cancelled?' I was trying to make a joke of the fact he had become my official bearer of bad news as well as our head of publicity, and his reply came as a shock.

'Well, actually, some guys have put out a story, and they're saying they have a video of you, Kimberley and Nicola partying in a hotel room in LA.'

'Jodeci? Oh God, no. I was howling drunk and had mascara all over my face.'

'It's worse than that.'

'Tell me.'

'They weren't Jodeci. They were a couple of guys making an American TV show called *Parking Lot Pimps*. Their job was to chat up as many pretty girls as possible and get them to say "Hi PLP" on camera, and you did it.'

'You *are* joking!'

'Unfortunately not.'

I knew it was all very innocent but I was still devastated when I eventually saw the film the guys had made, after it turned up alongside the story on the *News of the World* website. I was mortified, in fact, not least because I had kissed one of the guys on the top of his bald head, which sparked all kinds of stupid stories about how I was taking revenge on Ashley. It caused so much trouble, and Kimberley and Nicola's boyfriends went absolutely bazooka.

'You know what, only *I* could escape the paparazzi and walk straight into something like this,' I said.

It would have been funny if it wasn't so embarrassing, but there was absolutely nothing we could do about it but put it down to experience.

I got on with the tour and really threw myself into it. I loved every performance and totally lost myself on the stage. It did me good to spend time with the girls, talking about high heels and hairspray instead of my problems. We actually sold double the amount of tickets we had done on the *Greatest Hits* tour the previous year, which was an incredible achievement. I was buzzing for the first time in months, and I wondered what on earth I'd been thinking of to even *consider* leaving the music industry.

At the end of the tour we did a private gig in Monaco, and while we were all sitting round our hotel pool one day my phone rang and I saw the name 'Simon Cowell' flash up.

I'd met Simon briefly the year before when I took part in *Celebrity Apprentice* for Comic Relief. I was in the girls' team, and we had to phone people up and ask them for money. The first person I thought of was Simon and I wasn't afraid to call him. I was filmed asking him for a donation of anything between £1,000 and £10,000.

'I'll give you £25,000,' he said after listening to my spiel.

The deal was that the donors had to come down to a funfair we were running, or the money didn't count.

'Why did you give me so much money?' I asked Simon on the night.

'Because you were so blatant and have such a sparky personality,' he said. 'You're opinionated too. I like that.'

Not long after that he'd asked me to take part in his new show, *Britain's Got Talent*.

'Hi Cheryl, how are you, darling?' he'd said. 'Listen, I was wondering, how would you like to be a judge on *Britain's Got Talent*?'

It was a brand new show and I didn't know anything about it.

'No, I'm not sure that's for me ...'

'But Cheryl, you're perfect for it. I could see that as soon as we met on *Celebrity Apprentice* ...'

Simon had then started explaining how the show worked, with the judges watching a variety of acts and pressing a buzzer if they wanted to vote them off.

'I don't like the sound of that. I'm not sure I could do that to someone. I know what it's like to be up there on stage like that, being judged. It's nerve-wracking enough, without a buzzer.'

'That's *exactly* why you're perfect for the job. You can relate to the contestants. Trust me, you'll love it.'

'Anyway, I'm on tour right now,' I'd said to him, which was true as I was on the *Greatest Hits* tour at the time. 'The timing doesn't work.'

'Filming starts after your tour ends, I've checked.'

Simon had an answer for everything and was ridiculously persuasive, and by the end of that call I had reluctantly found myself agreeing to do it. I had no time to give it any more thought while I was still on tour, but as soon as we'd done our last performance I had started to deeply regret saying yes.

It was 2007 when all that happened. I'd been married for less than a year at that point and all I really wanted was to spend time being a wife. I just wanted to be able to relax and see Buster and

Coco every day too, because I'd missed them like crazy while I'd been away.

I remember I agonised for about a week about what I should do about *Britain's Got Talent*, and two days before I was due to start I phoned Simon and pulled out.

'I'm sorry, but I don't know the show, and I want more time at home,' I told him honestly. 'It's just not for me right now, I should never have agreed.'

'Shame that,' he replied. 'I was going to offer you *The X Factor*. What do you think?'

'I wouldn't do *The X Factor* for all the tea in China,' I replied without hesitation, as I knew the show well and always watched it with Ashley.

My immediate thought was that *The X Factor* would be an even harder job than *Britain's Got Talent*, because the contestants were all singers. That meant I wouldn't just understand how it felt to be up there on a stage being judged, I would know *exactly* what was going through their minds, because I had literally been in their shoes less than six years before. I couldn't take someone else's dream away. It would break my heart to do that, and I told Simon there was no way he was going to change my mind.

'As I've said, I wouldn't do it for all the tea in China,' I said each time he came up with another way to persuade me.

'But thank you for the offer.'

I'd felt very relieved when I finally put the phone down, but Simon obviously didn't like taking 'no' for an answer.

'Cheryl, hi! It's Simon Cowell,' he said now, as I sunbathed by the pool in Monaco.

It was June 2008 and apparently Sharon Osbourne had quit *The X Factor* the day before.

'Will you reconsider?' Simon said.

'What part of "no" did this man not understand?' I thought.

'Simon, I'm really flattered by the offer but I said last year…'

I don't think he let me finish my sentence before he started trying to persuade me all over again to join him on the judging panel, alongside Louis Walsh and Dannii Minogue.

'You'll love it,' Simon was saying. 'It's a buzz to mentor somebody and watch them flourish. I've heard you have a good ear for music and I know you're gobby. I like that. You're perfect. Trust me, I'm going to take care of you here.'

Simon was very clever. He knew how I felt about the judging element and ending people's dreams, so he shifted the focus onto the mentoring part of the job, which I had to admit did appeal to me. Then, once he had my interest, he came out with the line that really caught my attention.

'The best thing is, the focus is on the acts, not you. It couldn't be more perfect.'

I hadn't thought of it like that before. I'd been under so much scrutiny because of my marriage, and now Simon was telling me that this was a chance to do something that wasn't all about me for a change. It was all about the acts, not me, and I liked the sound of that.

'OK, I'll consider it,' I promised.

I think Simon took that as a 'yes', because it's what he wanted to hear.

I immediately spoke to all the girls, and Ashley of course, and everybody said exactly the same thing: 'Go for it – what have you got to lose?'

I had no answer to that, which was just as well because the press statement was out there almost before I'd drawn breath from calling Simon back.

'Cheryl Cole to replace Sharon Osbourne as *X Factor* Judge.'

As soon as I saw the headline I wondered what on earth I was getting myself in to. What's more, I only had four days to get myself organised before the first auditions started. This was crazy.

I remember my dad phoning me around this time, sounding a bit upset.

'Cheryl, sweetheart, I've just seen on a documentary that you've had a boob job. I'm that shocked, I can't tell you.'

'Dad! I haven't had a boob job,' I replied. 'How many times do I have to tell you not to believe everything you hear? They're always making up stories about me. It's doing my head in!'

'Well, thank goodness for that. I didn't think you'd do anything like that ...'

I'd had the worst hell ever from the media for six months at this point, and my dad's call added to my worries about what I was letting myself in for with *The X Factor*. Would the spotlight *really* be on the acts instead of me?

I was already in a daily battle with myself not to take out my frustration with the paps on Ashley, and there were times when I'd really had to bite my tongue.

'You stupid bastard! This is your fault!' I wanted to shout at him after the paps had camped outside the house or chased me down a street. One time I was literally running down an alleyway in central London, being chased by 30 strange men. I wasn't even working; I'd been for a dental appointment, nothing more exciting than that. If those men hadn't had cameras in their hands I could have called the police, but I couldn't because they were doing their jobs, hunting for a story, and Ashley's behaviour had turned me into one of their biggest targets.

'I'm having a sad day,' was all I said to Ashley whenever I was finding things hard.

There was no point in blaming him because it would only cause more trouble, and I knew he was struggling too. When I was away on tour he hardly dared to go out, and he started smoking for the first time in his life, to help deal with the stress.

'Everybody's watching, waiting for me to mess up,' he said.

On one occasion, when he had to attend a football function, a blonde girl had tried to sit on his knee. Ashley swished her away and was fuming afterwards, saying the paps had sent her over on purpose.

'They're out to get me,' he ranted.

'It can't go on forever, we'll get through this,' I said, though I really wasn't sure how.

I had days when every time I saw a blonde woman I panicked, thinking it might be that hairdresser. I didn't tell anybody that, because I didn't want my friends and family worrying about me. I didn't confide in anybody, in fact.

I remember just once texting my mam and telling her about how upset I was by the paps chasing me. She replied by saying, 'OK', which made me burst out laughing. My mam didn't know how to text properly, but even if she did she probably wouldn't have said a lot more than that. I hadn't been brought up to pour my heart out, and it was a big reminder to me of how I'd dealt with all my troubles in the past.

'Pick your chin up,' I could still hear my brother Joe saying to me, and that's what I was trying to do, every single day.

Taking the *X Factor* job was a good way of doing that, I told myself. It was something new and exciting, and what did I have to lose?

10

'Everyone loves you. You're a star. Well done!'

'Me dad would always choose the song off the album that would be a hit,' I said to Ashley as I tried to convince myself I could do the *X Factor* job.

'I've grown up with that. I can spot talent, can't I?'

'You'll be brilliant, babes,' Ashley said. 'And look at the other telly you've done – you're a natural.'

None of the other TV work I'd done was remotely like being a judge on *The X Factor*, but I knew Ashley was only trying to support me.

'Well, I'm doing it now,' I said. 'There's no going back. If it doesn't work out, at least I've tried.'

I didn't say this to Ashley, but my attitude to a lot of things had changed since his cheating. The way I felt in Thailand, when I didn't care whether I got eaten by a shark, was still with me. I'd been to hell and back, and nothing could ever be as bad as that. Not being a successful talent show judge certainly wouldn't come close, so what did I have to fear?

That's how I felt when I turned up for the first audition days later. I'd watched the last few series of *The X Factor* at home with Ashley and always really enjoyed the show. I'd always been able to pick out the winner too, and so it wasn't like stepping into something totally unknown.

'Just be yourself, that's all you can do,' Ashley said.

Simon came over to me with a cheeky, smug smile on his face. 'I'll guide you step by step,' he said, which was good to hear, but I wasn't even nervous.

Louis made it easy too. 'Let's forget everything that's gone before,' he said. 'Calling us fat, you mean?' I thought, but I just smiled and agreed with him. 'We'll let bygones be bygones.'

When I met Dannii I decided to get in first, saying to her, 'Let's not let the media make this a bitch fest.' She readily agreed. I didn't know what had gone on between Dannii and Sharon Osbourne at that point, but there were all kinds of rumours that they didn't get on, and that was why Sharon had left. I really didn't have the energy for all that rubbish and I didn't ask questions. I just wanted to focus on the job and pick out the best talent, and I imagined that was all Simon wanted me to do too. I had no idea at the time, but I came to find out later that Simon actually *loved* drama between the judges.

One of the first auditions I saw was in Manchester, and it completely threw me. I recognised the contestant the second he walked in the door. It was Nikk Mager, one of the boys who had made the final 10 in *Popstars* with me, six years earlier. He never made it into the boy band One True Voice, but he hadn't given up on his dream and was back, trying to win a recording contract, all those years later.

'I can't do this,' I said when he started to sing. His audition wasn't going well, and I felt like I was having a panic attack. I just knew I was not going to be able to say those words: 'It's a "no" from me.' It seemed so wrong, having once been on the other side with him, so I refused to vote. Simon was fine about it afterwards, because of course any drama was good for ratings, but that was something else I was too naïve to have worked out back then.

Once I got to know Simon a bit better I'd actually beg him not to make me be the one to say 'no'. 'It makes me die a little bit inside,' I'd plead.

'Sorry, Cheryl, it's all part of the show.'

'But you don't mind saying "no". In fact you enjoy it!'

'So-rry.'

The only acts I didn't having any problem saying 'no' to were the 14-year-olds. I didn't care how good they were, I considered them too vulnerable for the industry at that age and would point out what happened to Britney Spears and Michael Jackson to anyone who argued with me, Simon included.

'Come back when you're 16 and you'll have more experience,' I said to each and every one, and I'm pleased to say the entry age was raised to 16 for the next series because of me.

Another audition that sticks in my mind is the one by two Welsh boys, Ant & Seb, who came to see us in Cardiff. They told us they compared themselves to P. Diddy and Usher, with Rick Astley thrown in, so I had a feeling it wasn't going to be good. My instinct was right. Their version of 'Mysterious Girl' turned out to be hilariously bad, with one of the boys throwing the odd random word in while the other sang. Me, Simon and Louis all got the giggles and I swear I hadn't laughed so much in a long, long time.

I was quickly finding out that life on the judging panel was an emotional rollercoaster, although I seemed to be affected much more than the other judges. No sooner had I stopped giggling about something than I'd be crying my eyes out when an act tugged at my heartstrings. This happened in a big way when Daniel Evans first auditioned. He'd just lost his wife and had a teeny baby, and I found it incredibly distressing to hear him sing. He chose 'Sometimes When We Touch' and I just couldn't stop the tears pouring down my cheeks, because it was like he was singing directly to his wife.

I felt a real connection to him, and looking back it was probably because of what I was going through with Ashley at the time. Even though the allegations were a good six months behind us, it was like I was experiencing a sort of mourning process, grieving for the marriage we used to have, while at the same time trying to resurrect it. I can't describe it in a better way. Something had died in my life, and I was trying my best to revive it and carry on.

I couldn't even say 'yes' to Daniel when he finished his audition because I was crying so much, so I just had to nod my head to give him my vote as I sniffed and dried my eyes.

I got to know Simon quickly. He was true to his word and did guide me through as he'd promised. We took cigarette breaks together and he'd talk to me about things I knew nothing about, like the production side of the show. He got off on the incredible amount of power he has and was in his element playing the big 'I am' television executive, but he has such a cheeky way about him too that I couldn't help liking him.

One of the first things I learned about Simon is how ridiculously vain he is. The very first time we took a break together, at the Birmingham auditions, Simon spent the whole time looking over my shoulder. I had my back to the building, and it took me a while to realise that he was actually looking at himself the whole time we were talking, because the building had reflective walls. I took the mickey out of him when I realised what he was doing, but he didn't care and thought it was funny. It was such an unexpected, immature thing for a man in his position to do. I've always been fascinated by people with interesting characters, and I was definitely intrigued by Simon.

'You are literally one of the best people I've worked with, and I don't say that lightly,' Simon told me one day.

The edited auditions had started to be shown on TV, and it felt like the whole country had gone completely *X Factor* crazy. The show – and my part in it – was being written about and talked about everywhere, which completely took me by surprise. I was used to the documentaries and chat shows I'd done in the past being written about in the press, but most of my television experience consisted of going on promo with the girls and on *Top of the Pops*, and nobody ever wrote about that.

'So how do you feel being part of the show?' Simon asked. 'Aren't you glad you listened to me?'

'I don't really know,' I shrugged.

'You should be. Everyone loves you. You're a star. Well done!'

When I watched the audition shows myself for the first time I was surprised to see that I was being filmed even when I wasn't talking. In my naïvety I'd imagined the camera would only be on me when it was my turn to speak, and yet there I was whispering to Louis or giggling about something with Simon. According to Simon that was all part of my appeal. I was a natural, apparently, and that's why people had warmed to me. They loved the fact I wore my heart on my sleeve and wasn't afraid to show how I really felt, whichever emotion that was. 'You're doing what they're all doing at home,' Simon said. 'That's why you're such a hit.'

On a professional level I worked well with Dannii, but we didn't spend time one on one. There was no common ground at all. We were from different generations and both into totally different clothes and music. She's a child star from a showbiz family, so we certainly couldn't relate to each other's background either.

'What problems could you possibly have by the age of 25?' she commented during one audition, when the contestant had talked about some personal problems. I can't remember what the guy had said, but if Dannii had had a spare couple of hours – or days, even – I could certainly have enlightened her. I was only 25 myself.

There was a lot of gossip about Dannii's relationship with Simon. It was the reason Sharon left, so I heard, but I didn't take any notice. I didn't have the time to waste talking about it, and whenever I saw Dannii and Simon flirting with each other I turned a blind eye. I'm surprised Simon has since talked about it in his unofficial biography; he's a person who hates disloyalty.

Before the live shows started I went on Net-a-Porter.com and bought myself some dresses. I was responsible for my own styling, and so I also asked my friend Lisa, who had worked with Girls Aloud for years, to do my hair and help me with my make-up. It was at this point that I also asked the other girls if I could take Lily England out of the office. She was working as a PA to all five of us, but it had reached the point where I needed full-time help. The girls agreed to find somebody else, and Lily came to work exclusively for me.

I hadn't realised how all-consuming *The X Factor* would be. I'd imagined a few weeks of auditions and boot camp here, a short trip away for judges' houses and then the live shows.

It was obvious the 'lives' would be hard work, but I'd totally underestimated the rest of it. I had absolutely no idea how mentally and physically demanding it would be just looking after my acts, helping with song choices and dealing with their personal dramas, week in week out, so when Lily came on board to help organise *my* life, she was a total lifesaver.

I always gave myself two hours to get ready, but Simon had the dressing room next door and would be relentlessly calling for me. He was the boss and so I couldn't ever refuse, even if I was in a tracksuit and slippers with rollers in my hair and mascara on one eye.

'Nice,' Simon would say cheekily, eyeing me up and down.

'I think *she* looks awful, though. You need to change the outfit.' This was a typical criticism of his, directed at one of my girls. I had Alexandra Burke, Diana Vickers and Laura White in my final three and I was fiercely protective of all my acts. By that stage, having gone through boot camp and judges' houses together, we'd formed a strong bond and things were incredibly intense.

I was super sensitive to anything anybody said about my girls, to the point where Ashley would say to me when I got home, 'You shouldn't invest so much, babe,' because I was always emotionally wrung out. Ashley loved the show and thought it was great I was doing it. He told me that his mates all said, 'We love your missus on *The X Factor*,' which made him proud, but he could see it was taking a lot out of me.

'I know what you're saying,' I'd tell him when I got home feeling absolutely wiped out. 'But I know what it's like being left to fend for yourself. I'm seeing this through. I'm not doing what Louis did with Girls Aloud – I'm supporting my girls one hundred per cent.'

As I got to know Simon even better and the final got closer, I started answering him back more. If he had a last-minute go at me about song choices it really did my head in, because he'd usually known about them for most of the week.

'Why are you leaving it until now to say this to me?' I'd ask.

Sometimes I felt like I was going crazy I was so strung out, and Simon started this joke about me being like a puppy dog with big wet eyes.

'Come here then,' he'd tease, patting his thighs with the palms of his hands, like you do when you call a little puppy. 'Come here!'

He was so cheeky, but I just used to laugh it off. Nobody else could have got away with it, but Simon did.

'Why tell me this now? Why don't you just save it for the show?' I'd tell him as I flounced out of his dressing room in my fluffy slippers. I sometimes did that on purpose when I was genuinely panicking about not having enough time to get ready. Simon loved all that, and Louis would see me flapping in the corridor and burst out laughing. 'They should just film backstage, it'd make a better show,' he always said.

Louis was probably right. Simon's dressing room alone would have provided hours of gripping reality television. He had assistants bringing him all kinds of health juices and tablets and he'd sit there laughing at cartoons like a little boy one minute then gazing at himself in the mirror the next.

'I can't believe how vain you are, Simon,' I'd tease, but really I was gobsmacked by how this ridiculously wealthy and powerful man could be so fixated by appearances.

'Did you know they all liked Dannii's dress better than yours last week?' he'd snipe.

'And?' I'd reply. 'I'm not here for what the tabloids and magazines think about who had the best dress on. I'm here to find new talent and mentor the acts, remember?'

I honestly didn't care about all that 'battle of the babes' rubbish. There was far too much going on in my life for me to be poring over magazines, seeing who had a tick and who had a cross over her frock each week.

Simon always had women all over his dressing room, hanging off every part of his suit. Some of them I didn't recognise, but I got to know the more familiar faces like Sinitta, Jackie St Clair, Terri Seymour and Mezghan Hussainy. They were Simon's

s of the past, present and future. I really didn't pay much
to who was currently 'the one', and by the same token
ery rarely asked me about Ashley. He might occasionally
say, 'How's Ashley?' and that was literally as far as it went. He
never, ever talked to me about my relationship and he certainly
never tried to give me any advice – he knows I'd have told him
where to go.

Actually, Simon started to ask *me* for advice, all the time, but
only ever about work. He wanted to know what I thought of the
set and the show's format, and what could be improved. I think he
liked the fact I was looking through fresh eyes, and I always told
him straight. 'That part of the set looks cheap, I don't like it,' I'd
say, and the next thing I knew it would be gone, replaced by something bigger and better. 'I think we should have Beyoncé on,' I
also said, and then I couldn't believe it when she was actually
booked, and I was going to meet one of my all-time idols.

On the day of the final, in December 2008, I was a complete
and utter emotional wreck. Beyoncé was going to sing with
Alexandra, and I was totally starstruck when I got to meet her. I'd
been in the business for six years by now and was used to seeing a
lot of famous people. I never really got excited by it any more, but
Beyoncé was different. I used to sing along to Destiny's Child on
repeat in my bedroom, and this was the woman I took inspiration
from, so much so I'd bleached my hair blonde as a teenager.

Beyoncé has a star aura and an incredible presence and when
we were introduced I can't remember a thing we said to each
other. When she did her sound check with Alex I started crying
and didn't really stop for the rest of the day. I could see how overwhelmed Alex was too, and I knew exactly how she felt. It was a
huge, huge moment for the both of us.

As we waited for the final result, with Louis and his group, JLS,
on the stage beside us, I was shaking as much as Alex. It was exactly
like waiting for Davina to announce the members of Girls Aloud
back in 2002. I looked at Alex's anxious face and it was like looking
into a mirror. That was me, six years earlier, and it was also like

looking at a reflection of myself in that exact moment too, because I was sharing every emotion, every wave of nervous excitement and rush of adrenalin that Alex was experiencing.

The second she was announced as the winner I felt her body drop and I literally pulled her back to her feet. We were both absolutely euphoric, and Alex was so shocked she could barely speak. It was just the best, and I went backstage and cried my eyes out, sobbing more than I ever did on *Popstars*.

Ashley was so happy for me, but he also said he was relieved it was all over. He'd seen how much the show had taken out of me. In the end I was skinnier than I'd been in years, and I was absolutely exhausted, to the point of collapse. The show had been a huge ratings success though, and Simon was absolutely over the moon and was already talking about the next series.

'As I said to you at the start of this process, you are literally one of the best people I've worked with,' he told me. 'I knew you could do it. You're a natural. Well done.' Then he added: 'Thanks for being great, and most importantly, thanks for making me look good in choosing you.'

I'd never set out to have this part of my career and I was amazed by what had happened to me. *The X Factor* had dominated the past six months of my life, and I'd been so caught up with the acts I hadn't had any time to take stock of my own life along the way. It was like Simon had put me on a rollercoaster ride in June and I'd just stepped off with my head spinning, and gone, 'Wow! Did I really just do that?'

Over the past couple of months I'd performed 'The Promise', our new Girls Aloud single, on *The X Factor*, as well as on *The Jonathan Ross Show* and Children in Need. It was great to be on stage with the girls again. This was our nineteenth single, it went to number one and we partied just like in the old days.

That was all I'd ever wanted, my whole life; to sing on the TV and have a number one record. I could hardly believe it was still happening all these years after 'Sound of the Underground' had first made my dream come true.

I started being praised all over the place, and I found it really embarrassing. I was also winning all kinds of polls – crazy things like *Glamour* magazine's 50 Best-dressed Women in the World, or *FHM*'s World's Sexiest Woman. It was ludicrous, really.

'What do you think they'd make of me if they saw us like this?' I said to Ashley one day.

We were having a rare Sunday off together, and I was wearing a pair of comfy old trackies and no make-up.

'You still look gorgeous, babe,' he said, and I started pulling silly faces at him, to make myself look daft.

Ashley and I had moved house by now, because I wanted a fresh start after all the heartache. I didn't want to live in a house that had been filled with bad memories, and so we sold our place in Oxshott and were now living in Hurtmore House, a gorgeous six-bedroom mansion in Godalming, Surrey.

We were enjoying chilling out, eating grilled chicken salad and pitta bread we got from a restaurant up the road. After the *EastEnders* omnibus we watched a recording of one of my favourite shows, *Dancing with the Stars*. I loved the show not only for the dancing but for all the colours and sequins on the dresses, which I found really inspiring for costume ideas. Derek Hough was my favourite dancer, and every time he came on I said to Ashley, 'That guy is such a great dancer. He's the best one on there.'

Days like this reminded me of the early months of our relationship, when we used to spend time together in Ashley's old flat at Princess Park Manor. The only difference was, in those days it was Domino's Pizza on the menu and I was more likely to be dreaming about what I hoped to achieve than talking about success that had actually come my way.

'We're doing "The Promise" at the BRITs,' I told Ashley. 'We're nominated for Best Single. Can you come?'

'Yes, I'll be there, babe.'

The BRITs were in February, and last year's held bad memories, coming as they did just weeks after the cheating story first broke. Then, nobody knew whether I was going to stick by

Ashley. I remembered there had been almost as much publicity about the fact I wasn't wearing my wedding ring as there was about Nadine being missing from the group. It was a joke. That whole 'on–off' saga of my wedding ring was such a lot of nonsense and had really bugged me throughout *The X Factor*. 'It's a huge yellow diamond that doesn't go with every outfit I wear. Get over it!' I wanted to scream whenever paps tried to photograph my bare left hand.

This year I was definitely wearing it to the BRITs, and Ashley was coming to watch. It didn't take a genius to work out that this was going to attract a lot of publicity too, but we didn't discuss it. I didn't want to pick at old wounds, and Ashley certainly wouldn't have started a conversation along those lines. We both knew people were watching him and waiting for him to mess up again, but what could we do? He'd barely dared to go out in the whole past 12 months, and we couldn't live like that forever. He was my husband and I wanted him with me on such an important night.

All five of us girls were so scared on the night of the BRITs it was ridiculous. We'd done arena tours with incredibly complicated sets and played the O2 with all the bells and whistles, but this was different because it was a huge production number and we were doing it in front of all the music industry bigwigs.

Thankfully the performance went down a storm and I somehow managed to get down the huge staircase wearing incredibly high Christian Louboutins and a massive bright pink feather without breaking my neck.

We actually won Best British Single. This was an award voted for by the British public, and as I said on the night, it was the cherry on the cake for Girls Aloud after seven years together. I was bursting with pride when I posed for photographs with all the girls, and I couldn't wait to see Ashley after the ceremony.

'You smashed it! I'm so proud of you,' he said.

I felt ecstatic, like the pieces of my life were clicked back where they should be. I cuddled up to Ashley with a big smile on my face, and it seemed like a million pictures were taken of us together that night. For once I didn't care about the paparazzi. I wanted the world to see we had got through the past year, and that 2009 was going to be absolutely amazing for us.

11

'I just want to be a wife'

'Remember when you gave me money for charity when I did *Celebrity Apprentice*?'

'Yeeees …'

'Well, I'm raising money for Comic Relief again. Can you make a donation?'

'Sure. What are you doing this time?'

'Climbing Mount Kilimanjaro, with Kimberley and a few others.'

There was a long pause before Simon said, 'You're mad. I'll tell you what, I'll pay you *not* to do it.'

I started laughing but Simon was deadly serious, and for the first time I realised I didn't have a clue what I was letting myself in for.

Kimberley had asked me to do the climb after she had already agreed to take part and then took a wobbler.

'Please, Cheryl, I don't want to do it on my own,' she begged. 'I've asked Sarah and she said no, she couldn't cope. Will you come?'

I wasn't used to seeing Kimberley like that. Normally I was the one who was panicking and needed calming down, and she was always the sensible one who kept a cool head and took control.

'OK, I'll do it,' I said. 'I don't mind a challenge.'

To me it was just a charity walk. All I had to do was give up a week or so of my time and put one foot in front of the other, and we'd raise a load of money to help protect people in Africa from malaria. There were seven others taking part – Gary Barlow, Chris

Moyles, Alesha Dixon, Denise Van Outen, Fearne Cotton, Ronan Keating and Ben Shephard from *GMTV*, all of whom I'd met before. I wasn't bothered who else was going anyway; I was there to raise money for a good cause and help Kimberley do the same.

I was so busy in the run-up to the climb, in March 2009, that I had no time to prepare properly or even think about it.

At the beginning of the year I'd spent some time in a recording studio with Will.i.am, who had been telling me ever since I recorded my little part on his 'Heartbreaker' single 12 months earlier that I should record some solo material.

'You know you're gonna do a solo record, right?' he said to me over and over again before I eventually said 'yes'.

'I don't know how to do it on my own,' I'd protested the last time I saw him, when we met up in London.

'I'll help you, every step. I want to be involved with your career. Come into the studio, write with me. I know we can do some great stuff. Say yes. You won't regret it.'

He gave me one of his charismatic smiles.

'OK. I'll try, after *The X Factor*. But I'm really not sure about this.'

When the day came to actually go into the studio with him I was nervous but excited. I'd written songs before, but this was Will.i.am I was dealing with, one of the world's biggest producers. How could I go into a studio – just me, Will and a pen – and write music?

As I stepped into that recording studio my stomach was filled with a million butterflies but if Will noticed how nervous I was, he didn't say anything.

'You go first – you write your bit,' he said.

He was just so cool about the whole thing, while I was feeling very British and self-conscious. Physically putting pen to paper with Will beside me was one of the most daunting moments of my career. I was intimidated just to be there in the studio with him, but I took a deep breath and began to scribble down some lyrics.

'I like it!' Will said straight away. 'That's so good!'

I'd been worried about him not liking what I'd done but he got me straight away.

'You're good. I told you, you could do it.'

The next thing I knew I was in a booth, actually recording, and when I'd done it once it got easier each time. Will was so enthusiastic and encouraging that he made the whole thing seem so easy, and so much fun. We wrote six tracks together, and I loved working with him. It was exciting and new, and even though we hadn't really spent much time together at all, he already felt like a really close friend to me.

Around the same time, in early 2009, I was also working on new material with Girls Aloud and preparing for our fifth tour. We had our single, 'Untouchable', coming out soon, and the *Out of Control* tour was starting in May.

As a result, practically the only preparation I did for Kilimanjaro was to ask my mam to wear in my hiking boots, as she's the same shoe size as me. 'Can you just put some thick socks on and wear them round the house?' I asked her.

'Aren't you meant to wear them in yourself, Cheryl?'

'Yes, Mam, but I can hardly walk round recording studios in those, can I?'

I had a setting that was actually called 'Kilimanjaro' on the treadmill in my gym at home and so I'd have a go on that occasionally, even though I hate running and usually gave up before I'd completed the programme. Ashley thought I was crazy for agreeing to the climb, but he didn't seem worried like Simon was and he happily gave me some money and got his friends to make donations too.

'Good luck, babe,' he said. 'Hope it goes well.'

There was no fuss, and my mam was just as laid-back. 'Bye, Cheryl,' she said, just as if she was waving me off to catch the bus to town. Besides Simon, my brother Garry was the only one who was really concerned about what I was doing, as he watches all those extreme documentaries and knew that people had died on the mountain.

'I'll be fine,' I said, rolling my eyes. 'Statistically, what are the chances of things going wrong? We've got film crews with us and the best guides possible.'

We flew to Nairobi and had to take a little plane from there to Tanzania. Kimberley was taking the whole thing incredibly seriously, and she had lots of emotional calls from her family, who were all telling her they loved her and to stay safe. 'If anything happens to me, remember I love you,' I could hear her say.

A group of Maasai warriors appeared near the base camp, which was amazing as they literally came out of nowhere and started bouncing really high on their bare feet all around us. It was incredible, and seeing them gave me a sharp reminder of why I was there, to help people like them.

Kimberley told me that malaria kills a child every 30 seconds in Africa, when a £5 net could save them. They were the only numbers that lodged in my brain, because that was all that mattered to me. The fact the mountain is 19,340 feet above sea level and temperatures on the climb can range from 45°C to minus 25 didn't register with me at all, until I was actually there, finding that out first-hand.

'This is so scary,' Kimberley said on the first night. We were sharing a tent with Alesha Dixon, tucked up together like three sausages in our sleeping bags. I hadn't enjoyed the first day of climbing at all. I'd expected it to be more of a hike than a scramble up actual steep rock, but nevertheless I'd just put my head down and got on with it. I was relieved to finally be in the tent at our first camp, and I actually found it quite a novelty and was enjoying the feeling of being on an adventure.

Alesha is good fun and we had plenty in common, as she was in Mystique when we were starting out with Girls Aloud. We also had another link, though this one wasn't fun at all. Her husband had cheated on her with Javine, the singer who very nearly made it into Girls Aloud. I didn't know Alesha well but I knew that her ex-husband was MC Harvey from the band So Solid Crew, and that Javine had a baby with him. I remembered that Alesha had texted me to offer support when I went to Thailand after Ashley cheated, and I'd understood why, because she knew what I was going through.

I really enjoyed having a different girl with us, but Kimberley just couldn't relax at all. She was flapping and nervous and panicky about every noise outside and every detail of the climb.

'Lighten up,' I said. 'What's wrong with you?'

'I wish I'd never agreed to this,' Kimberley said. 'Anything could happen …'

'Stop it! We'll be fine. Get some sleep, we need all the energy we can get.'

As the days went on, I must admit I got where Kimberley was coming from. I had totally underestimated just how physically demanding it would be to climb and climb for hour after hour. My toenails were falling off and I had huge blisters all over my feet that absolutely killed me. I'd gone from being in sweltering heat at the start to enduring freezing temperatures like I'd never experienced before. Then the altitude started playing with my brain. The less oxygen there is in the air, the shorter your breath, and that affects how you function. My legs got heavy, I felt dizzy and light-headed and I became a bit delirious, laughing hysterically one minute and crying the next. It's like I wasn't in touch with my emotions, and I had next to no contact with the real world because my mobile signal cut in and out very randomly, so I literally felt like I was on another planet.

One night when we got to a camp I heard Fearne Cotton telling Denise Van Outen she was getting up to go to the toilet, and then I heard a loud crash as she keeled over. Fearne had severe altitude sickness and needed urgent medical help. Another time poor Alesha nipped out for a wee and actually fell down part of the mountain. I just couldn't go to the loo behind a bush; I got total stage fright, especially when I saw a camera pointing at me one time. 'Get out of me face!' I shouted, taking a huge hissy fit.

Chris Moyles gave me his huge coat one day when I was shivering, and Denise was very supportive the whole climb. She is one strong woman, I can tell you. I listened to Denise's words of encouragement and got on with it, but Kimberley was finding it much tougher. She would be all over the place, crying like a child does when you need to keep wiping their face and holding them.

The seriousness of what we were doing really hit me on the third day. We passed a guy from Leicester who was rocking on both legs and was so spaced out he was hallucinating. 'If he doesn't get down quickly he could die,' his guide told us.

I had a sudden, sharp realisation at that point. The reason Kimberley was suffering worse than me was because she was used to her life running so smoothly. She'd been with her boyfriend, Justin, for six years, and nothing in her life was extreme or scary. She'd hardly even changed her hairstyle in all the time I'd known her, let alone anything else, while I had gone through all kinds of crazy dramas. This was the first time Kimberley had felt so frightened and vulnerable in her life, while to me it was all part of the journey.

I was probably hallucinating a bit, but I imagined seeing my life as one of those 'colour by numbers' pictures, the ones I used to do as a child. It was a kaleidoscope of vibrant, clashing colours that were painted everywhere. I'd had so much colour in my life I wasn't daunted by this challenge at all. I'd gone through much more frightening things than this, and that was why this wasn't so tough for me. I'd not climbed Kilimanjaro before, but I lived my life climbing mountains of other kinds, and I'd learned to expect the unexpected, because that's what life always brought me.

My phone signal kicked in when I was literally up in the clouds, and I dialled my dad's number as quickly as I could.

'Hi Dad!'

'I thought you were climbing the mountain?'

'I am. You know when you used to say to me, "Cheryl, get your head out of the clouds?"'

'Aye.'

'Well, I'm ringing to tell you that I'm *in* the clouds!'

My dad was laughing his head off. The signal cut out, but talking to him really raised my spirits.

A bit later on, I was happy to see I had a voicemail from Ashley. We'd managed to speak once or twice, and now I dialled the number excitedly, looking forward to hearing his voice.

'Babes, it's me. Basically I've been arrested. I'm in the police station. Sorry. Call me …'

The battery died halfway through the message, and so did something inside me. I asked Denise if I could use her phone, telling her Ashley was in some kind of trouble. I couldn't believe he'd got himself arrested, especially when his reputation was already so bad.

I didn't get through straight away and I started getting agitated.

'What the hell has he done now?' I hissed. 'I'm climbing a mountain for charity and he's getting arrested. How does that work?'

'I got f****** arrested for telling a police officer to f*** off,' Ashley told me, when I eventually made contact.

I didn't get the full story, but I heard enough to know he'd been drunk when he did it. That was all I needed to know. I tried to hold myself together, telling myself at least he wasn't in danger, and that I would just have to deal with this when I got home.

It was emotional enough on the mountain without this. He wasn't even meant to be going out drinking. How could he do this to me, now?

We'd been going for four days by this time and the altitude sickness really hit me in a big way. I started projectile vomiting as soon as I smelt the food in the camp, and I needed an injection in my bum to stop the nausea. It worked, thank God, because this was the toughest day ever, even without Ashley's contribution.

The summit was in sight and it was minus 25 degrees.

I remember Denise talking about being in *Chicago*, the musical, to keep my mind off the pain in my feet. 'I can't do it,' I told her, 'You can, Cheryl. Get up! You're a Geordie, come on, you're meant to be tough.'

The wind was howling around me as I walked, and it reminded me of being in my grandad's high-rise flat in Newcastle. It made the same eerie whistling sound, and I felt I was actually back there, which was so bizarre as really I was walking on frozen gravel, surrounded by stars that were more yellow than I'd ever seen, and looking at the snow-capped summit shimmering against a massive moon.

It's very difficult to describe how testing it is to be up there, exposed to the elements. I used hand warmers to help me cope with the bitter cold, but nothing could help me deal with my emotions. I literally felt stripped bare, like my whole life was being tipped out around me as I took each step.

I had time to think about things I'd buried. Andrew, my brother, had given a long interview to a tabloid newspaper a few months earlier. I'd been too up to my eyes working on *The X Factor* to really think about it, and if the truth be known I really didn't *want* to think about it, but here on the mountain there was no escape. Andrew had told the paper how I'd visited him in prison and pleaded with him to turn his life around. I didn't read it myself, but I know he repeated what he had said to me: 'I'm too far gone.' That's what he'd told me to my face, the last time I saw him. I'd offered to help him, but he said he wasn't ready to help himself, and he didn't want to let me down. He had 50 convictions by now, and was as addicted to alcohol and drugs as he was to crime. It had broken my heart to see how low he had sunk, and now I was feeling incredibly hurt and let down that he had sold a story on me. I don't know how many thousands of pounds he got paid for it. Even taking a penny for his thoughts was insulting to me. I'd told Andrew I loved him and I would pay for him to go into rehab. He was my flesh and blood. The money was there to help him and all he had to do was agree to help himself, but instead he'd sold out. His life was bleak and hopeless.

I was crying as I neared the summit. Dawn was breaking, and the glacier was outstandingly beautiful, but when I actually summited it felt like an anti-climax. The landscape felt bleak and hopeless too, and I had to psyche myself up and tell myself it had all been worth it, because even if just one extra mosquito net could be bought because of me, it could save a life. I couldn't save my brother, but at least I might be able to save someone else.

Just as I'd underestimated the climb, I had not anticipated how tough it would be to get back down the mountain. It was so steep I was running down vertical drops taking really fast steps, like a little kid running down a big hill. My feet were frozen and I felt like I had pebbles in my shoes. It was a horrible sensation, so I took them off and shook them but there was nothing there.

I passed Kimberley who was still on her way up and I told her she had about 45 minutes to go to the top, and gave her the biggest hug ever. She cried, and the tears froze on her cheeks. It was impossible to stick together because you just had to do the best you could all the time, which meant one of us was usually ahead of the other. I barely recognised Kimberley as I waved her off, because she looked so emotionally zapped. We just looked at each other as if to say, 'Who *are* we?'

When we reached the next camp all the tents had blown away and we had to keep going for an extra three hours, which tested me in every sense. I was eating Kendal Mint Cake and Haribos for energy, and I was trying to keep myself mentally strong by think-ing about talking to Ashley and all my family and friends when I finally made it down to base camp. There were black trees and clouds rolling past me, and I remember begging Gary Barlow to get us a helicopter.

'We've done what we set out to do. We've summited. Please can't we get a helicopter to pick us up?'

'Cheryl, if you can get a helicopter to come out here, I'm in,' Gary said.

I knew there was no chance, but I was feeling desperate, and I knew Gary was suffering too as he has a really bad back that had plagued him the whole time. It had taken us four days to get up the mountain and I knew the descent would take about two days.

When we reached the second camp we still had 14 hours to go, and I'd absolutely had enough of everything and everyone. I was dreaming of having a shower and a blow dry and wearing lipstick, but I had to settle for sleeping in the dirt yet again, wiping my face with a flannel in the morning, padding out my shoes with anything I could find to stop my blisters rubbing, and then walking for another six hours.

'Keep going,' I told myself. 'Think how many mosquito nets we'll be able to provide for people.'

I filled up again when base camp finally came into view. I was desperate to use the toilet, as I'd not felt comfortable enough to go properly on the mountain for the whole week, but first I wanted to plug in my phone. It had been all over the news that we had summited. The cameramen had told us that, because they'd managed to get some footage out, and I knew everyone back home would have seen it. I wanted to listen to my messages and hear Ashley's voice and all my family and friends, because I knew they would have all got in touch.

My phoned started beeping wildly as soon as it had some power. There were absolutely loads of texts and voicemails from everyone who cared about me. The names kept flashing up. Mam, Dad, Garry, Nicola, Sundraj, Hillary … everyone was so relieved I'd survived the ordeal. 'Well done, Cheryl!' 'Proud of you, congratulations!' 'Ring when you can – can't wait to talk to you.' The messages were filled with love and relief.

'Thank God!' Hillary whooped in her voicemail. 'I've watched *everything*. So glad you made it. Safe journey home.'

As I listened to the last message and read the last text, I felt absolutely gutted. There was nothing from Ashley. We were in a hostel now, and I went and knocked on Kimberley's door and we both cried in each other's arms.

I should have been enjoying the sense of achievement because this was by far the most gruelling thing I had ever done in my life, but instead I just felt devastated. I didn't want to start unloading on Kimberley because she was already very emotional, but she knows me so well and I couldn't hide how I felt because it bothered me so massively. If it had been Ashley climbing the mountain I'd have watched every second of coverage on TV and I'd have been trawling the internet looking for any bit of information I could find. I'd have been sick with worry and desperate for news, but he clearly didn't feel or think like me.

'You selfish bastard,' I thought. 'It's two days since we summited. You've had all that time to send a message. Where's your support?'

I gritted my teeth and sent him a text that simply said: 'I'm down.'

'Well done, babe,' he replied, half an hour later.

Kimberley didn't appreciate that at all, and I knew I was not going to forget it in a hurry. We still had his arrest to talk about too, so I think it's fair to say I was deeply unimpressed by my husband.

We found out that our fundraising total hit £1.4 million when all nine of us summited, which was just incredible, so I tried to focus on that instead of my disappointment with Ashley.

'Good news, team,' Gary Barlow said. 'We've got a private plane for the last leg of the journey back to London.'

I don't think anybody cheered. We were all emotionally spent, and I for one would have got on any plane going, as long as it took me home as quickly as possible. I'd managed to have a shower in the hostel, but I still felt filthy and was itching all down my legs, and my face was a terrible colour and covered in a horrible rash. Poor Kimberley had cold sores on her lips that were weeping, and when we boarded the flight I was shocked to see she still couldn't stop crying.

'That has changed my life,' she sobbed. 'I've never, ever felt like that before. I was scared to death. I thought I was going to die. Cheryl, I just can't see the world the same way again.'

I didn't feel my life had changed, but I knew I'd learned something about myself. I'd been in the first group of four to reach the summit, pushing though gale-force winds on that final stretch, and that had nothing to do with my physical ability. I was mentally strong, I realised. I didn't crack easily under pressure, because I was so used to it. I'd spent my whole life careering from one pressurised situation to another, usually without much chance to breathe in between.

The journey home was torturous. It was a 12-hour flight, and I swear the little map and the clock showing our progress were moving in slow motion. It felt like a lifetime before we landed.

Mam had put up banners at the house to welcome me home. She and Ashley both started clapping when I walked in the door and the dogs were going crazy to see me. For a minute or two I felt quite strange; more like I'd just got off a spaceship than a private plane, because my home comforts felt so alien to me.

Mam had baked little sponge cakes in the shape of the mountain, which was really sweet, and Ashley presented me with a crystal vase, engraved with the date of the climb and filled with loads of flowers. I was glad to be home, and the worst of my disappointment about him not leaving me a message had passed. He didn't have a clue how devastated I had been, and I decided I'd try to let it go.

'Sorry about the whole police thing,' he said nervously.

This was clearly the thing that was preying on *his* mind, and I asked him to tell me the details.

'It was the paparazzi's fault,' he said. 'None of this would have happened if it wasn't for them.'

Ashley had been to a fundraising event with some of his Chelsea teammates on the night in question, and then he'd gone to The Collection bar in South Kensington. He told me he got annoyed because he was photographed talking to a blonde girl who came up to him, uninvited. He knew how this could appear if the picture was published and so he had a row with the photographer that continued when he left the club. There were police officers outside and Ashley swore at them when they got involved in the argument, because he was so frustrated by the paparazzi. He got arrested for being drunk and disorderly and was held for three hours and fined £80. I later discovered he had to pay a fine of £164,000 – two weeks' wages – to Chelsea. I'm glad I didn't know that at the time, because I'd have been more annoyed about how many mosquito nets that could have bought than about Ashley being arrested.

I just listened and didn't judge him. I didn't even bother questioning why he had gone out drinking after the charity event, as I knew it would have been one of those spur-of-the-moment decisions and not something he'd planned behind my back. I'd invested so much energy into the climb that I didn't have much left, to be honest. It was obvious Ashley felt ashamed of himself, and that was his real punishment.

When he'd said his piece I couldn't help telling him how I felt about the voicemails, because as I'd sat there listening to his woes I realised it was still bothering me, a lot.

'Can I ask you something? How could you not contact me after I summited?'

He looked at me blankly.

'I mean, how could you not know if I'd made it safely down? If it was me, I'd probably have a plane waiting for you.'

'Sorry, babe,' he replied.

He really didn't know what to say, but I felt better for getting this off my chest. I wasn't angry with him any more. I knew full well how bad he was at expressing his emotions, and I dismissed it as a man thing. In the past this would have eaten away at me, but I'd grown up a lot, and I'd learned to accept that other people see things in a different way to me. That was one of the lessons I'd learned on the mountain. Ashley hadn't meant to upset me, and that's what mattered.

I hadn't physically recovered from the climb when I had to go and shoot the 'Untouchables' video with the girls a few days later. I still had the rash on my face, which the doctor had told me was a symptom of me not going to the toilet for a week. I was literally toxic, and that's how my body had reacted. I had a black toenail

and massive blisters too, but when I saw Kimberley I could see she
was in a worse state than me. Her lips and feet were all a total
mess, and the pair of us had to have make-up on an inch thick to
cover our blemishes.

'This is a joke,' I said to Hillary when I realised we had to dance
on racks in high heels. 'We just can't do it.'

I was literally dancing on raw flesh, seething with resentment at
Hillary and threatening to walk out any minute. She knew I
wouldn't, and as usual we all just got on with it and got the job
done. On the advice of my doctor I washed the toxins out of my
system by doing the 'lemonade master cleanse', which meant
drinking a mixture of water, lemon juice, maple syrup and cayenne
pepper in place of meals for a few days. It did the trick, which is
just as well as our next tour was about to start and I needed to be
fighting fit.

The *Out of Control* tour was our most ambitious yet, with 32
dates booked between April and June. Rehearsals started a week
after the mountain and had gone well, and we were all very excited
about the set, which would see us being popped up from under the
stage on a mechanical device. I was particularly looking forward
to playing the Metro Radio Arena in Newcastle. We had two dates
in May there, and we were ending the tour with another two
Newcastle dates at the start of June.

'Who's that?' I said to Kimberley when Nadine brought a bloke
we'd never met before onto the tour bus.

'No idea,' she said. Nicola and Sarah didn't seem to know
either, and so we waited for Nadine to do the introductions.

'This is Bruce, my manager,' she said.

'Oh!' We all gasped.

It was no secret that Nadine was trying to launch a solo career
in America. She'd been living in the States for several years by
now and was forever travelling back and forth. My feeling had
always been that we were lucky she was prepared to split herself
in two, because we were a five-piece band and it took all of us to
make it work.

This was different, though. Having her manager actually on tour with us was crossing the line, and that's when I knew that it was finally time for us to take a break.

To be fair, I think we'd been heading that way for a while. Ever since Kimberley had appeared in *Les Misérables* for the *Passions* documentary she'd had her heart set on doing more acting and musicals. I knew that, as a woman, she was also just ready for a break, to have more time to herself and to spend with Justin.

Sarah also wanted to focus more on acting and had got herself a lead role in the latest St Trinian's movie, *The Legend of Fritton's Gold*, which she was shooting in the summer. She also just wanted to chill out, go on holiday, spend time with her new dog and enjoy just living for a change, instead of working all the time.

It was only really Nicola who looked at the rest of us blankly when the subject of taking a break was raised.

'Why would you want to do that?' she said. 'Am I missing something?'

Nicola just couldn't understand why anybody would want to stop while we were all still having fun as a band, and were enjoying a lot of success. I could see her point, especially as Girls Aloud ran like a well-oiled machine by now. Even though we'd reached the point where our costumes, videos and all the staging and production was more extravagant than ever before, every year we'd got better and better at managing how we did things.

Gone were the days when none of us could drive and we'd all turn up at the recording studio in one car and wait to do our individual vocals. In the beginning we'd often be sitting around doing nothing for two or three hours, but now we just went along to the studios in Kent separately. We'd stuck with Brian Higgins at Xenomania throughout, which is unusual, but there was no reason to change as he always came up with a new, winning formula and produced hit after hit for us.

By now Brian had a really good idea of who would be best suited to sing which vocals, which saved even more time in the studio. Once we'd all recorded our parts he'd decide whose vocals sat best in each part of the song. We wouldn't know how the track was going to sound until he delivered it, which was kind of exciting. It meant that lots of our records were recorded without the five of us ever being in the studio at the same time. That's how we'd managed with Nadine living in America. She would record all the demos and the rest of us would just add our parts afterwards.

'We're not splitting up,' I said to Nicola. 'It's just a break. It's not the end.'

She was still like the little sister I never had and I'm sure the fact she is the youngest in the group had a lot to do with her reaction, as well as that Nicola is so into her music she couldn't understand why anybody would want to do anything other than sing and perform and make records.

'We've gone from being teenage girls to being young women,' I said. 'I think we all need a minute to ourselves, space to do our own thing.'

'What do *you* want to do?' Nicola asked me. She knew *The X Factor* wasn't the reason I wanted a break, as I'd managed to combine the two things already. I'd already agreed to do the next series, which didn't take too much persuasion from Simon after I'd had a rest from the first. He'd given me a large pay rise and lots of compliments, and in true Simon style made it impossible for me to turn him down. 'People love you,' he said. 'You're unstoppable. Why would anyone in their right mind back out now?'

After my experience in the studio with Will, and how much I'd enjoyed it, I was planning on doing some more recording later in the year. Both of those things I could have done alongside being in Girls Aloud, though. What I *really* wanted was more time for my marriage.

'You know what,' I told Nicola. 'I just want to be a wife. Above all else, I want to spend more time with Ashley, and think about starting a family.'

I was nearly 26; in my mind the perfect age to start having children. Ashley had been telling me practically since we got married that I should live my dream first and we could have kids later, but now I was more broody and impatient than ever. Where I come from the women have their children young, and I never wanted to be an older mother. I'd look at my nieces and nephews and my heart would *ache* to be a mother.

'I just feel ready,' I said to Nicola. 'After all that's gone on, I finally feel more settled again now, and I don't want to keep putting it off.'

I also had another ambition, one I'd been thinking about ever since all the heartbreak with Ashley. When I was feeling really low, I'd found myself thinking about other people who were struggling with their lives too, in different ways. I decided that when I was stronger I would try to help them, and ever since the mountain I'd been thinking about this more and more, and wondering if I could set up some kind of charity.

I'd talked to Will about this recently, and he told me he was once paid $400,000 for a DJ-ing job and that he used the money to put three kids from an underprivileged school in his old neighbourhood of Boyle Heights in LA through college. That was so inspiring it gave me goosebumps, and I was starting to think about my own background and how I could bring a bit of light into the lives of disadvantaged kids in the North East, ones who were affected by drugs or poverty. It was definitely a challenge I wanted to take on.

For now, though, I was focused on the tour. I was determined to really enjoy it because in the back of my mind I was wondering if things would ever be the same again for Girls Aloud after this. We'd all had a discussion with Hillary and had agreed that we were going to take a break, but we hadn't decided on how long we were taking off, which was quite scary. We'd grown up together as a group and we were so used to consulting one another and making joint decisions, all the time. I couldn't imagine not having conversations about which two of us were in hair and make-up first or who was doing the sound check next, and I knew I'd miss the chaos of five girls all fussing with zips and tights and heels at

the same time before a show. I loved all that girly stuff. It was
bonding, and when we walked out on stage I always felt we were
really together and close as a group. It was a fantastic feeling, and
even when we'd decided to take a break I was very glad to find that
vibe didn't change.

We only had one disaster on this tour. It was when we played
the O2, and my platform ground to a halt. I could see all the other
girls getting higher and higher and I could hear the fans screaming, but only my head was popping up from underneath the stage.
It was really embarrassing and I just wanted to talk to the other
girls to find out what was happening, but I couldn't. Instead I just
stood there laughing, waiting until the machine started working
again, and then got on with the show feeling like a lemon.

'That was hysterical,' Nicola laughed afterwards. 'I would have
totally freaked out if that happened to me, but you just carried
on!'

Nicola had actually talked to a psychologist before the tour, as
she's terrified of heights and needed to get her head around the
fact the podiums rose to about 50 foot. She knew that I thought
seeing a shrink was a bit over the top, and it was so typical that I
was the one who ended up having the problem.

'At least I provided a little distraction for you,' I joked. 'I'm glad
you found it so funny.'

Playing Newcastle for three nights running was a really great
way to go out on a high. The Metro Radio Arena was somewhere
I'd passed on the bus every week as a child, always dreaming that
I'd be on the stage there myself one day. Every time we played
Newcastle over the years it was amazing. Members of my family
would come down to see me when we were sound checking, and
I just felt so at home hearing Geordie accents everywhere, or
walking past the kitchens and catching familiar cooking smells in
the air. Even the chips have a unique smell up there, and I remember one night the cooks made stottie, a type of bread, which took
me right back to my childhood. When I looked in the mirror in
my dressing room I honestly half expected to see my teenage self

looking back, and to find that this was all a dream, and really I was about to go on stage at Metroland.

The crowd went wild every night, and when they chanted my name I could just feel the Geordie pride filling the whole arena. It was an absolutely mind-blowing experience, and I felt so proud of us and myself. It was amazing to feel appreciated as a fellow Geordie. The way the media treated me, it was as if I wasn't a human being sometimes, but here I felt so different. I was Cheryl, a local girl made good. I was one of their own who was flying the flag for Newcastle, and that meant the world to me.

12

'Unfortunately, you're going to be number one next week'

'Was I right?' Simon asked.

He was talking about Kilimanjaro, and his advice that I shouldn't do it. I could tell by the way he was puffing out his chest and raising an eyebrow expectantly that he wanted me to say, 'Yes, Simon. You were right, as always. It was hell. I shouldn't have done it.'

'No,' I said. 'I'm here, aren't I? I did it, and we raised millions.'

'Mad,' he said, shaking his head. 'You are completely crazy.'

That conversation is typical of the way Simon and I spoke to each other. I always refused to play 'Simon says' and dance to his tune, but he refused to let me dent his ego and always made sure he got the last word in.

I was talking to Simon because the *X Factor* auditions were starting again soon and, just like last year, I was now wondering whether I'd done the right thing in agreeing to do the show. As planned, the girls and I had announced at the end of the tour that we were having a break from Girls Aloud, and I was now putting together my first solo album, *3 Words*. The record label wasn't at all sure about this, because statistically it doesn't work when one member of a girl band tries to go solo, particularly one who was not even the lead singer. Will.i.am was having none of it, though.

'I think you believe in me more than I believe in myself,' I told him.

'That's because I am right. You watch. You wait and see. You are going to be a big solo star, and you need to start believing it, because it's happening.'

Ashley was really supportive and encouraging too. He knew I'd always loved R&B and soul and he told me, 'This is your chance to do the music you love. It'll be amazing.'

I knew it was a great opportunity, but I couldn't shake off worries about how I would manage without having the girls around me. Team spirit spurs me on, and I've always found it easier to be strong for other people than for myself.

'Maybe I should have turned Simon down,' I fretted. 'Perhaps I should just be concentrating on my album.'

Ashley and I were taking a holiday in the South of France, between the end of the tour and the start of *The X Factor*. This worked out well, as June was the only month Ashley ever had time off in the football calendar.

'Will you stop worrying and chill out!' Ashley said. 'You've *got* to do *The X Factor*. You're too good at it.'

I'd learned that with footballers, the amount of money they are paid is directly linked to their level of skill on the pitch, like a reward for their talent. As Simon had given me a big pay rise to do this series, in Ashley's eyes that meant I was absolutely amazing at my job and therefore could not turn it down. I wasn't convinced. I knew that in Simon's world, money is seen as the biggest *motivator*, rather than reward. If Simon wants something he'll pay a high price. He expects to be able to 'buy' people because he can't understand why anybody would not be as motivated by money as he is. I had a different view to both Ashley and Simon. If something doesn't feel right, I turn it down, and now I really wasn't sure how I felt about *The X Factor*.

'Look, don't invest so much,' Ashley said. 'I told you this on the last series. Don't get so emotionally involved.'

'I can't help it,' I said, but I knew Ashley had a point, because I was already worrying about the competition before I'd even got there or met any of the contestants.

Thankfully, we had a few distractions on the holiday and I did manage to relax. One day we met Roman Abramovich, who told me he was planning to climb Kilimanjaro and asked me all about my experience. I could see he was a big fan of Ashley's, which made me feel very proud of my husband. It felt just like old times, actually. Ashley and I were loved up, having a laugh and soaking up the sun.

We also met up with Ashley's England teammate Wayne Bridge and his fiancée Vanessa Perroncel, who were on the beach with their very cute little toddler. Seeing Ashley play in the sand with him made me feel even more broody than ever. I *desperately* wanted to have babies with Ashley.

'Can't we just start trying now?'

'No, babe. Live your dream. Make your solo record. There's time for all that later.'

I was dying to be a mam but I also had commitments, and I reluctantly listened to Ashley because I knew that when I had kids I wanted to be able to take time out and bring them up myself.

When I got back to work on *The X Factor* I believed it was going to be my last series, because then I was going to get pregnant and start my family. That's what I wanted, more than anything else in the world, and thinking like that helped me deal with the madness of the next few months.

After the first auditions in Glasgow, Simon decided to change the format and bring in a live audience, which is something he hadn't done before at the audition stage of the show. This bothered me massively, because I imagined how I would have felt if I'd had to audition for *Popstars* in front of members of the public, and I knew the pressure would be immense.

I was right. I felt sick with worry when the contestants started coming out in front of the huge, noisy audience. My legs turned to jelly for them, just as if I were up there myself. Also, I hated being on show to the audience all day myself, because the auditions are long and tiring at the best of times, and you just don't want a camera in your face for that length of time.

I got over it after a while, and when some of the stand-out acts came on I really started to enjoy myself. I remember laughing my head off at John & Edward and thinking, 'You two are TV gold'.

I really liked Olly Murs and Stacey Solomon, and my heart melted when Joe McElderry first spoke and I found out he was from South Shields, the same neck of the woods as me. He even looked like my brother Garry, and I was willing him to be good. I'll never forget him singing the Luther Vandross song 'Dance With My Father'. I had goosebumps, and I was suddenly right back in the zone, emotionally immersed in the contest all over again.

'Why aye!' I said when it was my turn to vote, and I couldn't stop smiling. 'You just did me really proud,' I told Joe.

I got the boys' category that year, which I had mixed feelings about. I was really happy because Joe was in it, but I was nervous and felt out of my comfort zone because I'd never worked with boys before. When we went to Marrakech for the judges' houses stage, the gifts the boys bought me in the local market said it all. I got a size 20 T-shirt and a dried snake in a box. I remember laughing about it with Holly Willoughby, but deep down I was feeling very anxious about how the hell I was going to mentor boys, because I wasn't on their wavelength at all. Your relationship with your contestants is as important backstage as it is on the live shows, and I'd never worked that closely with boys in my life.

I also had something else to deal with while I was in Morocco: Jason Mack had done a story about me.

'What's he saying?' I asked Sundraj when he called to alert me. I was in the most beautiful surroundings, staying in a luxurious villa, but the second I heard Jason's name I was transported right back to our grubby little flat in Heaton.

I felt my stomach flip over, imagining all kinds.

'He's saying you pleaded with him to stop taking drugs, and that you were so worried about him, you couldn't eat or sleep. He also says you lost so much weight people thought you must have been on heroin …'

'Heroin? Sundraj, this is really important. What exactly does he say about heroin? I want to know precisely what he's saying.'

Sundraj was scanning the article again now and I made him read the quotes, word for word.

'When I first met Cheryl I was doing a lot of cocaine. Some days I'd blow £200 on the stuff. But she'd sit with me for hours to talk me out of getting drugs ...'

'Go on.'

'I went from having everything to living on a giro ... Cheryl stuck by us when I didn't have a penny ... but I started taking heroin because I wasn't getting any further forward.'

'Yes!' I shouted triumphantly. I felt an incredible, immediate sense of relief.

'Cheryl, are you alright?' Sundraj asked.

He was understandably confused by my reaction, and I had to explain to him that this was the first time I had *ever* heard Jason admit to taking heroin.

'You don't know how much this means,' I sobbed.

Tears were rolling down my cheeks now. It felt like an old wound had finally healed after all those years. I had not even real-ised how much it still bothered me that Jason had never made this confession before. He'd always admitted to taking cocaine, but continually denied he was on heroin. I *knew* he was lying, because I had seen the silver foil, the cold turkeying and the junkie friends he disappeared with for days on end. But I never once caught Jason red-handed, actually taking heroin, and he had used that against me time and time again, telling me and my friends and family that I was crazy and paranoid.

The truth was that I was a naïve, vulnerable teenager who thought she was in love and believed she could save her boyfriend from ruining his life with the devil's dust. I counted back through the years to when we split up in 2002 and I realised I'd carried this resentment around for seven whole years. The relief I felt now was absolutely indescribable. The fact Jason must have made money out of selling his story and had effectively betrayed me all over again hardly even bothered me. Nothing he did now could hurt me as much as his lies and mind games had hurt me in the past, and having the truth out there at last overshadowed everything.

*   *   *

There were all kinds of other dramas waiting for me when we got back to London for the live shows. I had Joe, Lloyd Daniels and Rikki Loney in my final three. Lloyd was only 16 and had some private stuff going on in his life that I was finding extremely difficult to cope with. Simon knew all about it, but he can completely separate himself from his emotions when the cameras are rolling. One week he criticised Lloyd's rendition of 'Bleeding Love' saying, 'It's like a mouse trying to climb a mountain. I'm going to put the blame for this on the girl on my right, who's not working with you properly.'

This was so mean of Simon to blame me, because he had actually told me to pick that song for Lloyd, and he knew I was struggling behind the scenes emotionally. I started to cry on the show, and I remember Rikki Loney making a comment about me being in more of a state than the contestants, which was actually true. All the boys would be trying to calm *me* down before we went on air, instead of the other way around.

Looking back, I was investing too much emotionally all over again, and I was also doing too much generally. I'd not long taken on my contract with L'Oréal, which meant scheduling in several days to make the 'Because I'm worth it' TV commercial.

'Wow, Beyoncé has done this!' I thought. It gave me the same buzz I'd had when Girls Aloud had Barbie dolls made of each of us, back in 2005. That was my all-time favourite product endorsement with the girls, because Barbies are just so iconic and were something I'd grown up with. I had the same feeling about this L'Oréal campaign. It was an honour to be chosen for it, and it was an offer I couldn't refuse.

I really enjoyed making the advert, but it happened at the same time as I was putting the finishing touches to my album, so I was working flat out. The record label wanted me to perform my first single off the album, 'Fight For This Love', on *The X Factor* too. I could totally see the logic. Artists were desperate to get on the show and I was in a position to walk straight out of my judge's seat and perform. I'd worked hard on the album and it would be foolish not to take the opportunity, but of course it was another pressure to worry about.

'You're nuts,' Simon said once it had all been agreed, and for once I couldn't argue with him.

It was also Simon's fiftieth birthday party around this time.

Unfortunately Ashley couldn't make it, as he was busy with Chelsea, so I was going on my own. I had no clue what to expect. Sir Philip Green had organised the party at Wrotham Park, where Ashley and I had our wedding, but when I turned up I didn't recognise the place at all. There was an enormous image of Simon projected onto the front of the building, and inside the Simon theme continued, everywhere. The waiters wore Simon masks, the toilets had Simon pictures on the walls, and even the wallpaper had Simon's face on it, complete with devil's horns.

'You're sitting next to me,' Simon beamed, steering me to the top table. His mother was on his other side, and Sir Philip and his wife and daughter, Kate Moss and her boyfriend Jamie, plus Naomi Campbell were also on our table. I'd met some of them before and had walked in a fashion show for Naomi once, but I didn't *know* them, and I just sat there quietly, taking it all in.

We were served soup that had Simon written in pasta in the bottom of the bowl, and a woman on the stage did a reverse strip, starting out naked and ending up fully clothed after pulling shoes out of her Afro and underwear from God knows where. It was totally surreal, and so far from my normality I felt quite unsettled. 'I'm in deeper than I ever knew existed,' I thought, looking around the room. This was a level of wealth and celebrity I wasn't even aware of.

'This is crazy,' I said to Simon.

'I know, tell me about it,' he laughed.

I sat there looking at people like Kevin Spacey, David Hasselhoff and Ozzy Osbourne, thinking to myself that they could have been in a film, because I felt so disconnected from them. It was so weird to be surrounded by so many famous faces, but I wasn't starstruck by them at all, it was just so weird. The decadence and the craziness was simply out of this world and so I sat there, at the head of this room, just watching it all unfold and thinking how strange it all felt.

I'd bought Simon a diamond watch from Harrods as a thank-you gift at the end of the last series of *The X Factor*, but for his birthday I decided to make a bit of a different statement. He laughed his head off when he saw the present. It was a grey T-shirt, a teeth-whitening kit, some fake tan, a can of hairspray and a mirror with a picture of Simon's head stuck to it. I also gave him a signed picture of me, which was a dig at the fact he'd given me a Simon Cowell calendar the previous Christmas.

'The difference is,' I teased. 'You were serious, and I'm having a laugh.'

'You know what, I can't always figure you out, but that's what I love about you, Cheryl,' he grinned.

A couple of weeks later Simon was back in classic, arrogant mode.

'You know you've done this to yourself, don't you?'

He was on the phone the night before I was performing 'Fight For This Love' on *The X Factor*.

'Why are you saying this to me now? What do you mean?'

'I mean you've only got yourself to blame. Good luck.'

I think Simon was nervous for me, and for himself and the reputation of the show, and that was his way of dealing with it. Everybody was nervous, in fact. Ashley had started saying to me, 'Are you sure you want to go through with this, babe?' and my mam, Nicola and Kimberley, Sundraj and Hillary were all phoning me, wishing me luck and crossing their fingers.

It was a big risk; I knew that. It was my first ever performance without the girls, it was my first solo single, and it was in front of millions. My acts were watching, and if I couldn't pull it off, how could I expect them to?

When the advert break came on, which was my cue to run from my seat at the judge's table and get into my costume, I felt sick to my stomach with nerves. It felt like the moment when I'd

watched Ashley take that penalty at the World Cup and I imagined the whole country was holding their breath at the same time
as me.

I was getting into the costume now, feeling my heart thud in my
chest as I pulled on my red and black military cap and tunic and
split harem pants. Even the lady who normally counts down
calmly for the contestants was nervous, because I could hear her
throat tightening as she rasped: 'Ten ... nine ... eight ...'

All my boys were wishing me well, and as I went on stage I had
this sudden panic about which of them might be going home
tonight. Oh my God, I didn't want to lose any of them! I'd have
to deal with that later, because now the spotlights were on me, and
I was suddenly right in the zone, singing and dancing and feeling
every word of the song. I really had to deliver.

It felt like I'd been on the stage for seconds rather than minutes
when I saw that Simon and Dannii were standing up and clapping.
'This is going to really pain me to have to say this,' Simon said,
smiling, 'But *that* was incredible! Unfortunately, you're going to
be number one next week.'

I was euphoric. I'd not only delivered, but I'd thoroughly
enjoyed myself, and I just knew this was one of those events in my
life where my dad was going to tell me afterwards: 'Cheryl, I was
so proud I could pop.'

Ashley came to the studio, which he didn't normally do as he
couldn't stand the chaos and drama of it all. 'You are nuts!' he said
when it was all over. 'What are you doing?'

'I swear I've been shaking the whole night,' I said. 'I don't know
what I was thinking putting myself through that, but I'm glad I
did. I'm absolutely buzzing now.' Nicola, Kimberley and Sarah
were there too, which was amazing.

Whitney Houston had been on after me but I'd been in such a
state I'd not been able to enjoy watching her. She actually fell
down a step and the strap on her bra snapped, but I didn't take all
that in until I got home and watched a recording of the show that
Ashley had set up.

Watching Whitney's performance just made the whole evening seem even more insane, because she was such a legend and yet it was only just sinking in that we'd shared the same stage.

'Fight For This Love' became the fastest-selling single of the year and went to number one in 10 countries. It felt like my life just couldn't get any better, but I had two more amazing nights in store that really made 2009 end on a high.

In the middle of December I hosted a one-off special on ITV called *Cheryl Cole's Night In*. I got to pick the guests and what I performed, and I invited Rihanna, plus Alexandra Burke, Will.i.am, Will Young and Snow Patrol onto the show. It was an incredible opportunity to bring together everyone I loved in the music world at that point in time.

I chose to perform my second single, '3 Words', with Will.i.am, plus 'Fight For This Love' and 'Parachute', which was to be my third single from the album. As soon as I heard 'Parachute', I knew I wanted to dance the Argentine tango on the video, and I had a stroke of luck because Derek Hough, my favourite dancer from *Dancing with the Stars*, agreed to choreograph the video, and he was also going to dance with me on this show.

I knew Derek was amazing at the tango and it seemed meant to be that we worked together. It came about because Hillary knows Bruno Tonioli, one of the judges on *Dancing with the Stars*. Bruno used to choreograph Hillary's old group Bananarama, and of course he knew Derek through *Dancing with the Stars*.

'We've had a word about "Parachute" and Derek's really excited to work with you,' Hillary told me, after explaining the connection.

'Wow, that's *amazing*,' I said.

I knew Derek was a world champion of Latin and ballroom, and I was really excited to work with him too.

Ashley thought it was really funny that I'd gone on about Derek for ages and suddenly he wasn't just a dancer I admired from afar on the TV, he was in London, working on *my* routine.

'You know what, you're lucky,' Ashley told me.

'I know,' I said, and I really felt it, on a personal as well as a career level.

Our marriage troubles were behind us now, that's how it felt. I would never be able to forget about the cheating and the allegations, but I could feel the dark days slipping deeper and deeper into our history, and I was looking forward all the time, not back. There was still a lot of speculation about us as a couple, especially if I didn't wear my wedding ring, and so at the beginning of November I got Sundraj to put a picture on Twitter of me with the ring on my finger, along with the message: '3 Words: Diamonds are Forever'. It was just a cheeky, spur-of-the-moment thing, something I felt like doing to put a stop to all the rumours about the state of our marriage. It felt right to do it, because I really did think Ashley and I were back together for good.

I hadn't done any ballroom dancing since I was a child, but as soon as I started rehearsals with Derek, I felt super comfortable. He was so talented and enthusiastic it would have been impossible not to be inspired by him. I loved the Latin paso doble-type routine he devised for us and I got to wear a gorgeous flamenco-style dress. I felt like a proper ballroom dancer in his arms, and I thoroughly enjoyed the whole evening, from start to finish. It was a total buzz, and I could hardly believe how lucky I was to have the chance to do something so special.

The night after the TV show was aired, it was the *X Factor* final. It was a crazy, crazy night and the whole atmosphere was much more chaotic than usual behind the scenes. I lit scented candles in my dressing room to try to calm myself down, but they didn't help. It felt like there was actually nervous energy trickling out of the walls. In the corridors it was a hectic blur of production staff, cameras and contestants running around and flapping. I tried having a glass of wine and a cigarette, but they didn't help either and my nerves were getting worse and worse.

I desperately wanted Joe to win. He was such a genuinely nice lad, and we'd formed a real bond. The innuendos in the press that he fancied me or we were having some sort of fling were ridiculously far off the mark. Joe had already confided to me that he was gay, and he was howling laughing about those rumours. Ashley didn't find it quite so funny; in fact he was disgusted. 'It just proves what crap they write. You're married, he's gay. It's sick.' I wasn't very amused either, but I shrugged it off. I had too much going on to let myself get wound up about something so stupid.

When decision time finally came, I could hardly believe I was on that stage again, breathless with anticipation, just as I had been with Alexandra the year before. I was absolutely *ecstatic* when Joe's name was called, and this time I didn't have to scoop the winner up off the floor, because Joe picked *me* up and spun me around. I could almost hear the Geordie voices in the air. I knew people were holding 'Joe' parties to support him all over South Shields, and this felt like a victory for the whole of the North East. I honestly could not have felt more proud.

After the show I got a message from Simon to say there was someone in his dressing room he wanted me to meet. I walked in and the scene was mental. There were women partying everywhere, and Simon was grinning like the Cheshire Cat.

'Cheryl! Say hello to Prince Harry,' he said, wafting his arms towards the ground. I looked over, and to my astonishment Prince Harry was lying on the dressing room floor, with his top buttons undone, relaxing with a glass of wine in one hand and a cigarette in the other. His girlfriend Chelsy was there too.

'Hi! How are you?' Harry said, grinning at me.

'I'm good, thanks,' I smiled. He just looked like a typical young lad, chilling out at a party, and he didn't even get up off the floor when we started to chat.

I knew Harry had said something in the past about being a fan of mine, and we had a little laugh about that. Then we talked about whether the press knew he was coming to the show this weekend. Harry didn't seem to care one way or the other. He told me that he and Chelsy had actually sat in the audience, and he said he probably didn't get scrutinised as much as me.

'I don't know how you cope with it,' he said, which was completely surreal coming from such a high-profile member of our royal family.

I could hear Simon laughing loudly, and afterwards he congratulated me on Joe's win.

'I have to hand it to you, you are incredible,' he said. 'If I knew what made you so special, I would literally bottle it and sell it.'

It was an enormous compliment, but as the words came out of Simon's mouth I was already wondering how I was going to break it to him that I was going to be focusing on my solo career and babies next year.

My album had been out for two months by now, and against the odds it was doing well. It debuted at number one and turned platinum in the November, which was way beyond my expectations. I was finally starting to believe in myself as a solo artist and I was picturing a future in which I had lots of children, and could slot studio time around my family life. That was my idea of a perfect world.

'Parachute' was to be the final single released off the album, and I shot the video with Derek in the middle of January 2010, at the historic Eltham Palace in south-east London. We worked for 19 hours, and just before the very last shot was taken the fire alarm went off and we had to evacuate the building. Derek never complained; in fact he helped keep everybody's spirits up with all his energy and enthusiasm. It was contagious, and I remember saying to Ashley afterwards, 'Derek is one of those people who makes the day more enjoyable,' because that was the truth. Derek and I agreed to keep in touch afterwards, and I said I'd call him when I was next in LA, where he lives. At the time I had absolutely no idea how soon that would be and I could never, ever have guessed how important Derek's friendship was about to become to me.

13

'Even if it kills me, I want to know it all'

'Cheryl! How do you feel about what's happening?'

It was a journalist, shouting to me across the car park of a London hospital. It was 11 February 2010 and Ashley had had an operation on his ankle that morning. He'd been under general anaesthetic, and he was only allowed out once he'd managed to hold some food down.

It had been a very long and stressful day and it was getting dark by this time. I was pushing Ashley to the car in a wheelchair, and now this journalist was heading towards us. I looked at the guy with disgust and just thought, 'What an absolute disgrace.'

Ashley was still sleepy, and he'd already had to put up with some nurses asking for his autograph in the recovery room, moments after he'd come round from the operation. He'd absolutely had enough by now. 'Liberty taker!' Ashley snarled.

'Can't you just leave him to have an operation?' I said. I was gobsmacked that anyone could behave so insensitively.

I helped Ashley out of the wheelchair and onto the back seat of the car, where he slumped down under a blanket. We were both fuming as we drove away, and at the end of the road there were loads of paparazzi who all took pictures of me in the front seat, with a face like thunder.

I honestly thought they wanted a story about Ashley's injury, and I felt super protective towards my husband. When we got home I helped him into bed, propped his leg up so he was as comfortable as possible, and made him a drink.

'You get some rest,' I said. 'Just let me know if there's anything you need.'

Ashley dozed off, and just before midnight I climbed into bed beside him. Minutes later the phone rang, and I answered it.

'I'm *so* sorry to be the person that's making this call ...'

It was Hillary, and my heart sank like a dead weight, making me feel instantly anxious.

'There's a story coming out in the morning. It's another girl, saying Ashley's cheated ... and ... she's got pictures.'

The penny immediately dropped about the journalist and the paparazzi at the hospital, and my heart sank even deeper, if that were possible.

'I see. Wow. Thank you, Hillary. I'll read it.'

My whole body felt heavy and numb. Ashley was awake now, and I relayed the conversation to him, stony faced.

'What the hell? When are they ever gonna leave me alone? I've just had an operation! This is beyond a joke.'

He snapped his eyes shut and I felt absolutely sick to the pit of my stomach. This was just too familiar and too painful, and I knew straight away that I wasn't going to get any more information out of Ashley. I'd been here before, except now it was worse, not only because he was recovering from an operation but because I knew from experience that the more he was pushed, the more angry and distant he would become.

Pictures, Hillary had said. 'She's got pictures.' How could *they* be made up? I had a sudden flash of anger and part of me wanted just to chin Ashley right there and then, like I'd done last time, but I forced myself to stop and think and stay as calm as I possibly could. 'It could still be another made-up story,' I told myself, though I was finding it very hard to believe.

'You know what, we'll just see in the morning,' I said to Ashley through gritted teeth.

He said nothing and eventually drifted off to sleep, while I lay in the bed beside him, wide-awake, the whole night long. I was dreading what I was going to see in the morning. Even if it was a

pile of crap there'd be hell to pay with the media. I was performing at the BRIT Awards in a few days' time, doing 'Fight For This
Love'. My God, the timing couldn't be worse.

I tortured myself thinking that the reason Sundraj hadn't
phoned me, rather than Hillary, was because the story must be
true. He'd delivered the bad news the first time and probably
couldn't bear to do it again. He'd been by my side through so
much, dating right back to the whole nightclub incident, and we'd
become good friends over the years. Maybe he couldn't handle
having to tell his friend something so devastating again?

I think I asked one of the drivers we used at the time to bring
me the newspaper the next day. I couldn't contemplate leaving the
house. There were paparazzi camped outside and, just like
the ones by the hospital, they must have known a lot more about
the story than I did. Nobody could have guessed that I'd spent the
night in the house with Ashley, yet I knew next to nothing. I didn't
go online because I just couldn't face it, and anyhow I'd learned
from the last time that the story on the internet isn't always the
same version as the one in the paper, especially when there are
pictures involved. I wanted to see the whole thing in front of me,
in black and white, to make no mistake about exactly what was
being reported.

I started to sob when I saw the newspaper. There, splashed all
over the front page of *The Sun*, was *my* husband, being accused
of cheating on me yet again. I could feel my heart aching and
breaking as I read the story. Ashley had supposedly sent this girl
'sex text' messages. That was the first thing I read. Not sex, just
text messages. That was a good start, I suppose. I was desperately hoping there was an explanation, or that the story might
have been dragged up from years before we even met, but the
girl was claiming this happened in June 2009 – the month we'd
been on holiday together to the South of France – and there
were several pictures.

There was one image of Ashley's face I'd never seen before,
and there was one of him with his England shorts on. They were

bunched up and kind of looked like a nappy. It was a horrendous picture, but what really caught my eye was Ashley's bare torso. He'd had a new tattoo since the first allegations in 2008, and I could see it clearly on this picture. That was a bad, bad moment, because I knew for a fact the photo had been taken within the last 12 months, in the time when Ashley was meant to be on his best behaviour.

I had tears dripping down my cheeks as I read that there was apparently a picture of him naked too, which was too X-rated to print. I think I blacked out, because I have no recollection of how I first confronted Ashley with all this. I just remember that his mother was in the house somewhere and so I didn't want to go too crazy and upset her, and then I have a memory of Ashley hobbling round the bedroom on crutches, saying, 'This is just a f***ing joke.'

My head was sore and everything in my mind was blurred. It was almost as if it was nature's way of protecting me, shutting off my brain because it was just so painful for me to be fully conscious. I don't have strong memories of the first conversations we had immediately afterwards, either. I can just see Ashley telling me something like: 'They're from my old phone. I was taking them to see what my tattoo looked like. I gave the phone away and forgot to delete them. It was a stupid mistake.'

I was asking him for details. I wanted dates, times and the why, when and how about everything. 'Even if it kills me, I want to know it all,' I said, but Ashley didn't have the answers.

'I've told you, this is just a f***ing joke. Why are they out to get me?'

I couldn't get any sense out of him whatsoever. It was just like the last time. He simply didn't have a clue how to communicate, and talking to him was like banging my head against a brick wall.

I had rehearsals and fittings all the next day for the BRITs, and so I somehow got myself together and went out to work, with the paparazzi chasing me everywhere I went, calling things out about Ashley. Even when I was locked inside my car there was no escape, and I had a pack of them in constant pursuit, running red lights to stay with me. I could see copies of *The Sun* everywhere I looked; thrown on lorry drivers' dashboards as I drove down the motorway, or outside newsagents and petrol stations.

I never considered pulling out of the BRITs, not for one minute. Just like when I'd had to do the 'Can't Speak French' videoshoot after the last lot of allegations, there were too many other people involved, and I just wouldn't cause that much disruption because of my personal life. I don't know how I got through the day, but somehow I did, by focusing on the job in hand and talking to people only when I had to, about the set or the chorography.

When I got back from work Ashley was still in the same place, lying in bed with his leg propped up, and I was stressed out and angry. It had been tough facing people all day, knowing they were all looking at me and thinking, 'Poor Cheryl'. Then I'd had the paps nearly knocking people over to get pictures of me coming home.

'Are you gonna talk to me now?' I shouted at Ashley. 'I *need* you to communicate with me. I *need* answers.'

I was worn out and very emotional too, and Ashley's reaction was not what I wanted to hear.

'This is just never gonna stop,' he snapped back. 'They're trying to break us up and they're winning.'

'You've said all that a million times,' I cried. 'I want detail. I want answers. I need to know the whole truth, not just some stupid excuse about you giving your old phone away. It doesn't add up, Ashley. It's just not good enough.'

'How are you ever gonna believe me when they've already damaged our relationship?'

'Will you *stop* saying the same stuff over and over again. Just tell me what happened!'

'Everyone's out to get me. This is so frustrating! They're trying to end my marriage because I left Arsenal and they're winning. *You're* letting them win.'

This was irritating beyond belief. He wasn't confronting the issue at all, and neither was he calling the girl a liar.

'Is that girl telling the truth or not? Have you been texting her like that? Can't you answer a simple question?'

That was met with total silence and so I started asking Ashley if there was something wrong with *me*, desperately trying to provoke a response.

'Is it *my* fault this has happened, again?' I screamed, but all Ashley did was shake his head.

'Did you make a mistake getting married to me? Is it something I did wrong? Is it my job that's the problem? Was I not here enough?'

'No, you're amazing,' he said finally.

'Why then? Was I too easy going? Did you not want to be a free spirit, to make your own choices? That's what I've always thought was best. Was I wrong? Did you want me to keep you under lock and key, and ask you where you were going and what you were doing every minute of the day?'

Ashley said nothing at all.

'Would it have been better if I was one of those wives who was forever saying "why didn't you call me five minutes ago like you said?" Well, would it?'

'No! You're the perfect wife.'

'Why then? Tell me why, Ashley.'

I was crying now, and he couldn't look me in the eye.

'This is such a lot of bullshit. They're trying to split us up and you're letting them.'

'You know what, Ashley, if you're not prepared to have an adult, married conversation with me, I haven't got time for you.'

Looking back the shock factor was nothing like the first time round. I didn't convulse or have panic attacks like I had two years earlier. I just don't think my brain would allow my body to go back there. It was quite surreal, actually. I was still managing to eat, and I got myself organised for work the next day, walking in and out of the bedroom where Ashley lay to get my things, but just ignoring him. I was almost on auto-pilot, playing a calm version of myself even though inside I was screaming and raging and hurting like hell.

I saw Sue, Ashley's mam, who was still staying with us and was making a cup of tea in the kitchen.

'These stupid girls,' she said, rolling her eyes, and I knew there was no point in discussing it with her, because she would always believe her son and defend him to the hilt. That's how she'd reacted last time, and I knew she'd be exactly the same again.

I was glad of the house being so big because even when people stayed with us, everybody had plenty of space to themselves. After that I kept out of Sue's way as much as I could.

That night I got into bed, next to Ashley, and quietly soaked my pillow with tears while he slept beside me. I eventually cried myself to sleep, wondering how the hell this was ever going to be resolved if my husband couldn't even hold a conversation with me.

The phone rang, at 5 o'clock in the morning.

'I'm so sorry. There's another story in the press today.'

'About the same girl?'

'No. Different story, different girl.'

'OK. Thank you, Hillary.'

I decided not to read this one.

'I'm going to work,' I told Ashley later. 'By the way, there's another story today.'

'I can't handle this,' he said.

I could see he was boiling with frustration and I knew that if I pressed him now he'd go absolutely berserk, so I just went to work.

'*You* can't handle it?' I thought. 'What about *me*?'

I'm not sure how I functioned that day. There were dancers over from America to perform 'Fight For This Love' on the BRITs with me and I think that helped, because I assumed they knew nothing about my personal life.

I was dying inside, but when I was working I didn't have to face it. I focused on the music and just threw myself into the choreography for the whole six hours we rehearsed. I was exhausted, but I didn't even enjoy taking my lunch break, because then I had time to think about Ashley.

That night I went through the same routine as the previous night at home, doing my own thing in the house and then lying beside Ashley in bed and crying myself quietly to sleep.

I didn't think about moving into another room. It was the least of my worries, to be honest. I don't know if I thought 'why should I?' or whether I still held out a tiny, teeny bit of hope that he might talk to me if I was there beside him – but he didn't.

The phone rang, at 5 o'clock in the morning again.

'Hello, Hillary. Another one?'

'I'm afraid so. I'm sorry, darling.'

'Thank you. I'll not be reading it.'

I told Ashley and went to work.

'I can't handle …'

I slammed the door and went out. It was actually Valentine's Day, though I didn't realise it until later. On previous years Ashley had taken me out to gorgeous restaurants and given me the most beautiful presents, like diamond necklaces. It was never important to me where we ate or what gifts he bought me; being with him was what mattered. He was my best friend as well as my husband, and when things were going well I just absolutely loved being with him. There was a natural chemistry between us and we always laughed and had a lovely time together, wherever we went and whatever we did. Our friends were always saying what a perfect couple we made, and if I'd had a magic wand I'd have turned back the clock, I thought. I wished none of this had ever happened, and I just wanted my man and my marriage back, the way things were before.

Unfortunately, as the week went on it became more and more obvious that wasn't going to happen. The routine of taking 5 o'clock-in-the-morning calls from Hillary went on for four days, and every day it was like Ashley put another brick in the wall between us. I tried a few more times to get him to speak to me, but the more I tried, the thicker the wall became. In the end it was so thick that Ashley had closed himself off completely.

I still hadn't read anything after the very first story, and I banned Hillary, and everyone else, from telling me anything at all about any of the other stories. I wanted to hear it from the horse's mouth, or not at all.

'Just keep it all away from me,' I said as the BRITs drew closer. 'I can't go on live TV with all this information in me brain. And there's no way I want to ruin that performance. He's not taking me music away from me on top of everything else.'

I had calls from the girls and from my family, who were all saying the same thing: 'I can't believe he's done this to you, again. Keep your chin up.'

Nobody I spoke to was questioning whether the stories were true, and I wondered what the hell had been said that I didn't know about. I knew it had to be bad, but I wasn't ready to face it.

I hated the fact that people I loved were suffering too. Part of me wanted to know what they had read that I hadn't, but even just being near a newspaper made me feel ill. If there was one on the table when I took my lunch break I had to move away from it, because the smell of the newsprint made me feel physically sick.

Until now, newspapers had always reminded me of puppies. Hearing my dad's voice brought back a very strong memory of when we first had our Dachshund Monty as a tiny puppy. I could see my dad putting newspapers down when we were training him, but now I felt like even that memory was tainted.

The night before the BRITs I had a final fitting to do. The stylist came to the house and we used the room next door to our bedroom, but I don't think I even told Ashley what I was doing because I wasn't speaking to him at all by now, or to his mam. I literally just walked past Sue if I saw her in the house, because I couldn't deal with talking to her, knowing she would be fiercely loyal to Ashley.

I didn't speak much to my own mam either. I just needed space to think for myself. I didn't want anybody else's opinion, and I didn't want everybody's eyeballs on me. I needed to get away, to make up my mind about what I was going to do next.

I had warned Ashley the last time that I would divorce him if he ever cheated on me again. I could remember my exact words: 'If anything like this *ever* comes up again I'm divorcing you. You're lucky I've come back this time and if you *ever* disrespect me like this again, it's all over.'

Ashley knows I'm a woman of my word and I started to think that my warning was the reason he had clammed up. He knew what he'd done, and the more he said, the more he would be making me leave him. That's what was going through my head. Our marriage was over. I could feel it, but I hadn't had the chance to breathe, and I needed time to myself before I made the decision.

By the day of the BRITs I had already planned my escape. I'd prepared to fly to LA, because when I'm there, or at least once I've got past the paps at the airport, I don't generally get chased. The American press is very different to the British tabloids; it's a much more positive relationship. They're not looking for dirt or for an angle on a story that doesn't really exist, they just want a nice glossy picture and when they have that they generally leave you alone. The American public didn't know me, and so I'd be able to have my freedom back, and space to think away from the madness at home.

When I told Hillary my plans I also said to her, 'I told you last time and I'll tell you again, I'm leaving this industry. I'm out. I do not want anything to do with it.'

'Cheryl, just get through this show, have your break and we'll talk again in two weeks.'

Of all my friends and family, Hillary was the only person who was not telling me to leave Ashley at this point. Even my mam, whose powers of forgiveness are superhuman, told me she couldn't bear to see me go through any more pain. 'Cheryl, you've only just got back on your feet again and started putting on a few pounds and looking like your old self,' she said. 'I don't want you to suffer any more.'

Hillary was a lone voice, telling me: 'Don't do anything rash or you might regret it.' Hillary's a very wise woman, and she knows me very well, so I did my best to listen. She knew I'd be having a mental freak out as soon the BRITs finished, and I guess she was trying to slow me down, and stop me doing anything crazy, like instructing divorce lawyers as soon as I touched down in LA.

I can vividly remember stepping out on that stage at the BRITs to sing 'Fight For This Love'. 'You've ruined our marriage, Ashley, I'll not let you ruin me career.' That's what I thought.

It was the thirtieth anniversary of the BRITs, I was on after Jay-Z and Alicia Keys and there were 40 dancers on stage with me. I was just thinking, 'Like hell I'm gonna mess this up. I'm getting through this performance, I'm giving it my best shot, and then I'm out of here.'

The song is all about strength, and I was so determined to be strong that night I think you can almost see the power coming out of me. I'll never forget it, and I was buzzing when I came off stage. I'd felt half dead all week, but it's impossible not to put on a show like that without feeling an adrenalin rush, and mine lasted for hours.

After the show I packed my suitcases instead of going to the BRITs after party, and I told Ashley early the next morning: 'I'm out of here.'

If he'd have said, 'I'm sorry, Cheryl, I'm ready to talk to you honestly and openly,' it would have been different, but he didn't. He had let me lie in bed beside him for five nights now, crying myself to sleep, and he hadn't given me one word of comfort. It was absolute hell not knowing the truth and he must have known that, but he did nothing to ease my pain. There was no trust and no communication left in the marriage, and so I had no choice but to leave.

14

'I'm divorcing you'

'I don't want you to leave. Please don't,' Ashley texted, but it was too late. I was boarding the flight to LA and now it was *his* turn to be left in the dark, because I didn't tell him where I was going or how long I was going to be away, and now I had to switch off the phone.

Lily travelled with me to LA. She didn't ask questions or say anything at all about Ashley; she was just there for me. She understands that I'm not one of those people who wants to talk and talk; I just like to deal with my own thoughts and feelings.

I had some peace and quiet in my head for the first time in days, and tears started rolling down my cheeks as I thought about my life. I was angry and hurt and upset, but I was also very proud that I'd done the BRITs and got on this plane without falling over. I think one of the few emotions I *didn't* feel was humiliation. I knew it was something that must be being talked about – how humiliating it was for me after taking Ashley back last time – but I honestly didn't feel that. *I* had been loyal in my marriage, and I hadn't done anything to humiliate *myself*, so why would I feel humiliation?

It was a 12-hour flight, and so I had a lot of thinking time. I thought about Ashley lying there in bed, not knowing where I was going, or when I was coming home. He had looked absolutely exhausted when I left, even though he'd been lying down for the best part of a week. It was mental exhaustion. He must be going through some kind of a breakdown. How could he not communicate with me when it was obvious our marriage depended on it? You absolute *idiot*, Ashley, I thought.

It was a blessing that I had to switch my phone off on the flight, or I would definitely have been tempted to start texting him. Despite what he'd done I actually felt terrible for leaving him there, worrying, because I knew how horrible that was.

I had no idea how much I would need Lily with me until we arrived at LAX Airport. There had been one or two paps when I left Heathrow, but here there were at least 50, some with video cameras and TV crews. They all crowded in on us at once, calling out: 'Hey, Cheryl! What's happening in your marriage?'

I held Lily's hand tight and the two guys who were picking us up literally had to barge their way through and squeeze us into the car. Lily and I ended up squashed into the same seat, it was all such a scramble. It was terrifying. I was close to tears and panicking like mad, and I didn't breathe properly again until we got inside our hotel in West Hollywood, which thankfully had an underground car park with direct access to our rooms.

I went on a bit of a crazy one once we got there, calling up all the friends I had in LA and going out drinking and clubbing every night. I was running here, there and everywhere, running fast, trying to escape. I figured nobody in LA knew my business and nobody would be judging me, so I could just let my hair down. The paps at the airport would sell their pictures to the British tabloids, because the American public didn't know me or have any interest in me.

One night I went out for something to eat with a guy I'd met when I was doing Will's 'Heartbreaker' video. We talked mostly about music, because that was what we had in common. He said nothing about Ashley, and I assumed he didn't know a thing until right at the end of the meal when he looked me in the eye and said, 'Your husband's a douche bag, by the way.' I was a bit drunk by then and I just laughed it off. I knew it was only his way of offering me support, but I wasn't impressed. *I* was allowed to criticise my husband, but I didn't appreciate someone who'd never even met Ashley getting involved.

On the Saturday night I went out clubbing with Brian Friedman, the *X Factor* choreographer who's a good friend, and I also met up with Derek Hough, having called him as I'd promised to do next time I was in LA.

'Wow, I didn't think you were coming out here so soon!' Derek said, as it was only a few weeks since we shot the 'Parachute' video.

'No, nor did I,' I replied. 'I'll explain later.'

Of all the people around me, Derek was the only one I felt comfortable confiding in. We'd worked together for about four or five days in total on 'Parachute' and had called and texted each other a few times since. We'd also done a gig in Munich together a few days after making the 'Parachute' video and enjoyed each others' company, but really we hardly knew each other. I just followed my instincts, because he seemed such a genuinely nice person; someone with a good soul.

Derek listened as I unloaded over several drinks, and I felt myself relax a little. I remember it was a Saturday, because at the end of the night I had a look at the *News of the World* online. The time difference meant it was already Sunday morning in the UK, and I'd had a text from someone back home alerting me to another story, one I was told I couldn't ignore. I was drunk by then or I wouldn't have looked at it, and I'm sorry I did.

There was a picture of Ashley with an American girl sat on his knee. Ashley was kissing her cheek and had a stupid, soppy drunken look on his face, a look only I would know. The girl said it was taken in Seattle, when Ashley was on a tour with Chelsea in July 2009, and while I was busy working on *The X Factor*.

Until this point I'd only read the initial story about the sex texts, supposedly sent to an English glamour model. I hadn't known what to believe, but this was very different. This girl, whose face I was staring at, was saying she had sex with my husband. And, even though I hadn't read all the stories in between, it was clear from this one that she wasn't the first to claim to have slept with Ashley.

There was another horrible truth I was facing too. This girl wasn't saying that Ashley was so blind drunk he didn't know what he was doing. That's what had allowed me to forgive him in 2008, but he clearly knew what he was up to this time. 'High-spirited' was the phrase used to describe him in the article.

'High-spirited? Are you absolutely joking after what I've been through?' I shouted as I read the story. 'I'm out of here! That is IT. It's over.'

That photograph was the decider. I was getting divorced now, and that was final. Even for Ashley to allow that girl to sit on his knee like that at a time when he was meant to be on best behaviour was disrespectful, and I wasn't going to be disrespected any more. It was time to press the button.

'F*** you!' I shouted at Ashley's face in the picture.

Derek was still there with me, which was awkward.

'Are you alright?' he asked. He had a look on his face that said: 'This is kind of crazy.'

'I'm fine,' I replied. 'In fact do you know what? I'm more than fine, because now I *know*. I can stop torturing myself and just deal with the decision.'

The relief I felt as I said that was huge, but from that moment on it felt like I was buckled into a rollercoaster ride that was mixing up my emotions whichever way I turned. I was sobbing uncontrollably one minute, laughing hysterically the next, and seething with anger and aching with pain all at the same time.

I didn't want to speak to Ashley at all, but he called me a day or two later. When I saw his name flash up on my phone I thought twice about taking the call, but I did pick up.

'Cheryl, the house has been broken into,' he flapped. 'I was lying in bed and the next thing was, there was this man crawling towards me in a balaclava. I whacked him with one of my crutches. It was terrifying …'

'You know what, you deal with it,' I told him, and switched my phone off.

I couldn't bear to speak to him, and I thought it was just a pathetic attempt to get me home. I texted my mam and said, 'You'll never guess what, Ashley's saying the house has been broken into. As if that's going to get me running back.'

'You know what, it has,' Mam said. 'I'm here.'

It turned out that the burglar had seen pictures of me leaving Heathrow without my wedding ring on and must have assumed Ashley was playing football, because Chelsea had a fixture. The crackpot had not taken into account Ashley's broken ankle, thought there'd be nobody at home and had tried to rob my jewellery. Apparently Ashley screamed like a girl as he clonked the guy with his crutch, which I could just imagine him doing after his performance with the lizard on our honeymoon, not to mention that cat that broke into his flat.

'Wow!' I thought, not knowing whether to laugh or cry.

I was in LA for 10 days, and my emotions were all over the place the whole time. Derek was brilliant. In the short time I'd known him I'd been bowled over by the spontaneous, free-spirited way he lives his life. 'I'm just snowboarding in Utah,' he'd said one time I called. Another time it was: 'I'm partying in Miami. Mary J. Blige is here – do you want to talk to her? She's really cool and I'm going to teach her how to tango ...'

Now he was taking me out for coffee or to the cinema, trying to keep my spirits up, and one night he asked me out to dinner.

'We can't go for dinner, they'll say we're dating,' I said.

'What are you talking about?' he laughed. 'It's just *dinner*.'

Even though Derek has family in the UK and had lived in England for 10 years as a child, he is from Utah and there are some parts of British life he just doesn't get. The tabloid press is, or should I say *was*, one of them.

He is very famous in America because of *Dancing with the Stars*, but he was only used to receiving happy, positive publicity because that's largely what the public wants over there. Derek simply didn't understand why anyone would want to photograph me

Coming close to being eliminated after singing Shania Twain's
'You're Still the One' during week two of the live shows.
I was nineteen at the time.

With newly formed Girls Aloud, just after we'd won the second
part of the *Popstars* competition by beating the boy band, One True Voice,
to the Christmas number one.

This picture was taken on our 'What Will the Neighbours Say? Live' tour in 2005, our first ever concert tour. I was twenty-one and I loved every minute.

Here I am with Victoria Beckham at the World Cup in Germany in 2006, enjoying supporting our men together.

Ashley forgot his shorts when we went on holiday to Dubai and had to buy these, and of course the paparazzi caught us off-guard . . .

Smiling with Ashley after our wedding in July 2006, with me dressed in a Roberto Cavalli gown at Wrotham Park in Hertfordshire. I was twenty-three, and felt like a princess.

At *The X Factor* final in December 2008, when winner Alexandra Burke got to perform with Beyoncé. This was *amazing* – Beyoncé is one of the people who inspired me to do what I do today.

he girls performing 'The Promise' the 2009 BRIT Awards. We were l very nervous performing in front f music industry bigwigs, but we on Best British Single.

Climbing Mount Kilimanjaro for Comic Relief with Kimberley in March 2009. I had no idea what I was letting myself in for, and it was unbelievably testing.

Performing 'Fight For This Love' on *The X Factor* in 2009. The military-themed costume really caught on with the fans, who we now refer to as soldiers.

A victory for Geordies! In 2009 I got the boys category in *The X Factor*, and when Joe McElderry won he jumped all over with excitement.

Dancing Latin ballroom with Derek on the TV special *Cheryl Cole's Night In*, December 2009. This is how we met and became really good friends.

Trying to escape LAX airport after the second revelations about Ashley in 2010. It was a terrifying experience.

Derek was photographed leaving the London Hotel in West Hollywood. He'd brought his friend's dog to cheer me up, and we had a good laugh about this picture afterwards.

On tour with The Black Eyed Peas in May 2010. Will would sometimes perform '3 Words' with me, but I never knew if he was going to appear on stage or not.

Me and my final four girls – Cher Lloyd, Katie Waissel, Rebecca Ferguson and Treyc Cohen – on *The X Factor* in 2010.

Simon and I joking about in our usual fashion on *The X Factor* judging panel. There was always a lot of banter between us, both on- and off-screen.

In February 2011 I had the honour of meeting Prince Charles at Clarence House after setting up my charity, The Cheryl Cole Foundation.

This is the FOX Upfront party to reveal the line-up of presenters and judges for *The X Factor* USA. I'm with Steve Jones, Nicole Scherzinger, LA Reid, Paula Abdul and Simon.

In September 2011 I went on a morale-boosting visit to Afghanistan to present a *Daily Mirror* Pride of Britain award. I have the greatest respect for our soldiers.

It was such an honour to perform at the Queen's Diamond Jubilee Concert in June 2012. When we all stood on the stage together after the show the atmosphere was incredible.

walking into a restaurant to have a quiet dinner with a friend, especially when my life was in such a mess.

'It's just not news,' he said. 'Honestly, I don't get it.'

'Trust me, it would be. It's not worth it.'

In the end Derek decided to just turn up at my hotel, bringing with him his friend's Yorkshire terrier, as he knew I was missing Buster and Coco like mad.

'I've brought you some doggy love,' he said.

I'd been crying but I started smiling, and I thought it was really sweet and thoughtful of him. Derek was like a breath of fresh air. He had no preconceived ideas of me. I wasn't a famous person to him; I'd just come into his life through a video, that was all. He told me about himself, and the fact he was brought up as a Mormon, and I felt I could trust him and talk to him about anything, because he just was so dignified and well mannered and easy to be with. I was used to being surrounded by girls, but I was now starting to get very mistrustful of women, which is probably another reason I confided in Derek.

'I'm questioning the sisterhood,' I told him. 'I'm a girls' girl, always have been. I would never sleep with someone's husband knowing they were a married man. I don't understand those girls, those hangers on who sleep with someone just because of what they do or how famous they are, or how much money they have. What about the sisterhood?'

Derek let me ramble on, and he moved the conversation on to lighter, brighter things whenever I got too tearful and distressed.

I hadn't wanted to talk to Nicola and Kimberley, or anybody else I was close to, because I felt they'd already been there for me once in this situation, and it was embarrassing to be in it again.

Derek was a new ear, and he was the perfect person to speak to. It was like he was a little angel, sent to help me through this testing time. I looked at him and honestly half expected to see a halo around his head.

It was the early hours of the morning when he left, and sure enough he got photographed leaving the hotel, with a funny smirk on his face and carrying the dog in his arms. The stories that accompanied the picture insinuated that Derek and I were having some sort of relationship.

'Like *what* are you doing?' his friends said, and Derek couldn't believe the photo was absolutely everywhere, all over the internet and the British press.

'My God, I've never looked so gay in my life! What they thought I was trying to do with you in that hotel room with the dog and the funny smirk I have *no* idea!'

The suggestion we'd met on a video just weeks earlier and were now having a 'relationship' as he watched my marriage crumble was a joke. From Derek's point of view I'd turned from a perfectly normal singer he was doing the tango with one minute, into a crazy drunk woman who was weeping and wailing and shouting and screaming the next. It's not exactly relationship-building stuff, is it?

I called Ashley from LAX Airport before I boarded my return flight to Heathrow.

'I'm divorcing you. I want you out by the time I get home.'

He was clearly dumbstruck, so I carried on talking.

'I literally want you to be out of that house, with your stuff, and I don't care if you've got to hobble. Get out before I get home. It's over.'

'Right. OK,' he stuttered. 'I won't be here. I'll be out when you get back.'

Hearing those words brought me no peace of mind whatsoever. I was willing him to fight. Even now I wanted him to say, 'No, you're my wife and when you get home we're gonna talk about this,' but he didn't.

'What a *wimp*,' I thought.

I got Sundraj to put out a statement that said: 'Cheryl Cole is separating from her husband Ashley Cole. Cheryl asks the media to respect her privacy during this difficult time.'

I thought that making an announcement would at least stop the speculation and might take some pressure off, but I knew that landing at Heathrow was still going to be horrendous. Before I got off the plane I put on big sunglasses and took a deep breath. I just wanted to get to my car and get home as quickly as possible.

The amount of paparazzi and TV film crews was absolutely unbelievable. There were scores and scores of photographers and cameramen, all pushing and shoving and shouting to get a shot of me. I felt tiny and vulnerable, and it was a total shock to my system. I was going through hell, and I was being treated like some kind of performing animal. It was inhumane. I felt like one of those caged bears who's prodded with a stick to make it dance. How could other human beings treat me like this and think it was acceptable?

Mam was at the house when I got back, and she told me Ashley had left just a few hours before I arrived.

'I gave him a hug before he went,' she said.

'What did you do that for?' I asked angrily, because I didn't think he deserved a hug, especially from *my* mother.

'I can't bear to see anyone in that much pain.'

I texted Ashley and thanked him for going, and giving me my space. He'd taken a few bags but his stuff was still all around the house, and I could smell him everywhere. I couldn't face looking at our wedding pictures, and I turned them all to face the walls.

'Mam, by any chance do you have the stories?' I asked.

I was jetlagged and felt dizzy, but I knew it was time to read them.

'Yes. I knew you'd ask for them. I have them all.'

Mam brought them out, put them in a pile in front of me and left me alone.

As I started to read, I felt numb inside. I was freezing up, protecting myself, to try to deal with the pain. I read each and every story, one after the other. There were four different women, all making different allegations. I knew about the first girl, the sex-text one, and now I was turning the pages in horror, reading that all the other three were saying they had sex with Ashley.

I was subconsciously looking for something that wasn't true. I read a text message that didn't seem real. 'Would Ashley *really* write that?' I thought.

One claim went back six years and I just thought: 'Why would you come out with that now?' This girl was saying she was with Ashley the night we were first photographed together at the Funky Buddha nightclub, but I knew *I* had been with him then. I didn't believe her and I was looking and looking, hoping I could find flaws in every story, wishing that somehow Ashley was right, that this was some kind of media vendetta against him that had got dangerously out of hand.

I didn't get my wish, of course. Another girl said they drank rosé wine in a hotel bedroom together, and that Ashley smoked. He does like rosé wine, and at first I told myself she could have seen him drinking it in the bar rather than sharing a bottle with him in the bedroom, as she claimed. The smoking, though? He's a footballer and this wasn't something he did in public. Hardly anybody knew he smoked.

There were other little details in the stories nobody could have known, nobody *should* have known, except me. Holding hands in the bed. That hit a nerve, a big one. That was *my* husband that someone else was talking about. The description 'like relationship sex' was so painful to read I blocked it out totally; I just couldn't deal with it. The fact that he'd been cheating on me when he was away with Chelsea also made my blood run cold. I'd always thought I didn't have to worry when Ashley was at work, because the club wouldn't tolerate that kind of behaviour, but I had a sudden, horrible realisation that if I ever did get back with him, I would end up being one of those horrible, paranoid wives I never wanted to be. I'd already banned him from socialising with certain friends, but I couldn't stop him going to work, could I? I'd be worrying myself sick the whole time.

When I'd finished reading I stared at the papers in disgust and disbelief. It was as if I'd been physically attacked by them, because I felt winded, like the pages and the words had punched me in the stomach. I pushed them away, feeling sick at the smell of the newsprint, and then I actually vomited.

I didn't believe everything I'd read, but I'd seen enough to know that the trust had completely gone out of our marriage, and I was doing the right thing divorcing Ashley. It was almost like payback time. He had hurt me so very badly, and divorce was the only way of getting back at him, of showing him how much damage he had actually done.

I sat alone for ages, thinking to myself, 'I have no idea who my husband is any more. I don't recognise him. The man I've just read about isn't the man I married.'

Seeing the papers had given me another, very unexpected shock too. I'd been so caught up in my own problems that the whole scandal about Wayne Bridge's fiancée, Vanessa, having an affair with John Terry had literally passed me by. It had clearly come out in the press just before the stories about Ashley. Thinking about being on the beach with Wayne and Vanessa and their child the summer before just added to the pain and confusion I was feeling. It was like the world had gone mad, and I couldn't understand what made people cheat and cause so much chaos and upset.

I spent the next few days moping round the house and crying. Ashley was trying to phone me all the time but I didn't answer. I had no idea where he was staying and I didn't want to know. If he was in the papers again I didn't have a clue, because I'd made a decision not to read any of them ever again.

So many things were going through my head. One minute I'd be panicking, thinking, 'If I believe the stories are true then I married a stranger, and how can I ever cope with that?' The next minute I'd think, 'How can anybody hurt someone who loves them so much?' It was agony.

When I hit a really low point one night I phoned Ashley and begged him to talk to me, to give me an explanation.

'You know you said I did nothing wrong, well I don't believe you,' I sobbed. 'There must have been *something*. You have to tell me. It's driving me mad.'

'Nothing,' he said. 'You've done nothing wrong.'

'Ashley, I don't think you get where I'm coming from. You can't just keep saying nothing. It's not fair. Tell me what I did wrong and at least I can deal with my flaws.'

'It's not you. There's nothing like that.'

'But there *is*. Can't you see that by saying nothing, or saying it has nothing to do with me, it's like saying you're guilty of the whole lot. Is that the case, Ashley?'

'I don't believe this …'

It was like talking to a brick wall all over again. I would have preferred him to say: 'You know what, Cheryl, I slept with them all and I loved it.' That would have been less of a torture than not knowing the truth.

When I put the phone down I started sobbing hysterically, like a little child does, crying so hard I was gasping for air and wanting to be sick. The house felt huge. It has six big bedrooms and it's spacious at the best of times, but now I felt like a tiny, teeny person who might get lost inside it. I tried to get ready for bed but I got angry seeing our bedroom and thinking how Ashley had wrecked our life together.

'How *could* you?' I screamed, kicking a pair of his shoes. 'Why did you do it, Ashley? What did I do to deserve this?'

If anyone had heard me they'd have thought I'd finally cracked up, because I was ranting and raving and talking to myself. When my head hit the pillow I started screaming and crying into it. I'd got some sleeping pills off the doctor, and they were a lifesaver. I actually felt good just for 10 minutes before I fell asleep, but in the morning I had to face the whole nightmare all over again. It started the minute I woke up, and the horrible realisation that Ashley had gone and this was my reality hit me all over again.

I started smoking 20 cigarettes a day when I normally only have one or two, and I was drinking too, just to try and relax and knock the sharp corners off my feelings. I was well aware I could fall into a dark depression again. If I'd gone that way after having my heart broken as a teenager I knew it was a strong possibility I could go back there now. In hindsight, the pain I felt at 16, after splitting up with Dave, was absolutely *nothing* compared to what I was suffering now. It wasn't even one-thousandth of the agony I was going through, yet at the time I'd thought I could never feel any lower.

For days I didn't want to see anybody, even my close friends and family, and I could feel myself retreating into my shell. I was protecting myself, I guess. I didn't trust anyone or anything around me, because I didn't even know who I was any more.

I had to get back to work, though. I had studio time booked for my second album, and Will had asked me to be the supporting act on some of the European dates for the Black Eyed Peas' spring tour.

I'd been frightened of doing it at first but Will had more or less repeated what he'd said to me about me recording solo records. 'I know you can do it. Trust me. You *will* be amazing. It's the next step for you. You are going to be a huge solo star.'

We had rehearsals coming up, which I knew was a good thing as moping around the house was doing me no good at all. The tour excited me, and I imagined I could focus completely on my work instead of my pain. It was a way of escaping, I hoped.

I remember going into the Metropolis recording studios in London to work on the album and thinking, 'This is the one thing I've got left. I'm not going to stay at home and wallow in all those horrible feelings and thoughts when I could be doing what I love and making music.'

I'd smile at the security guard on the way in and go through the motions of acting normal, but inside I was dying, and I mean dying. Every day I was getting worse. I thought I was actually going to fall apart it was that bad, and being chased around London by photographers certainly didn't help. I began to really loathe and despise the paps, more than ever before. I couldn't understand how one human could do that to another. I'd felt like a hunted animal for a long time, but now I was so badly wounded the chase felt more inhumane than ever.

Derek was in constant touch, calling and texting. I'd tell him how I was feeling sometimes, but I didn't want to be a burden. He was still like my little angel though, giving positive advice and cheering me up by telling me he looked forward to seeing me when I went to LA, as I had some recording time booked out there too.

'Can you make it to the tour?' I asked him hopefully, as soon as I knew the dates for the Peas. 'You could dance with me on "Parachute".'

'I'll be there for the last week,' Derek said. 'How does that sound?'

I was delighted. The tour was going all round Europe and I was really looking forward to it, for lots of reasons. The main one was that it would be like going back to the early days with Girls Aloud, as I'd be performing to different territories, to people who didn't know me and would have no preconceptions. It would be pure performing and not too much pressure, as I was only the support act. It would be great to work with Will again too, and whenever I felt like I was cracking up I'd try and visualise being on the tour, dancing with Derek, being inspired by Will, and being happy because I still had my music, and nobody could take that away.

About a week after Ashley had left he came round to the house one night to collect some of his stuff. I'd answered his calls a few times by now, and every time he'd told me he didn't want our marriage to end. He sounded torn apart, completely. I felt sorry for him, because despite what he'd done he was still a human being, a person I'd loved more deeply than I'd ever loved anyone before, and he was suffering.

As soon as he came into the house I gave him a cuddle. He squeezed me and clung to me like a little boy. There was no screaming and shouting and I asked him nothing, because I knew it was pointless. Actually, it reminded me of the last time I had seen Andrew in prison, when I reached the conclusion that if he wasn't going to help himself there was nothing more I could do.

It was exactly the same with Ashley. He knew I was there, willing to talk. He knew that divorcing him was not what I wanted, not really. But I couldn't do any more. It was just like with my brother. In order to move forward Ashley had to take responsibility, but he didn't seem capable of doing that. He didn't stay long and was so tongue-tied we barely spoke, and when he left I fell on the bed and howled into my pillow.

I felt like I'd taken a big step, but it wasn't a pleasant one. Seeing Ashley had drawn a line under the pointless rows, but it was also a step closer to the end. Ashley hadn't said sorry for what he had done, or accepted responsibility, not once, not ever. In one way I felt empowered by what had happened, like the victim who finally stands up to the bully one day, goes crazy and shouts 'STOP'. For me, it felt like the mental abuse, the going over and over the same things again and again in my brain, had finally stopped. There's only so much a human can take, and I had reached the limit and was not going to keep asking for more.

When I woke up the next day I felt bereft. There is no better way of describing it. My marriage had died, and I was properly grieving for it. It *is* like a death, but the only thing is you're still alive, living after the death of something that was such a big part of both of you. I could still see Ashley and talk to him, and I knew he was grieving too, and that a part of him had also died. It was just the worst feeling in the world.

15

'Yes! *This* is what I live for'

'I'm nervous,' I said to my mam.

'Why?' she asked.

'Have you got some kind of a shield around you where nothing touches you?' I joked.

She looked at me nonplussed and said, 'Calm down, Cheryl, everything will be fine. What are you worried about?'

It was the beginning of May 2010 and we were on a flight to Dublin, where I was playing to a crowd of 14,000, all by myself. That was nerve-wracking enough and as I reminded my mam, I was also supporting the Black Eyed Peas – one of the biggest bands in the world, one I'd listened to and loved for years.

'It feels like only yesterday I was singing their songs in my bedroom, and now I'm going on tour with them. It just feels so surreal.'

'I know you'll do a great job, Cheryl,' my mam said. 'You make sure you enjoy it. It'll do you good.'

'Mother, I wish I could bottle whatever it is you're on,' I smiled.

Her calmness must have rubbed off on me, because I sat back and thought of all the positive things about this tour. I was really looking forward to working with Will.i.am again, and it would be great to get to know Fergie and the rest of the band, because I'd only met them briefly before.

Will is such an intriguing, charismatic person and I've always loved a character. There is absolutely nothing boring or regular about him, from his geeky glasses and dreadlocks to his intuitive, warm personality. From the moment I met him we had just clicked. I was in such a vulnerable place when I did his 'Heartbreaker' video. Will was this massive superstar, but he was doing his first solo record without the Peas, and so he felt vulnerable too. I hadn't realised that until later, but we had some common ground there, which really connected us.

I hesitate to talk about fate, because I once said in an interview that I'd seen a psychic who told me I was going to meet a footballer. This was actually true, and it did happen not long before I met Ashley, but the number of times that story was recycled was just ridiculous. I am not one of those people who relies on clairvoyants to guide me through my life, but I do have a belief in destiny. How else could I have known from when I was a child that I was going to be a performer? Anyhow, without making too much of it, I'm sure fate was on my side when I chose street dancing for the *Passions* documentary, because it had led me to Will, and now he was a very important part of my life. It was almost as if he looked at me, the very first time we met, and was able to see into my future, to see what I should be doing. He had a genuine belief in my talent and ability that nobody had ever expressed to me before.

When I arrived in my dressing room at the Dublin venue I found flowers, sent from all the Peas. 'My God, they're actually here, in the building,' I thought. 'I really am on tour with them!' I could already feel my adrenalin starting to pump, and it was only about two o'clock in the afternoon. There was also a big Jo Malone hamper from Will, containing scented candles, room spray and perfume. He knows I love all that. It makes me feel at home in a strange place, and it was such a thoughtful gift. Knowing Will, he had already thought about the fact I was used to getting ready to go on stage in a cloud of hairspray, with four other girls who were all having little dramas with sequins and lipstick. It wasn't like that any more. I was all on my own, in more ways than one.

*   *   *

Ashley and I had been separated for two months now, and I was still mourning my marriage in a big way. I'd cried every day, sometimes hysterically, sometimes just shedding a tear when I made a cup of tea and sometimes silently, into my pillow, all night long. The initial stabs to my heart were not quite as sharp but in their place it felt like I had big bruises that ached and throbbed and would never, ever go away. I'd told Ashley I was filing for divorce.

I can't remember the time or the place, but when I was feeling strong I'd called him and told him I was starting the divorce proceedings.

'OK. What about the house ...?'

'Shove it up your arse. I'm taking the dogs. I don't want anything else.'

I instructed my lawyers to deal with it and told them I wanted as little to do with the divorce process as possible. They'd phone me up from time to time asking me whether there were certain ornaments or pieces of furniture I wanted from the marital home, things like that.

'No, thank you. I'll get me own tables and chairs. Why would I want to take memories from there? I don't want anything but the dogs and the divorce papers, and I want it to be quick.'

I knew I was still fragile and vulnerable, but having to perform helped me cope. I was determined to take my mother's advice and really enjoy the tour.

Stepping out onto the stage for the very first time as a solo artist was nerve-wracking but absolutely amazing. I just thought, 'Yes! *This* is what I live for.' I'd divided my set up into three sections: strength, femininity and independence – the three words I chose to reflect me, and the songs from my *3 Words* album. When I got to the independence section I was wearing crystallised Ray-Bans that fogged up, so I did the last two songs peeking out from underneath the glasses, desperately hoping I wouldn't crash into any of the dancers. It all worked, and the sense of achievement when I came off stage was just the best.

All of the Peas came to my dressing room on their way to the stage to say congratulations. I was blown away, completely. It was like a dream.

That first night set the tone for the whole tour. I loved every minute of it. At the O2 Will came on to duet with me for '3 Words', which totally took me by surprise. He'd said that he wanted to do it but I'd told him he was crazy; it would spoil his big entrance with the Peas. When he appeared I was buzzing though, and the crowd went wild. After that I never knew if he was going to pop up or not. The band and the dancers had to be on standby to adjust things slightly if Will was there, and sometimes he was and sometimes he wasn't. It all added to the excitement on stage.

Every night I'd watch the Peas perform after I came off stage, get drunk and go to bed. I didn't want to think about the divorce and so I made sure I didn't have time to let myself get too sad. It didn't matter where we were – London, Zurich, Milan, Berlin, Prague, Antwerp, Paris – I did the same thing every night for the whole month I was on the tour, and it was great.

One evening I walked into my bedroom and *Sky News* was on. Chelsea had won the Premiership and the FA Cup, and all of a sudden there was Ashley, celebrating on the pitch. Other players' wives were there. I should have been there too; that's what I immediately thought. I could barely breathe. It was a massive event in Ashley's life. Chelsea had won the Double; it was such a momentous occasion, but I wasn't a part of his life any more. The next minute I saw Ashley's mam and his brother and his nephew on the pitch congratulating him, and I suddenly felt like I'd lost a whole family as well as my husband. I was separated from them all. What hurt the most was that when I looked at Ashley's face I just knew he would be thinking the same as me; that I should have been there too.

Will's support helped me no end. He would text me out of the blue saying things like: 'You're amazing!' or 'Your strength makes me proud!' He could sense when I was having a bad day, and I'd tell him if I felt particularly sad. Will is one of those people who doesn't just say, 'Are you OK?' without really meaning it. He would look me in the eye and ask me very directly. 'You *OK*?' He never interfered and he never said anything about Ashley unless I mentioned him first, which I appreciated. He isn't one of those people who would say, 'Your husband's a douche bag.' Will isn't like that at all. He's very open-minded and looks at the big picture, rather than pointing the finger and being judgemental.

'It's one of those things that happens in life,' he said to me more than once when I told him how sad I felt or mentioned the divorce.

Each day, I'd receive another gift from Will to put a smile on my face. One day he even sent me some goldfish, which really made me laugh. There was a black one and a gold one – me and him! Only Will could do that. When Derek came over to dance with me on 'Parachute' he gave me another escape, because he was as fun and upbeat and inspiring as ever. I felt surrounded by people who encouraged me, believed in me as a person and as a performer, and wanted me to succeed, and that was so liberating. It was the same when I did a private gig at the Cannes Festival in the middle of the tour. Everyone was charming and incredibly complimentary. It was like being on another planet compared to being back home, where I was constantly hounded by paps and scrutinised by journalists who seemed to actually enjoy pulling me to pieces and dragging me down.

I confided in Derek much more than I did in Will, because Derek had been there with me in LA when everything had started caving in. I would never have got him involved in my marriage crisis deliberately, but he had happened to be there and now he was actually one of the few people I was really talking to, honestly, about how I felt.

'I'm scared of going back home and being hounded by the press,' I told him. 'I'm not sure I can handle it all over again.'

Derek would listen and reassure me, and then he usually tried to move the conversation on to more positive things. We got talking about animals one day, because he knew how much I loved my dogs and he's an animal lover too, and out of nowhere he said,

'You know what, I'd love to go on a safari. Wouldn't it be *amazing* to see a lion face to face?'

Derek's eyes were shining at the thought of it.

'Let's do it,' I said.

'Are you *serious*?'

'Yes. Why not?'

I think I surprised myself a bit, but I really wanted to do it. If *anyone* I really cared about had been so enthusiastic and passionate about something like that I'd have tried to make it happen for them. Normally I wasn't this spontaneous, but my whole world had been turned upside down, and it felt like all the rules had changed. I had no husband, no responsibilities, so why shouldn't I go on safari with Derek if I wanted to?

We booked a trip to Tanzania for when I would have four days off during the *X Factor* auditions in June. 'One last series,' I'd said to Simon. I wasn't doing anything with Girls Aloud that year, and I wanted to be busy, busy, busy.

I was dreading the end of the tour because I was enjoying myself so much, and after my last performance I actually broke down and cried. It felt like I had only been on tour for five minutes and suddenly it was all over. It's common to get 'tour blues' because it's always a bit of an anti-climax when the last show is over, but this was like nothing I'd ever experienced before. It was like crashing down from a huge high, and before the *X Factor* and the safari, I knew I had to go home and deal with the divorce, which made it even worse.

The divorce papers had been lodged at the High Court on 25 May, while I was still with the Peas. Ashley was in Austria, preparing for the World Cup, and the *X Factor* auditions were starting on 9 June in Glasgow. That meant we were both in the spotlight because of work *and* because of the divorce, and the media attention was intense. There was a lot of speculation about my friendship with Will at this time too, because we were so close on the tour. The press didn't believe I could possibly have a friendship with a person with different body parts to me, but any sexual relationship was all in the mind of the media and it sickened me that they were scrutinising us like that.

I think one of the reasons Will and I had become such good friends was because of our backgrounds, as he's from the street and had lost friends to prison and drugs like me. We had an understanding of each other and a common bond, but most of all we just like each other a lot and enjoy each other's company – it's that simple.

Back in London I was chased by the paparazzi everywhere, and I mean everywhere. One day I went for a sexual health check, which was traumatic enough without having a pack of men pointing cameras at me and following me to the clinic. I had to face the fact that Ashley's infidelity had been putting me at risk for a long time, and I had to put my mind at rest. 'This is so cruel on so many levels,' I thought as I gritted my teeth and pushed my way through the paps. 'I don't deserve this.' I was given the all clear, but my emotional health was still in so much danger, having to deal with crap like that.

Another day I went to a meeting with the divorce lawyers and was literally chased down the street by 25 paps who were all calling my name and asking, 'How's Ashley? How do you feel, Cheryl?'

I sobbed so much when I arrived at the office that the lawyer asked me, 'Are you sure you want to go through with this?'

I was in such a state I really wasn't sure, even at that stage. I wished someone I trusted would tell me I was doing the right thing, but I knew that only I could make the decision, and yet I wasn't sure I trusted myself.

'Yes, I'm sure,' I said eventually. 'I'm not crying about the divorce, I'm crying about the paparazzi. They're scaring me.'

I wanted it all over as quickly as possible, but all the time I was in that office I was looking for a sign, wishing someone, somewhere would validate what I was doing. I hardly listened to a word the lawyer said. She was explaining how the divorce happens in two parts, with the decree nisi coming first, then the decree absolute.

I tried to focus but inside I was silently begging God to guide me. 'If you're up there, show me a sign. Let me know I'm doing the right thing. Nana, Dolly? Is *anyone* looking down on us?' Honestly, I was that desperate I was looking for guidance from anyone who might give it. I half-smiled to myself when I thought about Dolly. 'I told you it would never buckin' work,' she'd probably say. 'Buck him, Cheryl. Get rid!'

That's what it was like inside my messed-up head, but if I thought *I* was cracking up, people were telling me that Ashley was in an even worse state.

'Cheryl, it's terrifying,' one friend said, and what she described made it sound like Ashley was going through a mental breakdown. 'He's literally talking nonsense, he's got a beard and he's smoking and drinking loads.'

Somebody else told me that Ashley had said something like: 'I don't want to be here any more.' I didn't believe he was seriously suicidal, but I was relieved to also hear that the club was trying to get him some help.

I'd ignored most of Ashley's texts and all of his calls for weeks now, and when I heard how bad he was I felt incredibly sorry for him. I know a lot of people couldn't understand that after how he'd treated me, but it was one of the most overwhelming emotions of all that I felt at that time. Whatever Ashley had done I couldn't just stop caring for him overnight, but at the same time I couldn't bear to see him in that state, and so I couldn't offer him any comfort.

I knew he didn't want us to get divorced. He'd made that clear many times, but that was about all he did say. He had still never once, in all those months, opened up and come anywhere close to having a proper conversation with me about the cheating.

'So you don't want to divorce me but you can't tell me *anything* that might explain why?' I'd think. 'I just don't get it.'

I was in pieces. In hindsight what I really needed was a relaxing holiday in the sunshine when I finished with the Peas, which is what I always did when I came off tour with the girls. I should have been taking time out to come to terms with what was happening and to contemplate my future, but instead I was now straight into having fittings for *The X Factor*, trying to choose 15 outfits to wear for the auditions.

The 'dress wars' Simon provoked on the last series between Dannii and me meant I now needed a stylist to help me deal with this part of the job, because our clothes were always under the spotlight.

This really annoyed me because it wasn't what I signed up for. The daft thing was I didn't see Dannii as a rival at all. I just chose dresses that I liked and I thought suited me, and I took a few risks with some new designers, because I like to help people who are making their way.

As I tried on the clothes I reasoned with myself that at least *The X Factor* would keep my mind off the divorce. I hoped it might also make the paps focus on something other than my personal life, too, and I told myself that the safari break with Derek would make up for not having a proper holiday. By the time the auditions started I was really looking forward to throwing myself into the new series.

'Well, isn't this fun?' Simon smirked as I got into a helicopter with him and Louis and headed into Glasgow. Dannii was heavily pregnant, so we were having some guest judges filling in for her at this stage. I knew the helicopter was one of Simon's new ideas to rack up the drama of the auditions, but I couldn't help teasing him.

'What's all this in aid of? Are we supposed to be like the Three Musketeers swooping in, or what?'

'Be. Quiet,' Simon said slowly. 'I know you love it really, Cheryl. Be a good girl and smile for the cameras.'

The days were long and draining, especially as Simon had insisted on holding the auditions in front of a live audience again, like the year before.

'You know this makes it crap?' I said to him. 'It makes a mockery of the whole process. You should have just kept it with us in a room.'

'What are you talking about? It's fantastic!' he replied.

'It's too nerve-wracking to be instantly judged by a whole audience.'

'But it's great telly!'

'But it's mean!'

I thought we only found one little pop star during the first three days we did in Glasgow and Birmingham, and that was 16-year-old Cher Lloyd, who I told was 'right up my street' as she looked a bit like I did as a teenager, and she had attitude.

On the whole I enjoyed myself, though, and I was in a great mood when I flew to Tanzania with Derek on 17 June. Just picturing his face lighting up when he saw a lion was giving me a buzz, before we even got there.

'Isn't this *exciting*?' he said.

'You know, it really is,' I replied.

We stayed in the bush in a safari hut, literally sleeping amongst the animals. You could hear them howling and moving around in the night. For four days we had 5am starts, heading out in a rickety jeep with our binoculars as the sun rose, looking for the 'big five'. We weren't disappointed, and we got to see them all: lion, leopard, rhino, elephant and buffalo, as well as giraffes, warthogs and impalas.

'I will never, ever forget this,' Derek said.

'Nor will I,' I replied.

I have always enjoyed giving presents more than receiving them because I love to see the look on people's faces, and being there with Derek and seeing his face light up was such a privilege it brought a tear to my eye.

Being surrounded by so much nature also made me feel very emotional. One minute I'd be laughing my head off, watching in fascination as a baboon ate a peach like a little old man, staring back at me. The next I'd have a sad moment, like when I was looking at crocodiles on a river safari. 'I should be scared of you but I'm not,' I thought. 'If I fell in, so what?' It was like when I flew to Thailand with the girls, and I didn't care if I fell out of the plane because I was already swamped in so much pain, nothing else could hurt me any more.

Every night I cried myself to sleep. I remember that very vividly.

I didn't unload on Derek on that trip, and I had no signal on my phone in the bush so I couldn't have spoken to anybody else if I'd wanted to. This was an escape, somewhere I had time to myself to think, and whenever I thought about Ashley and what had happened to us, the tears poured down my cheeks.

On the last day I was really ready to get back to the UK. It was like I couldn't wait to do the trip, and then when I was away I couldn't wait to get home. In hindsight, I can see that I was so unhappy deep down that no amount of running, here and there, could change things. I couldn't run away from myself and my thoughts and feelings.

I mustn't have been thinking straight when I packed, because when we got to the little local airport to take our internal flight to Dar es Salaam I didn't have my passport. It was an 80-minute round trip to go back on a little charter plane and collect it from the hotel safe so we missed our flight back to London, and then the next one was cancelled. I had to be at the London auditions the next day, and I started panicking. I hadn't told Simon where I was, and I knew there'd be war if I didn't turn up. I phoned Lily in tears.

'I'm stuck. You're gonna have to get me a plane, somehow, to get us home.'

Derek was trying to calm me down, and I was apologising to him for getting him involved in another one of my dramas.

'Don't say sorry. It's been *amazing*,' he told me. I knew he meant it, but I still felt terrible.

In the end we got a rusty, smelly old plane to take us to Nairobi and from there Lily got us booked on a BA flight to Heathrow, which would get in at 7am. There was no airport lounge and we sat on these plastic chairs for three hours waiting for the flight, with me wondering how I was going to survive a whole day of auditioning straight after this.

When we finally took off I noticed I had three mosquito bites that weren't there before. There were two on my foot and one on the right side of my face, and all three were really painful and itchy throughout the whole flight. I couldn't rest at all and I had a massage as soon as we landed to try to make myself feel awake and alive for the auditions, but I knew I was going to have to explain myself to Simon. The bite on my face was absolutely huge by now and there was no way he wouldn't spot it.

'A safari! Are you mad?' he said. 'I could *never* go on one of those things.'

'Well, you should go. You're on your phone all the time, constantly stressing, and you can't do that on safari. It would do you good – and you love animals. You'd love seeing them in their natural habitat.'

'No, I couldn't think of anything worse. As for dressing in safari gear – just no.'

'Well, you might have a point there. I couldn't see you in the hat …'

I was tired, but I enjoyed the next week of auditions, particularly when we went to Dublin and met Mary Byrne. She told us she was 50 years old and worked on the till at Tesco, and then blew us all away with the huge Tom Jones' hit 'I Who Have Nothing'. It was people like her who made me love my job, and I told her I really enjoyed her audition, and that I could feel myself getting goosebumps when she sang.

It was my twenty-seventh birthday two days later and I woke up feeling a bit ill. I hadn't planned a party, because it was my first birthday without Ashley and I didn't think I'd be in the mood. Lily got me two puppies from Harrods to play with – a little pug and a Chihuahua – because Buster and Coco were in Newcastle with my mam while I was away doing the auditions, and Lily knew I missed them. Buster and Coco love it up north, although Buster always comes home like cock of the walk, with what I call his 'council estate swagger'. He's a nuisance for days afterwards, but

I'd much rather he was with my mam up there, seeing the kids, than being put in kennels.

Derek came over in the evening and cooked something, and he'd made me a photo album of our safari on the computer, with *Lion King* music playing in the background. I had about three vodkas, ate loads of birthday cake and really enjoyed myself, despite not feeling one hundred per cent.

The next morning I woke up with what I thought was the worst hangover ever. I felt really sick and my whole body ached and throbbed. My skin was sore, too, which was really weird. It was actually painful to touch, and I thought I must have completely overindulged the night before.

I had to go to a photoshoot for some false eyelashes I was endorsing with Girls Aloud, and I remember apologising to the driver who collected me, because I just had to lie down in the back of the car. When I got to the shoot Lily had laid out a red carpet as another surprise as I hadn't seen her on my birthday. She'd also got a giant cupcake birthday cake for me, but I couldn't face eating any of it.

I was drinking water, thinking I was dehydrated, and then I tried eating a couple of sweets, hoping the sugar hit might give me a boost, but I couldn't stomach them. I decided I must have eaten too much cake the night before, on top of the alcohol. People were asking me all day if I was OK because I must have looked half dead, but I just kept telling them, 'I'll be fine,' because I was sure this was self-inflicted, and I didn't want to moan.

The next day I was in Cardiff for more *X Factor* auditions, and I was really struggling now. I hadn't really eaten anything for a couple of days and I'd practically collapsed into my bed after the photoshoot, then dragged myself here. I felt unbelievably ill and tired, and when I looked in the mirror my face looked puffy and different, like there was something seriously wrong with my skin.

'I'm so sorry,' I said to Pixie Lott, who was the guest judge and must have thought I was quite weird because I hardly spoke to her. 'I'm not myself at all. I feel really ill.'

As I was sitting there I started to sweat, and then every five minutes my arms would go freezing cold and I got these huge, super-hard goosebumps all over them. I showed Pixie and Simon. 'I did have a drink on my birthday,' I said. 'And I've not felt the same since.'

Nobody knew what to say because I didn't look as bad as I felt, and I started to think I might have flu. I texted Derek, who was with his nana, and he told me that she'd had flu and it sounded like classic symptoms. As the day wore on I was finding it painful to even keep my head up and when we took a break the smell of food sickened me. By the evening my lips were deep purple, my finger-tips were blue, and I was almost passing out. I now wondered if this was a combination of flu and exhaustion.

'Lily, I need to schedule in some days off. I'm just wiped out.'

I felt emotionally and physically shattered by this point, and it also crossed my mind that this could be my body reacting to everything I'd gone through this year, telling me it couldn't take any more stress.

I think Lily thought the same. She called Hillary, who said, 'If Cheryl needs a week off, we'll just have to tell Simon. It's tough.'

'Don't say anything yet,' I said. 'I've got the *Vogue* shoot to do, and I'm not letting them down.'

I'd done a *Vogue* cover before and it was a big honour to be asked a second time. Besides, I'd already done the interview to go inside the magazine and I knew they had a renowned photographer travelling from Paris, so cancelling was just not an option.

Nevertheless, I woke up and cried on the day of the shoot because I felt so ill. Sundraj met me at the studio, took one look at me and said, 'This isn't right. You can't do this.'

Unfortunately, we found out that the photographer had taken the Eurostar to Ebbsfleet in Kent instead of to St Pancras. It wasn't his mistake and it meant he'd had a long drive to get to us, which made me even more determined to carry on.

'Sundraj, I'll get through it,' I said. 'As long as it doesn't take too long, I can do it.'

I've never done a photoshoot so quickly in my life before. I remember the make-up artist looking at my purpley blue lips and saying, 'Right, what are we going to do with *those*?', there was a guy pulling at my hair and someone else was painting my nails, all at once. The smell of the nail varnish was super strong, like Andrew's glue in the house back home, and I sat there feeling horribly nauseous and wanting to vomit. Unbelievably, just 15 minutes and four costume changes later, everything was done.

'I'll just lie down for a minute,' I said, and apparently I was out cold for a full hour.

Sundraj lifted me up and I was drenched in sweat. Even my hair was soaking wet.

'You're going home and you're having a week off,' I heard him say.

I agreed, because I knew there was absolutely no way I could carry on. I forced myself to eat a handful of cashew nuts when I got in. There was nobody in the house, and I literally collapsed on my bed.

16

'You're tryin' to kill me!'

'Tell me everything,' I said to Derek. 'I want to know all the details.'

I was delirious when I was admitted to the Cromwell Hospital the week before and I couldn't remember a lot of what had happened in there. I knew this was going to be embarrassing, but I'd learned by now that you have to forget about your dignity when you go into hospital. You leave that at the front door and pick it up on the way out.

Derek started to laugh mischievously. 'Honestly, Cheryl, do you not remember how *scandalous* you were in the Cromwell?'

That was typical of Derek, teasing me and looking to make light of a situation. He was only trying to cheer me up but I still cringed. Some of the things that I could remember myself were embarrassing enough.

'You're tryin' to kill me!' I shouted at the first doctor who examined me. A blood test taken at home had confirmed I had malaria and Derek and my mam had rushed me into hospital for emergency treatment in the early hours of the morning. Just a few hours before that, on the Sunday afternoon, I'd been trying to convince Derek I was fine even though it was only the day after I'd collapsed on the *Vogue* shoot. It was the fourth of July and I know what a big deal that is for Americans. I begged him to go out and watch the fireworks. 'I'll be alright,' I said. 'Don't let me ruin your Independence Day.'

'No way,' Derek replied. 'Enough's enough. You need to see a doctor.'

I was lying on the rug in front of the fire at home. Derek said my lips were blue, and I was sobbing and crying. I'd phoned him up that morning and said, 'Please can you come over. I feel seriously unwell.'

I can only remember flashes of this, because by now I was starting to get delirious. I'd been so ill for days already but I was still trying to convince myself I had the flu, and was exhausted. I'd get over it with a bit of rest, that's what I was saying.

Derek was having none of it. He got a taxi to the local chemist and bought a thermometer, and when he took my temperature it was 104. He had to keep doing it because he couldn't believe the reading.

'This is ridiculous,' he said. 'I'm calling the doctor myself. I think you might need a blood test.'

I went crazy, shouting at him that I hated needles. I associate them with pain; emotional pain. They make me think of heroin addicts. Just the thought of a needle can transport me back to a dark, terrifying place in a heartbeat. I didn't tell Derek all that, but I pleaded with him not to pick up the phone.

'How do you know what I need?' I shouted. 'What are you on about blood tests for?'

He rang Lily, who rang my doctor. She agreed to come over, even though it was a Sunday. I can remember the doctor trying to take blood, but I was going in and out of consciousness.

'I can't find a vein,' I heard her say. The thought of a needle going in my arm made me want to vomit. Apparently I had no visible veins. The doctor couldn't even get the tiniest baby needle in my arm.

When she failed to take blood, the doctor asked me to provide a urine sample. I struggled to do it, and what I produced looked brown and as thick as honey. Disgusting, I know, but that's the truth.

'This is serious, and I mean serious,' the doctor said.

She called her partner and he arrived with his wife, who is South African. Derek called my mam and told her to get on a train down from Newcastle straight away.

All the while I was crying and drifting in and out of consciousness.

They tried again with a needle, tying a tourniquet around my arm to raise a vein. It sickened me, and I was so angry with Derek for making me do this. Finally, they got a little spot of blood out of my arm.

I heard Derek tell the doctor, 'We've just got back from Africa – could it be related?' Derek had been paranoid about malaria while we were in Tanzania. He'd taken his tablets religiously, and had taken them for longer than me. I just took them for the four days we were away and for a few days afterwards. It was far less than you're meant to do, but the area we stayed in was not actually a malaria danger zone and I wasn't concerned. Derek told me afterwards that something was telling him that day it was malaria, even though we'd actually been home for two weeks by now.

'Oh my God, this is classic symptoms of malaria,' the South African lady said as soon as Derek mentioned Africa. 'It takes two weeks for it to take hold.'

The blood sample was rushed off for testing, and the next thing I remember is hearing the phone ring, and my mam being there and answering it. Hours and hours must have passed by now if she'd managed to get herself from Newcastle to Surrey, but I'd lost all sense of time.

Apparently it was 1am when my mam said, 'Cheryl, you're gonna have to get to hospital. They've had the results and you've got malaria. I've called a car.'

I staggered into the night with her and Derek supporting me. I was too weak to think straight or even to have much of a reaction to the diagnosis. Part of me was just relieved to know what it was, and that I was going to be treated.

I must have slept in the car and I remember waking up in the Cromwell Hospital, delirious. That was when I started accusing the doctors of trying to kill me.

'You were just *so* scandalous,' Derek taunted me now. 'Are you *sure* you want all the detail?'

I told him to tell me everything because, as embarrassing as it was to listen to, I wanted to be able to piece his memories to my own so I knew exactly what had happened in there.

Doctors were trying to take my blood again as soon as I arrived. They were also covering my body in freezing, wet towels to try and lower my temperature, which I flung back at them. That's why I was screaming at them. First they were struggling to find a vein, then there was blood pumping out of my wrist. My body was blowing up. By now my face was so puffy my eyes were like slits, and I was so swollen I looked nine months pregnant.

Someone was trying to take off my bra, saying they didn't want to cut it off.

'Just cut it!' I screamed.

'But it's a nice bra.'

'I don't care. Just cut it off!'

A guy was trying to hold an oxygen mask on my face but I wouldn't let him. I told him, 'I know what you're doing. You're all trying to kill me. Don't think I'm stupid.'

Derek said he couldn't help laughing, but in an incredulous 'is this really happening?' kind of way. He said that when I shouted the only thing that moved beside my lips were my eyeballs, which was very unnerving. At one point Derek watched me breathe and tried to breathe at the same pace. He was shocked to find he couldn't keep up, because my breathing was so quick.

Both my lungs were filled with fluid. There was about an inch or less left in each of them for air; that was all. My liver was three times its normal size and I was five minutes from having to have kidney dialysis for the rest of my life. I wasn't aware of that at the time, thank God. There's no way I would have coped with that.

I have random recollections, and I remember seeing a doctor's face right up close to mine. I could smell and taste the oxygen and the plastic of the mask, and I could hear the whirring and beeping of the machines. All my senses were heightened. Everything was super sharp and noisy.

They tried to give me a drug called quinine to flush my system out but it didn't work, and I was getting angrier.

'You're not a doctor, will you please leave?' I said to Derek. 'I don't know what you're doing in here but you're getting on my nerves!'

I then flung a towel at him and swore at him to get out of the room. He said my language was absolutely shocking. Derek never swears, which makes it all the more shameful.

They put a catheter on me and I heard someone say, 'If she doesn't get rid of some of this fluid in the next 24 hours we've lost her.'

I heard my mam's voice, and then somebody told her, 'She may have left it too late. She should have come in sooner.'

'She'll be fine, Cheryl's a fighter,' my mam said calmly. She never, ever flaps. I don't know how she does it.

I had the worst strain of malaria you can get. George Clooney has the other one, the one that isn't as severe initially but lives with you and resurfaces from time to time. I had falciparum, the one that hits you like a steam train but when it leaves your body it's gone for good. It was attacking my liver and new blood cells. That's what it does. The body tries to shut down and your veins shrink, which is why it was so difficult getting the needles in.

My malaria count was rising rapidly. They were taking blood all the time, and the parasites in my liver were doubling.

'We can't facilitate her here. She needs to go to the Hospital for Tropical Diseases.'

My mam kept strong. She said there was no way she was letting any negativity in.

'Cheryl's tough. I know she'll pull through.'

I was aware I had to move, and I heard someone say it wouldn't take long to do the short journey, especially on a blue light at 5 o'clock in the morning. 'There'd better not be paparazzi,' I thought. Even in that state I was scared of the paps. That's how bad it had got with them.

There was a young woman tending to me when I came round in intensive care at the Hospital for Tropical Diseases. She explained that they were waiting for me to pass water. 'That's a vital sign we're looking for. It will show your kidneys are still prepared to flush waste from your body.'

It was so frightening, and I felt absolutely exhausted too. I just wanted to go to sleep and make everything stop.

I can clearly remember asking the nurse if I was dying, and feeling relieved when she told me, 'It's a possibility.'

'Make this end,' I thought. I just had nothing left.

Afterwards I said to my mam, 'I'm gonna write me will. Bring me some paper in. I need to tell you what to do. Gillian can have most of it and Andrew – don't give him a thing.'

I was matter of fact. I was so over it by now. The exhaustion was overwhelming, and I was too tired to take any more.

'Cheryl, you'll be fine,' my mam said. 'We'll be laughing about this in the future.'

She told me afterwards she would slip outside and pray to God, to nature, whatever might help. 'Please God, don't take her,' she would say. I was moved when she told me that. My mam's never openly affectionate and rarely shares her feelings, and on the few occasions she's said she loves me I've practically fallen off the chair in shock.

I was given loads of different drugs and I couldn't take the oxygen mask off or within minutes I couldn't breathe. My left lung was filled the most with fluid, and if I lay on that side or rolled over on to it by mistake I couldn't breathe at all.

Derek slept on the floor beside me, refusing to leave. He also started to blame himself, saying we would never have gone on the safari if he hadn't said he wanted to see a lion in the wild.

'It's not your fault,' I told him later, when I could talk. 'I'm the one that said, "Let's go", and we weren't even in a malaria region. How can it be your fault?'

When I thought about it, I was sure the mosquito bites I got at the airport must have been the ones that had done this to me because they were so extreme, but we'll never know. 'It was just really bad luck,' I told Derek. 'I won't have you beating yourself up. You saved my life.'

One day a nurse tried 10 times to take blood. It was horrendous. It felt like she had a massive needle that was digging into the bone in my left wrist, and I really lost it.

'I'm gonna call the police!' I threatened. I called her names I'm too embarrassed to repeat, and Derek said you could hear me right down the corridor.

When the nurse failed to get the needle in my wrist she told me it would have to go into a vein in my neck.

'No way, I'd rather die! There's no way you're poking that big thing in my neck.'

'Can't you go in higher up her arm?' Derek suggested.

'You're not a medic,' the nurse told him. 'Please get out of this room now.' The nurses were fed up with Derek because he was poking his nose into everything, trying to make sure I was getting the best possible treatment.

He laughed about it later, telling me they all hated him but he didn't care what they thought. He was there for me, not to make himself popular.

I was so grateful to him that day, because the nurse did manage to raise a vein in my left arm, halfway up, and so my neck was spared. She fitted a tap to it so that the next time they needed to take blood they could just switch it on instead of using a needle.

'I won't have any blood left in me system because you lot are taking it all,' I accused her, but that's exactly what it felt like.

The minutes dragged, and a ticking clock on the wall in front of me started to drive me insane.

'Can you hear that tick-tock, tick-tock, tick-tock? It's cracking me up!'

Derek sprung to his feet and took it off the wall. When the nurse came in she went mental and kicked him out yet again, but it wasn't long before he was back.

At last a few drops of urine appeared in the bag I was attached to. This is what we'd been waiting for. Derek took a photo of it and I started going mad at him.

'Are you crazy? You're worse than the paparazzi!'

'It's a happy moment,' he laughed. 'Be joyous!'

I didn't know whether to laugh or cry.

I finally started to feel a bit better once I was passing water again. It was my third day in intensive care by now. I wasn't eating anything yet and was being fed though a tube that pumped stuff into my arm, but I definitely felt less poorly.

Mam brought in a bottle of Victoria's Secret perfume so I could smell something clean, and a nurse gave me a foot massage and bed bath which helped me sleep.

When I was drifting off I could hear my mam and Derek talking about the paparazzi and about *The X Factor*. Because I wasn't at the auditions everybody knew something was wrong, and the doctors had had to give out a press release. It bothered me. I was starting to worry about what was happening outside the hospital walls.

Simon texted: 'Thank God you've pulled through,' and I found out later that Louis had been an idiot and told the press I didn't have malaria but just wanted time off, so I hope he ate some humble pie. The girls and Will were all sending messages, but I didn't want to see anyone but my mam and Derek. I just couldn't have coped with visitors and I couldn't bear anyone else seeing me looking the way I did, because I knew it would upset people.

At the end of my fourth day in intensive care I managed to breathe without the oxygen mask, and I was suddenly so ravenous I felt I could have eaten my hand. Derek got me a load of sandwiches, crisps and chocolate from the canteen, but I could only take a few mouthfuls without feeling full. Still, it meant I was now well enough to leave intensive care, although the doctors said I would need a further week of respite care.

I begged them to let me recuperate at home, but they convinced me the London Clinic was the best place for me. They made it sound like a hotel with room service, so when I got there and a nurse arrived to take a blood sample I was horrified and started kicking off and shouting all over again.

'I thought I was just here to rest! This is just another hospital. I've been conned!'

I had another stupid tube put in my hand for drugs and I was under observation. Every hour someone would stick a thermometer in my ear and check my pulse by clipping a plastic thing on my finger.

'I feel like an old woman,' I complained to Derek. I was all frail and bony, and I hadn't walked for days and days.

I had a craving for raw tuna and Derek got a big carry out of sushi from Nobu. I'd always hated that type of food but I tried it and loved it. I started eating tubs and tubs of Häagen-Dazs ice cream too because my blood sugar was seriously low and I needed building up, and every day I felt a little bit stronger. After about three days someone would come and get me up and try to make me walk a few yards.

'Ashley's here,' my mam had said at one point, while I was still in intensive care. 'He's beside himself. Do you want to see him?'

'No.' I replied. 'I do not want him anywhere near this hospital.' I didn't even think about it for half a second.

The thought of the paparazzi taking pictures of both him and Derek at the hospital made me feel physically more ill. That's what made my decision. That worry overshadowed everything.

Now, I look back and resent how the tabloids interfered in my life to that level. It was a ridiculous decision. What if I'd have died and Ashley never got to say goodbye? However badly he had broken my heart, I would never have wanted him to suffer like that. It would have destroyed him and I wouldn't wish that on any anybody. I just didn't want another media circus kicking off when I was in no fit state to deal with it.

The days went by very slowly at the London Clinic, and as my brain became more and more alert, I was doing a lot of thinking. I was making connections in my head I'd never thought of before, and they disturbed me. The most profound one will always stay with me. I thought back to when I was a teenager, taking out a loan for £100 with the 'Provi' man so I could buy an outfit and some shoes for my *Popstars* audition.

Then, in the blink of an eye I saw myself buying a pair of Christian Louboutins. They were the most gorgeous shoes I had ever seen and they cost £800. I was clicking buttons on Net-a-Porter, spending thousands of pounds.

'What could me mates buy for that back in Newcastle?'

That's what price tags like that used to make me think, but I was over thinking like that now. I'd discovered what the term 'retail therapy' meant when Ashley cheated on me, and being on *The X Factor* took away any guilt I may have had in spending that kind of money. The shoes were not a guilty pleasure; they were a pleasure I'd earned and deserved.

'I might have the shoes, but I can't walk to the shops in them.'

That was the very next thing that came into my head, and it hung there like a big, black rain cloud. I opened my eyes in that hospital room and everything still looked black.

'I might have the shoes but I can't walk to the shops in them.'

I couldn't get that thought out of my head. It was so true. Even though my whole brain felt sore and dizzy, the words were crystal clear in my mind.

'Who the hell am I?' I said to Derek eventually. I don't think he knew what to say. He must have been thinking to himself, 'How am *I* here, in London, with this girl I haven't long known, who's nearly just died.' He mustn't have known what had hit him, but it was just so typical of me to be in a situation like this. My whole life had been like a mad rollercoaster ride. I was so used to experiencing extreme highs and extreme lows; it was all I had known, all my life.

Being in here was just the latest example. Who else climbs a mountain to raise money to protect children against malaria and ends up nearly dying from the disease the following year? It was just *so* typical of me. Who has a number one record and gets locked in a police cell, all at the same time? All these crazy combinations of events flashed in my head. Walking the red carpet one minute, visiting my brother in prison the next; marrying the man of my dreams in a fairytale wedding and then seeing him splashed across the newspapers exposed as a 'love rat'.

You just couldn't make it up. I'd had enough. I wanted to be floating around on the carousel now, not watching my knuckles turn white on the rollercoaster. I just had to work out *how* to change my life.

17

'Do they not think I'm a human being?'

'Simon, don't worry what everyone is saying, I'll be there for judges' houses.'

'Good, I'll see you there then,' he replied.

I'd finally been allowed home after a week at the London Clinic and Hillary had told me I wasn't doing *The X Factor* any more and my album would have to wait until next year.

My initial thoughts were, 'D'you wanna bet? *The X Factor's* one thing, but I'm doing the album. I've lost my husband and my health, but I'm not losing me album. No way. It's all I've got left.'

I reacted that way because *The X Factor* meant less to me personally than my album, but after a couple of days of sitting around at home, watching the telly and trying to build myself up by eating Sunday roasts and my mam's home-made mince and dumplings, I was starting to feel bored and sorry for myself.

I wanted to be busy, and I thought that going to the judges' houses stage of the competition would do me good, especially as Will had agreed to help me.

The truth was I didn't want to sit still, because then I would have to face how I felt. I was so sad and disillusioned with my life it was easier to run away and keep running, even though I was nowhere near fit. I was all skin and bones, my muscles had wasted and my hair was falling out in clumps. It took me an hour to take a shower in the morning because I was so weak, but I didn't care. At least I was out of hospital and on the mend.

I told Simon I'd be there when filming started again in a couple of months, and plans were made to hold my part of judges' houses in Ascot instead of Cannes, just in case I wasn't fit to fly.

However, in the meantime I'd already made up my mind that I was going to beg the doctors to let me go to LA, as I already had studio time booked.

'I'm sorry, it's out of the question,' the doctor said when I laid out my plans, which completely shocked me. 'Your haemoglobin is far below what it should be. In fact, I'm afraid that for the time being, the only place you're going is back into hospital. You need a blood transfusion.'

I'd been out of hospital for about a week when I was given that news and I was horrified at the thought of going back. The doctor explained that I didn't have sufficient 'adult' blood cells and that to wait for my 'baby' blood cells to mature could take three months, so a transfusion was the best course of action. I went back to the London Clinic very reluctantly, but the thought of having some-one else's warm blood running though my veins made me go cold.

'I can't do it,' I said at the very last minute. 'What if I don't have the transfusion?'

'You'll be suffering a little while longer. You'll feel tired and weak for about three months.'

'OK, I'd rather suffer than have the transfusion.'

They gave me an intravenous B-vitamin through the tube that they'd intended to use for the blood transfusion, to give me a boost. They also kept me in overnight, and I actually felt better than I had for weeks. The best thing of all was that I asked one of the hospital doctors if I could go to LA and he agreed, saying I could travel in two weeks' time, provided I wore surgical socks on the flight and made sure I listened to my body, ate well and tried to relax.

'I promise,' I said, but as far as the 'relax' part went, I was already struggling. There had been a pack of photographers outside my house all day, every day, and they were really making me feel stressed.

I couldn't understand how they could hound me like this, know-ing I'd been severely ill. Some of them had actually followed me home from the hospital that day, and when my car pulled in it felt like I was in the middle of a lightening storm as so many flash-bulbs popped all around me.

'Are they not gonna give me time to recover?' I thought. 'Do they not think I'm a human being?'

When I shut the front door behind me, I felt like a prisoner in my own home. I wanted to leave the country, immediately, and the thought of spending another two weeks holed up like this was making me crazy.

'They're ruling my life,' I said to Derek one day. 'I just want to go out and have a walk in the sunshine, but I can't even do that in peace.'

'Just do it!' Derek said. 'Where do you want to go?'

'I'd be happy just to go to Starbucks down the road.'

'Then go!'

I was in a dark, dark hole, and I knew I had to climb out of it. I listened to Derek, and I changed out of my pyjamas, threw on a white T-shirt and a pair of jeans and decided to go for it. I'll never forget it, actually. Every day, I'd been feeling like the walls were closing in on me a little bit more. The pressure of having the paps outside made me feel like I was trapped in a furnace. There was a wall of fire to get through to get outside into the fresh air, that's how it felt. I had to brave the flames to break out of the hell I was stuck in, but I had to do it or I'd lose my mind.

The scrum lunged towards me, shouting and closing in on me. 'Cheryl, how are you feeling?'

They all got their picture, but they didn't go away. I was followed to Starbucks and photographed getting a freezing cold strawberry Frappuccino. When I drank it, I had a brief moment when I didn't care about a thing. It tasted like the most amazing drink I had ever had, because I was out in the fresh air, doing what I wanted to do, paps or not.

I made plans to go to LA, and I was absolutely *determined* not to be followed. Ashley had texted me one day to ask how I was, but I didn't feel strong enough to reply. I kept thinking about how I'd refused to let him come to visit me in hospital, and I felt gutted. He was still my husband, because my illness had delayed the end of the divorce proceedings. How could I have turned him away like that? I'd behaved like that not because of our relationship, but because of the media.

That's when I knew, once and for all, that the paps had to get out of my life. They had crossed the line, a long time ago, and they were not just cataloguing my life with pictures, they were interfering in it and ruling my decisions. I was honestly so scared and paranoid about them by this time that I really thought I would crack up if I had to put up with any more scrutiny.

I spoke to my lawyers about how I could go about getting an injunction against the press, and then I chartered a little private plane to take me to Paris, so I could fly from there to LA and avoid the paps at Heathrow. I literally had to sneak over the back wall of my house to get in the plane, and Lily helped me set up a whole decoy car at the front to make absolutely sure the plan worked.

My heart was thumping and I felt sick with nerves as I climbed into the plane, but it was so worth it when we took off, with the paps, the malaria and the feeling of being trapped all left behind. Unfortunately, when I landed at LAX there was another pack of paps. I just wanted to scream at them: 'F*** off, you're a f***ing disgrace, each and every one of you!' but of course I didn't. I had to remain composed and keep my dignity, otherwise I would spark another whole load of stories about how I was cracking up.

I never wanted to have to do that again though, and I told my lawyers I was prepared to do whatever it took to prove to the courts I needed that injunction, for the sake of my health.

When I quietly checked into one of my favourite hotels in West Hollywood later that day, I started to breathe again. My skin was an awful yellow colour and my hair was still falling out, but the sun was on me, I was eating coconuts cut fresh from the trees and every day I could feel myself healing. I got a doctor to do the routine blood tests I still had to go through, and Derek would come over and hold my hand sometimes when the needle went in. He was still blaming himself for my malaria and was super panicky if I didn't get in touch with him for even a day, but I told him not to worry, and that I needed some time to myself, to work on my music.

This was true, and I also needed time to think. Each day my head was so full of thoughts it was throbbing. The malaria had changed me as a person, I could already see that. Things I would have stressed about before now mattered less. So what if my hair was falling out? It would grow back eventually. Who cares, really, if I've missed *The X Factor* auditions? I'll be there for judges' houses.

My BlackBerry was constantly beeping with messages of support from friends and family, but I felt completely and utterly lonely. I was about to get divorced, and it really hit me that for the first time in years I was a single person, standing alone in the world. I'd never felt like that before. I'd gone from living at home to being in Girls Aloud and being married to Ashley. Now it was just me, making a solo album as a single woman, living alone in a house in London and a hotel in LA. Even when I was surrounded by people I felt lonely. Looking back, I had cut myself off from family and friends, isolating myself from them because they were just another thing to deal with and I felt nobody really understood what I'd been through or was going through now.

After a month I was ready to get back home and prepare for *The X Factor*. I'd done the 'lemonade master cleanse' again, which helped me feel I'd flushed the malaria totally out of my system, and though I wasn't yet strong enough to work out, I was eating more healthily than I ever had before. I'd start the day with porridge or poached eggs and I'd eat lots of fish, prawns, sushi and avocado. I think my craving for tuna and sushi in the hospital had told me something. My body was craving good things like fish oils, lean protein and B vitamins, because it knew how bad junk food and sugars would make me feel when I was at a low ebb. I've pretty much stuck to that diet ever since, although I still have bad days when I just want to eat burger and chips. I don't stress about it. I feel I deserve it, because I'm so good most of the time.

Heading home, I felt healthy. I'd finished recording and I needed another purpose and something else to occupy my mind, so I was glad I had *The X Factor* waiting for me.

'I'll send you the tapes,' Simon told me when I texted him to say I was coming back. I didn't have a clue what I'd missed in the auditions or boot camp because I'd deliberately avoided all news. I hadn't even touched a paper for well over six months, ever since I read the last reports about Ashley's cheating.

Nicole Scherzinger had stood in for me on the show and I didn't feel a part of it at all. Looking at the tapes, it was like watching as a viewer, which was odd. I was given the girls to mentor, including Cher Lloyd, Katie Waissel, Rebecca Ferguson and Gamu Nhengu, and as soon as I met them all I felt some of my old spark return. I wanted to find a little star, and I felt confident that I could do it, especially with Will by my side at judges' houses.

I'd seen Katie's first audition before I got ill and couldn't stand her, but Simon had spent the past two years drumming into me that we needed acts who would be 'good TV'. When I saw Katie perform this time, I had to admit that she was certainly that. She was quirky, intriguing, and busting to succeed. In short, she had the character and drive it took to withstand the pressure of the show, and so I put her through, even though she messed up when she sang in front of Will.

As for Cher, I absolutely loved her and had done from the start. She reminded me of myself, coming from a similar background and being gutsy, putting herself out there. She felt poorly at judges' houses and basically broke down when it was her turn to sing, but I still put her through because I believed in her and I felt sure she'd blossom as the competition went on.

'Don't put her through,' Simon said. There was a lot of talk behind the scenes about Cher's health because she looked so frail, but I had a strong instinct that she was going to make it.

'Trust me,' I said. 'I know how to navigate her through.'

'On your head be it,' Simon said, because he always had to have the last word.

Rebecca Ferguson was such a beautiful and enchanting singer I had to pick her despite the fact she was so shy, but I decided not to keep Gamu. I hadn't been there for her first audition, but I'd met her behind the scenes and I saw what the cameras didn't. I couldn't see a spark in her eyes and I just didn't get her, even though she was lovely and had a nice voice. I believed very strongly that the audience would vote her off in a couple of weeks, whereas my instinct on Cher's potential was so strong, which is why I chose her over Gamu.

I was completely unprepared for the amount of outrage that decision caused. 'Cheryl, it's time to tell the truth,' I saw splashed across a newspaper front page that flashed up on TV in my bedroom a few days later. It completely floored me. 'What the hell?' I said to the television. I couldn't believe I'd apparently caused a national uproar just by doing my job on a television talent show. It was insane. Will had totally agreed with my choices and had picked exactly the same girls I had. We'd chosen the acts we believed could win the competition; it was that simple.

'I can't handle this. It's just unbelievable! I'm not even completely well again.'

I honestly didn't know anything at all about Gamu's background when I decided not to take her any further in the competition. I had absolutely no idea she had an issue with her visa and was worried about deportation. All of that came to light afterwards, and yet now I was being accused of booting her off to get rid of the problem for ITV. It was horrific, absolutely mortifying.

I knew full well from past experience that once a story is out there it's impossible to take it back, and giving an interview to the press to try and correct inaccuracies usually just fanned the flames.

Over the previous few weeks, Piers Morgan had been in touch to ask me to go on his *Life Stories* show. I liked Piers, but going on his show didn't appeal to me at all. I couldn't understand why anybody would want to be interviewed at length like that on national television, especially someone like me who was trying to stay *out* of the media spotlight. After the Gamu scandal, though, I suddenly saw it through new eyes.

'You know what, I'm going to do it,' I told Lily. 'There's nobody twisting your words on there. It's just going to be me, on camera, speaking. I can set the record straight.'

Once I'd made the decision it felt liberating because it wasn't just Gamu I would be talking about. My decree nisi had been granted the month before, while I was in LA, and the divorce would be finalised in a couple of weeks. I started to see the show as the perfect opportunity to say my final piece about the marriage, and to shut the door on all the speculation about it, once and for all.

I knew from friends that Ashley had been really bad lately. He'd been drinking a lot and his flat had been ransacked, and he was basically in a real mess. I didn't feel hatred towards him. It was very painful to think of him like that, and I knew exactly what I wanted to say on television.

'You have no idea what I've been through. I'm not celebrating the end of my marriage. I still have feelings for Ashley and I wish none of this had happened and I was still married to him. I feel at the end of my tether. I've been through a divorce and nearly died, all in the space of a few months. It's too much for anyone to cope with, and I just want us both to be left alone to deal with it.'

That is what I had running through my mind as I prepared for the interview, but when the cameras started rolling it felt too difficult for me to say everything I wanted to. I did manage to tell Piers that Ashley had been my best friend, that a part of me would always love him and I was a heartbroken girl, but it was so hard to speak.

'I wasn't a footballer's wife in an ivory tower with all the lovely things and so thinking it will all be alright,' I managed to say.

My shoulders felt like cardboard I was so full of stress, and my chest was caving in. The amount of sadness I felt as I spoke was really overwhelming, and it shocked me. I started to cry, and when Piers went on to ask me about the nature of my friendship with Derek, I told him I was never going to talk about it, ever.

I said this because I'd made the mistake in the past of talking about my private life. Having my wedding in *OK!* magazine was the worst mistake of the lot. It made it impossible to ask for privacy afterwards, and now the marriage was over there was speculation all the time about who I might be dating.

'I've got a magazine on asking if you're going out with 50 Cent,' Sundraj had said one day.

'Well, I'm not. I met him once when I was 21.'

Another time it was: 'Are you going out with Andre Merritt?'

'Sundraj, I know he wrote "Fight For This Love" but I've never even met him.'

'Er, I have someone asking if you're going out with a billionaire who Derek introduced you to.'

'No! I wish I was!'

'What about your hairdresser? Any truth in that rumour?'

'Sundraj, please! I was out with him and his boyfriend!'

I wanted all that rubbish to stop, and I knew that whatever I said about Derek would only increase the speculation, so I made that pledge never to speak about our relationship, or any other I may have in the future. I have stuck to that pledge, and I will always stick to it.

I honestly hoped that by doing Piers' show I had said the final sentence, and I really thought I had.

Back on *The X Factor* I felt like an emotional wreck after the ordeal of talking to Piers, but I didn't want anybody to know how fragile I was and so I put on a feisty front. When Simon said to me on the show one night, 'I would like to start off by saying Cheryl, you look much better tonight – less orange,' I felt like knocking his head off. My complexion was still a touchy subject after the malaria, but I didn't want to say that and play the victim. 'You too, and your teeth look whiter,' I replied instead, to a gobsmacked Simon.

He loved it really when I answered him back like that, and we were actually getting on better than we ever had done. I'd told Piers that Simon was one of the most important people in my life, and it was true. Inviting me on *The X Factor* had changed my life and taught me so much on so many levels, and I was grateful to him and saw him as a friend as well as a colleague.

Sometimes I'd take Buster into the show with me, and Simon would go all gooey over him. For this series Simon had a whole floor converted into a huge dressing room. It looked like a really flash bachelor pad, with white leather sofas and black wood everywhere, and one time Buster did a wee on his floor. I'd had to stop taking Coco in because she did that all the time in my dressing room, but Simon just laughed about it.

That's what it was like. One minute we'd be crossing swords, the next we'd be giggling together like a couple of naughty school kids. We often took a break together, running off down the corridor to sneak outside and have a cigarette. To me, Simon was exactly like an annoying but charming older brother, the type who winds you up and makes you want to scream sometimes, but you love him really. There was nothing sexual between us, and there never has been. Why he came out with that line in his book saying he would have liked an affair with me, I'll never know.

'I felt like a mouse being played by a beautiful cat,' he apparently told Tom Bower, his unofficial biographer. 'She would drop her eyes and play the soulful victim to get around me. She played me.'

Honest to God, I don't recognise either the scenario, or Simon, there. I think he must have been going through some kind of mid-life crisis when he spoke to that guy. We sparked off each other and we 'got' each other, but there was never anything sexual going on between us. I never, ever felt like Simon was trying to hit on me, and despite what's been written I have never called Simon 'creepy' for what he said about me, because as far as I'm concerned he is not creepy. He is just Simon, and I knew what he was like and how to handle him.

I laughed it off, and Simon texted me afterwards and said, 'I'm so sorry if this has caused you any embarrassment, I didn't write the book.' He also told me that he meant it as a compliment that I 'played' him.

'You're saying I manipulated you?' I asked, because I was genuinely confused. 'What have I ever got you to do that you didn't want to do?'

'You had me wrapped round your little finger,' Simon said. 'Whatever you used to do to your eyes to make them big and wet …'

'What? I have no idea what you're talking about,' I told him, and I still don't.

I remember having a huge row with Simon one night, during the lives. Before we went on air he was really critical of Rebecca's song choice. That stressed me out a lot, but when the cameras were on us he was all sweetness and light, as if the song choice had never been much of a problem at all.

'It's all a game to you, isn't it, Simon?'

'No, it's business, Cheryl,' he replied.

I was fuming with him, because I'd taken his criticism completely to heart. I understood that we needed to make 'good TV', but I hadn't been so tainted by Simon that I lost sight of other peoples' feelings. He, on the other hand, was quite happy to toy with me to get a good reaction for the show. I don't think he once stopped to consider if I was emotionally strong enough to be doing this job, but looking back I definitely wasn't.

There were terrible girl dramas going on all the time, and Cher in particular was always kicking off and needed a lot of attention. It was draining and I'd be in tears at some point each week, but Simon never spoke about feelings. With him it's all about work, and if I was being feisty and tearful, it was good for ratings. I'm sure if he'd have known exactly how close to the edge I was he'd have been concerned, but I was obviously doing a very good job of hiding it.

'We work so well together I'd love to have you in the US with me,' Simon said one night.

It was November 2010. I knew some of the big bosses from Fox had been in the audience, watching how we did things over here. A couple of them had even been to my dressing room to meet me, and now I realised why. This was typical Simon. He's the manipulator of all manipulators, and he'd obviously known about this possibility for a while and chosen to pull strings behind the scenes instead of being up front with me.

'If you're trying to get me on American *X Factor*, then do us a favour ...'

'What?'

'Please will you be the one to tell me if I'm doing it or if I'm not. I know what you're like, and I don't want stuff all over the press before I know myself.'

'Agreed.'

I wasn't excited or nervous or anything at all, to tell the truth. I just thought I'd wait and see what happened.

Not long afterwards I got a phone call at home from Simon.

'You know that conversation we had about American *X Factor*?'

'Yes.'

'You've got the job.'

I didn't speak.

'Cheryl, are you there?'

'That's cool,' I said.

Simon had never actually asked me if I wanted the job, but he had already confirmed with Fox that I was doing it. He said he wasn't telling the press anything at all, and I was to keep it a secret. In Simon's world, the idea I might turn the job down didn't exist, because it was a huge career opportunity, and didn't everyone want to become an even bigger star and earn even more money?

I put the phone down and felt absolutely nothing, again. No excitement, no fear, no nerves, just absolute numbness. Literally the only thought that ran through my head was: 'If I become famous in LA, where will I be able to escape to?'

I was in the process of moving out of the marital home by now. Ashley was going to move back into Hurtmore House when I was gone as it was close to Chelsea, and I had rented a place in Hadley Wood, North London, which was nearer to Kimberley, Lily and Hillary.

I stuck to what I'd said at the start of the divorce process and I didn't want any possessions from the house at all. I'd told the lawyers to just deal with the split, and I'd signed the papers, asking for nothing except the dogs. I just wanted to get out of the marriage and out of the house, but as the day of the move got closer I became more and more emotional. I hadn't anticipated this. It was heartbreaking packing up my clothes and still seeing some of Ashley's in the wardrobe. Every room held a memory, and I cried every night when I got home.

I didn't realise it, but I think I was actually going through a nervous breakdown. Throughout the live shows I was cracking up, in fact.

After the Gamu nightmare I'd started asking the production staff to give me the heads up on what was being said in the press and on Twitter about the acts each week. I needed to know what the public thought about my girls and their song choices and image, to help me steer them through the process, but I didn't get the help I needed and felt constantly wary and in the dark.

For instance, I began to worry that if Simon didn't like a particular song choice he'd make sure they didn't make a good track for it, to prove the point, but that would never have happened. I was totally paranoid because I was in such a weak place, mentally.

A waxwork of me was unveiled around this time, and I remember going to Madame Tussauds to see it and just staring at the model in bewilderment. 'Why am I here?' I thought. There were already models of Simon, Louis and Sharon Osbourne, grouped together, and I said, 'Do not put me near Simon Cowell, I want to be on my own.'

It is so freaky to see yourself in life form when you're only used to seeing a reflection of yourself in a mirror, or on the TV, and I felt unnerved. 'Who *are* you?' I thought. It took me back to when I was in hospital, asking myself: 'Who the hell am I?' The question had been on my mind ever since, but I hadn't had time to find out. I hadn't dealt with it, and I still didn't know the answer.

It was at this point that I asked my brother Garry to join my team. I wanted to promote Lily from PA to personal management as she was doing so well, which meant her old job would be available. Garry had recently left university and split up from his long-term girlfriend, and I thought it would be a good time for him to do something new and see a bit more of the world. For me personally it meant I got to spend more time with my little brother, and I wouldn't have the worry of hiring a stranger and wondering if they were going to be trustworthy.

'Why not?' Garry said. 'Yerl have to teach us the ropes though, Cheryl. I'm not used to all this celebrity hoo-hah.'

Just hearing his accent was always refreshing, and I knew straight away that Garry would be a reality check for me, too, which could only be a good thing.

I also decided I would need a manager in America; someone I could trust. My second album, *Messy Little Raindrops*, was coming out soon and it would have been impossible for Hillary to deal with everything I was doing once I was living in LA and working on American *X Factor*. Will was the person I turned to. He brought me into his team, and eventually his manager, Seth Friedman, became my US manager. This came into effect in March 2011.

On the face of it, I was coping. I was preparing for my new life and making some good decisions, but I was still close to tears all the time. It was like my nerves were always close to snapping, and I felt permanently on edge. I was making practical plans to keep my mind busy, but emotionally I wasn't functioning properly at all.

I remember going to a fancy dress party that Sarah threw for Halloween and feeling in a perfectly good mood at the start of the night. Kimberley and I went as the grim reapers and Nicola was dressed as Lady Antoinette. The girls came into *The X Factor* to get ready and we all walked directly past the paps outside, which had us in hysterics.

Nobody knew it was us when we arrived at the party either, because our heads were still covered. Once we got to our table we took the masks off and the fashion designer Julien Macdonald joined us. He was dressed as the devil, which turned out to be very apt. First he made a rude remark about Kimberley's weight, referring to her as 'not quite' the skeleton he had as company. Then he started throwing unnecessary insults out in every direction, and it was soon my turn to be in the firing line.

'*You*,' he said in his Welsh accent. 'What is that red hair all about? It is horrible, and I mean *awful*!'

I'd dyed my hair red not long before, just because I felt like a change, and I couldn't believe this man was criticising me in front of friends and strangers like this.

'I take it you don't like it then?'

'No, it's one thing if you're being paid for it, if it's a L'Oréal thing or something, but if you're not being paid for it you need to dye it back.'

'Actually, L'Oréal red hair dye sales have shot up by 600 per cent since I did this, so you should do your f***ing research.'

It didn't stop there. Julien then went on to tell me that I'd been looking terrible lately, and Dannii had been looking better than me in the previous weeks.

'I suggest you sack your stylist immediately,' he said.

As you can imagine, with the fragile state of mind I was already in, I was not going to put up with this at my friend's party, so I gave *him* a suggestion.

'You know what you should do? I suggest you leave this table. F*** off!'

While all this was going on Nicola was sat there in her Lady Antoinette dress and white face looking like something out of our 'Can't Speak French' video, gobsmacked at what was being said.

Looking back, we all laugh our heads off when we remember the scene. Around the table there was an assortment of fancy dress characters, some splattered in blood and all in elaborate costumes and make-up. Julien was stunned at my reaction to his rudeness, and all the grisly-looking and gruesome characters stared at him in disbelief as he slunk away from the table.

I was meant to be wearing one of his dresses the very next week on *X Factor* but I never did, and I have never worn his clothes since. How could I? He tried to drag me down when I was already feeling at my lowest ebb, and it was totally uncalled for. He sent me flowers to apologise afterwards but the damage was done, and at a time when I really didn't need it.

In hindsight this was quite a pivotal moment for me. I'd been running away from my feelings for a long time, and now my emotions were catching up with me and everything was coming to the surface.

My mam said she would help me finish packing up the house, and on the night of the *X Factor* final all my possessions were in boxes, ready to go. I'd just watched Matt Cardle win the show. I liked him, because he was a decorator and he reminded me of my dad when I was growing up, always singing a tune while he was painting. Of course I was delighted for Rebecca when she came second too, but I'd be lying if I said I was ecstatic.

I was wearing a beautiful long red dress and I was smiling on the stage, but inside I felt too stressed and anxious to enjoy the moment, and all I could think was: 'I'm *so* glad it's over.'

I broke down when I got home and saw the house packed up. It felt so final. 'It's really over,' I sobbed to my mam. 'I know, Cheryl,' she said. 'But things will work out, you'll see.'

My mam went home to Newcastle for Christmas and I slipped up there on Christmas Eve to deliver presents to all the family, then returned to my new house alone. I told everyone I wanted to unpack and settle into my new place, but the truth was I felt so miserable I didn't want to spoil Christmas for everybody else.

'You don't seem yourself,' my dad had said as soon as he saw me. 'I'm worried about you.'

Everybody was saying the same thing, but nobody could help me. 'I'll be fine,' I said, but really I wanted to say, 'Help me. I can't live like this any more. I hate the lifestyle. I wish I could come back home and walk to the corner shop in my pyjamas but I can't. I'm miserable as hell.' That phrase that first came to me when I was in hospital was ringing in my head: 'I might have the shoes, but I can't walk to the shops in them.' How true that was.

A month earlier, on Children in Need, Sir Terry Wogan had introduced me as 'the nation's sweetheart', which blew me away. Sir Terry was someone I'd watched on telly from when I was a kid. It was very kind of him, but to me *he* was the national treasure, not me, and if this was what it felt like to be the nation's sweetheart, I didn't want the title, not at all.

On Christmas Day I cooked myself a ready-prepared turkey in a baking foil tray that I carved with a butter knife, as I had no kitchen utensils. I ate it with some vegetables and it was quite nice actually, but just as I finished eating it I got a text from Ashley's mam.

'We miss you,' it said. It was harsh to read that, and I started sobbing uncontrollably. I broke down completely, in fact. It was like one of those scenes in the movies. I collapsed on the stairs and was sobbing so hysterically and was so out of control I couldn't breathe.

I did that three or four times in that house. One time it happened after I texted Ashley in a moment of desperation and weakness, telling him how low and alone I felt. I knew he'd been at rock bottom too, and I thought that if he knew how bad I was he might find it in himself to talk to me about what he'd done, to help me understand and move on.

'Can't you tell me why?'

'I don't know what to say. It's too painful,' was all he said.

This was unbelievably hard. I'd hoped Ashley might give me some kind of closure after the divorce, but this told me that he's just not articulate enough to put into words what had happened. I had to face the fact he might never grow up enough to be able to talk to me in the way I needed him to.

I tried to pull myself together for New Year, when Derek and I went to stay with my good friend Janine and her family in South Africa. I'd met Janine when she did all the interior design in the houses I lived in with Ashley. She knew me very well, and she could see I wasn't myself at all.

'Where did Cheryl go?' Janine asked when she saw how miserable I was.

I couldn't answer her. I'd spent six years of my life being half of a couple with Ashley. Even Janine admitted she missed him, and I really felt like half of myself had gone. Derek did a good job of entertaining everyone, and also tried to get me to calm down about the fact there were paparazzi following us everywhere.

'Just go and walk on the beach and pretend like they're not there,' he said.

'No. I feel invaded. I hate them so much. I don't want to give them anything when they're hunting me like an animal.'

I'd put on weight after the malaria because I'd been eating more to build myself up as the doctors advised, but my body hadn't stabilised and I was now bigger than I wanted to be. I couldn't bear to get on the scales, and that was another reason I didn't want to be photographed, especially on the beach.

I could see that Derek was thinking I was going over the top and was worried about how paranoid I'd become, but I didn't confide in him and so he couldn't help me. I was losing my head all the time and I'm sure I'd been having a nervous breakdown for months. I can see that now.

One day I went absolutely mental when the paps took photographs of Janine's young children through her glass balcony that overlooks the beach. 'I'm so, so sorry,' I sobbed. 'I can't believe they're invading your privacy too. It's inhumane.'

'I can't bear to see you cry,' Janine said. 'Don't let it get to you so much. You need to try to relax. There's nothing we can do about it now.'

'How can I relax? To relax I have to accept that the paps are going to violate me. I just can't do it!'

We were there for 10 days and that's how I was the whole time – sad and paranoid and a shell of my normal self. The pressure of keeping the secret that I had the job on American *X Factor* was adding to my stress, but at the same time I was relieved I wasn't starting until May, as I knew I had a lot of preparation to do, both mental and practical.

I also had a couple of other projects on the go. I'd talked to Will about doing a little eight-track album, and I was making progress with my plans to do something for charity and help the kids back home in Newcastle. Through climbing the mountain for Comic Relief I'd met a lady called Kristina Kyriacou, who now worked for the Prince's Trust. She suggested I could set up a foundation that could work alongside the Prince's Trust, helping disadvantaged youngsters in the North East.

The whole thing sounded perfect, not least because I remembered asking the Prince's Trust for help myself as a teenager. I wrote in and asked for money so I could do gigs. I never got it, but the whole idea that I could help kids like me from council estates was incredibly appealing.

I was invited to have lunch with Prince Charles at Clarence House in the middle of February, when the Cheryl Cole Foundation was officially launched. I'd been a big fan of the Prince ever since he was accidentally caught on mic on a ski slope, being rude about the press and telling his boys he couldn't bear one of the royal correspondents. I'd also sung in front of him at the Royal Variety and shaken his hand at several red carpet events before, but clearly this was very different.

Before the lunch I was briefed at length on the etiquette of dining with our future king, and it was explained that I must always address him as 'Your Royal Highness'. We had 45 minutes scheduled, and I was feeling quite nervous when I was finally escorted into a reception room and invited to sit on a sofa opposite him.

'Do you like hip hop music?' he asked me very unexpectedly after the formal introductions had been made, which instantly put me at ease.

'Harry has it on upstairs and I can't understand a word they're saying. It's just banging noise to me.'

'I like it,' I told him.

'You do?'

I couldn't help smiling, imagining Prince Harry in his bedroom blasting out 50 Cent, with Prince Charles shouting up the stairs, 'Turn that noise off!'

Prince Charles then told me he enjoyed listening to classical and orchestral music, and went on to say he was also a big fan of ballroom dancing.

'We all love watching *Dancing with the Stars*,' he said, which was a surprise, and had me smiling again.

'Derek is our favourite dancer, actually. Camilla and I would love to learn the Argentine tango. Maybe Derek could teach us?'

'I'll ask him if you like, I'm sure he'd love to.'

I was really enjoying myself. I completely lost myself in the conversation, in fact, and when Prince Charles told me that he enjoyed watching the ballroom dancing in some of the old movies, I totally forgot myself.

'They don't make them like that any more, Charles,' I replied.

'*Why?*' I said to myself immediately afterwards, hearing the word 'Charles' hanging in the room.

Honest to God, I wanted to pull that whole sentence out of the air and put it back in my mouth! Lily was sitting across the room and I could feel her wanting to laugh, but Prince Charles was absolutely brilliant. He changed the subject again very skillfully, and didn't draw any attention to my mistake at all. He spent an hour and a quarter with me in the end, and I left feeling really positive and excited about what we could achieve.

In fact, working with the Prince's Trust and making music with Will were the only things that did inspire me at that time. Whenever I thought about the American *X Factor* I still felt absolutely nothing. It left me totally numb. Even thinking about the move to LA did nothing for me, although I had to start making arrangements.

I applied for passports for Buster and Coco, I started organising my clothes for the show and I went house hunting. I was looking at fabulous condos worth millions of dollars up in the Hollywood Hills. It should have been a real treat and a pleasure, but I felt no buzz whatsoever.

'What are you doing driving around LA having your forehead photographed?' Simon said to me one day.

I was really annoyed by that. It was his fault my American *X Factor* job was a big secret, and I was sticking to my side of the bargain and trying not to let the world's press know that I was buying a home in LA.

There was speculation all the time about me being desperate for the job and wanting to 'crack' America, which was really irritating too, as it had never been an ambition of mine, ever.

'Can't you just make the announcement? You're letting the press toy with me.'

Simon just laughed. In his world, he would send his 'people' to buy him a house and he couldn't understand why I was doing all this myself, or why I even bothered to try to hide from the paps, which is how come I had my forehead photographed through a car window. To him the speculation simply added to the hype of the show and it was all fantastic publicity.

'You're mad, you know that, don't you?'

I didn't answer, because I always avoid letting Simon know when he's right, and I thought he was spot on this time.

'Yes,' I thought to myself. 'I think I am completely crazy.'

18

'Cheryl, I know you're laughing but this is really bad'

'Good luck,' Simon said. He was on the phone to me the day before I was starting work on American *X Factor*, in May 2011.

'Thanks,' I replied. 'I'll see you tomorrow.'

I should have been so happy. I was about to start work on this massive show and Simon had made it sound like my dream job.

'This is the perfect next step for your career,' he told me. 'And you're so good at spotting talent.'

I hoped he was right. I wanted this job to be more about the talent and less about me, and from what Simon was telling me, that was how it was going to pan out. I wasn't known in America. People didn't know all about Ashley and the divorce. It was an opportunity for a fresh start and I should have been on cloud nine, but I felt dead inside, just as I had when the job was first given to me. There was not one spark of excitement, nothing at all. I wasn't even particularly nervous. I'd picked out an outfit for the first day that I was comfortable with – purple trousers and an orange top – and I'd decided to have big hair. I felt ready to start, but that was about it.

It had been tough leaving England. I asked Ashley if I could see him, to say goodbye. He was apprehensive but agreed when I explained to him it was important to me. I thought it would be like laying my ghosts to rest before I went, something that would help me to move forward in my new life in America. I knew it would be painful, but something was telling me to do it, to make that final break.

I felt really nervous as I drove up to the house. I had not seen Ashley's face for over a year, literally, and I wasn't sure how I was going to react, especially as we were meeting in our old marital home, where he now lived. My heart fluttered as the front door opened, and when I saw Ashley standing there I felt so emotional. He took me by the hand and led me inside, calling me babe, just like I was still his wife. It was heartbreaking.

'It's like we've never been apart,' I thought. 'And I still love him.'

There was no awkwardness at all. It felt like I'd just been away from him for a few weeks. Ashley's mam was there and I went to say hello to her before Ashley and I went and had a cigarette together, alone.

'I'm moving to LA,' I told him. 'I'm doing American X Factor.'

'WOW! I'm so proud! I knew you'd always do big things.'

His eyes were shining with excitement. He reacted the way I should have done, and I thought that was very sweet. Ashley looked skinnier than before and the house had a different smell about it, but apart from that, it was like time had stood still since we'd last been together.

'I'm sorry for how it's all turned out,' he said, eventually. I wasn't going to ask him any questions about the cheating because that wasn't why I'd gone there, and I knew I wouldn't get any answers.

I asked about his football instead, and told him how sad I'd felt when he won the Double and I wasn't there with him.

'I felt the same,' he said. 'I locked myself in the dressing room and cried afterwards.'

We also talked a bit about my malaria and the fact I hadn't let him visit me.

'That hurt a lot,' he told me. 'I was so annoyed.'

'It's partly why I wanted to see you. I wanted to explain. I wasn't in my right mind and I wish I'd never done that.'

'I really appreciate that.'

I was there for an hour or so, and Ashley asked me if I would come back the following week and say goodbye to his brother, Matthew, and sister-in-law, and Sue. I agreed, and when I arrived the next week he'd laid out nibbles and really made an effort. We played pool and it was a really enjoyable night. I was so happy to spend time with Sue again. We'd always got on really well and she still felt like family to me. They all did, and driving away was painful. I felt like I'd stepped out of a parallel universe. Ashley and I lived totally separate lives now, but in that house it was like nothing had changed.

I couldn't sleep that night. I felt like I'd suffered a shock to my system. The same thoughts kept going round my head. How could we have said those vows and lost it all like that? We should have been going through life together, but we were missing out on so many big things in each other's lives. It seemed so sad and pointless, and I felt bereft all over again.

'Cheryl! Cheryl!'

I was standing on the pavement outside the Galen Center in LA on 8 May 2011, about to start my new job. I was in the purple and orange outfit, smiling and waving at all the photographers and film crews. It was literally just days since I'd seen Ashley and left England, but in that moment my old life seemed a million light years away. I was here, in LA, a judge on American *X Factor*. I still didn't feel anything like excited, but I had made a commitment to this job and I was going to give it my best shot. I took a deep breath and went inside the auditorium.

I had no idea what I was letting myself in for, but I just did what I always did in these situations. 'Do your best, that's all you can do,' I heard my mam's voice saying in my head.

I introduced myself to LA Reid, one of the other judges, and he gave me a big smile and welcomed me warmly.

'We're waiting on the two divas,' a member of the production team I knew from the UK *X Factor* whispered to me. 'Both notoriously late.'

That meant Simon, of course, and Paula Abdul. I'd never met Paula before, and in fact she didn't even know she was doing the show until the day before. Nicole Scherzinger and Steve Jones, the two presenters, were up on the stage, so I went over and said 'hi' to them. Steve was normal and friendly but Nicole was singing and dancing to her own songs, and I found that a bit crazy and odd.

'Hi! Cheryl!' She beamed. 'SO good to see you again!'

I wasn't sure the feeling was mutual. The first time I met Nicole was when she was performing on *The X Factor* in London.

'Oh my God, Cheryl! You're just as pretty in real life! I just heard your song on the radio!' she had gushed. It was really embarrassing. Then she started singing 'Promise This' to me, and I swear to God the woman sang the whole song, to my face. It was just so awkward, and every time I stood next to her she started singing it again. I thought how that would be like me going up to Britney and singing the whole of 'Baby One More Time' in her face. Can you imagine how weird that would be?

'Hi Nicole,' I smiled, relieved that this time she was too occupied with singing her own songs to start on mine.

As I walked off the stage, Richard Holloway, the *X Factor*'s executive producer who I'd worked with for years at home, came up to me.

'How are you feeling?' he asked.

'I'm getting there,' I replied honestly, meaning that I'd got through the press, met LA Reid, Nicole and Steve, and was about to meet Paula.

She and Simon appeared minutes later, and Paula was really lovely and seemed genuinely pleased to meet me. I had a good feeling about her, but Simon was acting like a weirdo, puffing out his chest as we went through to a holding area, where the contestants were waiting nervously.

'Good luck to all of you,' Simon said. 'We're looking for stars ...' It was the same spiel I'd heard him say countless times in the UK, but something was different. He seemed more arrogant than ever, and he began speaking quite rudely to the contestants as he told them what to do and where to go next.

'Are you OK?' he said to me briefly. 'Yes,' I replied, because I felt absolutely fine. I was just thinking to myself, 'I'm not sure *you* are.'

That first day of auditions went well. I put my work head on and got on with it. 'It's just like the UK auditions but with American accents,' I said to Lily at the end of the day. 'I've enjoyed it, actually.'

Even though I still didn't feel particularly thrilled by the whole thing, I was pleased I'd got off to a good start. Quite unexpectedly, Simon strode up to me, chest puffed out again, and told me in no uncertain terms: 'The crazy hair goes tomorrow', before turning on his heels and walking off.

'What's all that about?' I thought.

He called me later that night to make the same point again. 'The crazy hair goes tomorrow and you need to be more yourself.'

I was really annoyed now. 'What happens to your f****** hair, and when do you start being *yourself*?' I retorted.

I had already planned what I was wearing for the second day of auditions – a cream sleeveless top and dark trousers – and I decided to have my hair plaited loosely on one side, because that's what suited the outfit. I had no idea if Simon would like it or not, but quite frankly I didn't care what he thought. Nobody had told me he'd suddenly become a fashion expert.

I enjoyed myself more on day two, and I forgot about Simon's comments. There was a great atmosphere in the auditorium and I felt a connection to the audience, and to the contestants. Simon seemed fine, so I assumed he'd just been a bit stressed on the first day.

There was a break of a few days after the LA auditions, which suited me as it meant I could go to the Cannes Film Festival for L'Oréal, as they'd asked me to walk the red carpet for them.

Before I left, Richard Holloway came up to me and asked, 'Who do you think we should have as judges in the UK?'

'I don't know. Who are your options?'

He gave me a few names and I gave my opinion. I was just going 'yes, no, yes, yes …' It was just like that. I knew Simon valued my opinion, so this wasn't an odd conversation.

I was looking forward to Cannes, and when I got there my red carpet moment turned out to be one of the most memorable ever, for an unexpected reason.

'Oh my God!' I said just moments before I stepped out in front of the waiting photographers.

I'd had my nails painted at the last minute and, not realising they were still wet, I'd accidentally smeared burgundy-coloured nail varnish all up the side of my white Stephane Rolland dress.

'What am I going to do?' I panicked. I was meant to be a glamorous ambassador for L'Oréal, and this was just not acceptable. I didn't have another dress, and even if I had it would have been too late to change as I was literally expected on the red carpet any moment.

'You'll just have to hold your clutch back at an angle, over the worse of it, and hope nobody notices,' a stylist said, and that's what I did, the whole night long.

I laughed when I saw the photographs the next day, because the bag was in exactly the same place on every shot, no matter where or how I was standing, and when I waved at the crowd it was always with my left hand as my right arm was glued to my side.

Simon called me while I was still in Cannes, which immediately wiped the smile off my face.

'Do you want to go home … and be a UK judge?' he asked me.

I was absolutely stunned. By that time I'd already told everyone I wasn't doing the UK *X Factor* again. I'd made that clear when it was finally announced I was going to America. I'd done three years and enough was enough. I wasn't going back.

'No, Simon. I've been there and done it. Three times. Why are you asking me this question now?'

This was irritating beyond belief. The only reason I was doing the American *X Factor* was because Simon more or less told me I was doing it.

'I'm just wondering … if you would consider it?'

'No. Absolutely not.'

'So you definitely won't. You want to do the American one?'

I felt like screaming at him: 'Why have you left it until *now* to ask me this? Are you crazy?' but I simply replied, 'I've started now, haven't I, Simon?'

'OK. Seem more like yourself when you get back then,' he warned.

The conversation really annoyed me but I tried to put it down to Simon being under a lot of pressure himself, which I'm sure had also accounted for his odd behaviour in LA.

I was relieved that when we met up again, this time in New York, he seemed to be a bit more like the old Simon, although he did have the cheek to come up to me and say, 'You look more like yourself today,' with an approving smile on his face. By anyone else's standards this was very rude, but for Simon this wasn't untypical, and I let it go.

We were with the other judges and presenters to do a promotional event. It was called 'Fox Presents *The X Factor*' and was a kind of showcase for the series. Everything ran smoothly, and afterwards we all flew to Chicago for the next round of auditions.

As soon as I arrived at the Chicago venue I spotted a female producer from the UK who I knew had not long recovered from cancer. I went up to her to see how she was doing, and we ended up having a big conversation about how it feels to be poorly. I hardly ever talked about my malaria but I did on this occasion, because we were two women who had a connection.

I could sense Simon watching me, and looking back I imagine he was thinking I was not being myself again. This wasn't a typical conversation for me to have, I admit, but I didn't see what it had to do with Simon.

'There's something weird going on with Simon and Nicole,' Lily whispered to me later that day.

I had to agree that something didn't feel right, but I wondered if Lily was being a bit paranoid. She didn't think she was.

'I swear they're whispering and stuff. Something's not right.'

I focused on the auditions, which went really well. One of the contestants stood out for me because he could sing, he was good-looking and he had charisma. I told him, 'You've got the package.' Everyone burst out laughing, because the guy was wearing really tight jeans which obviously made people focus on the word 'package'. I hadn't meant for that to happen, but it was all good fun. I felt the same vibe I'd felt in the UK. I was enjoying myself, and the audience seemed to be really enjoying what I was doing.

We had a two-week break after the day of auditions in Chicago, because Simon had to be back in the UK for *Britain's Got Talent*. Before we left, Richard Holloway came up to me and asked where I was spending the time, and when I told him I was going back to England he asked if he could meet me there. He made it sound like a casual thing, as if we might just go out for dinner or something, and I happily agreed.

He phoned very shortly after we got back to London. Lily took the call and asked if we could arrange a date for the following week.

'Er, not really,' Richard replied. 'I need to see her sooner than that. We need to meet as urgently as possible.'

Alarm bells were ringing, and I agreed to see him in a hotel near my house in Hadley Wood a couple of days later. My mam was down, and I didn't want him coming to the house with her there, because I could sense this was bad news.

'Something's off,' I told Lily. 'If this isn't a social visit, why hasn't he rung management?' That's how it worked, and that would have been the polite thing to do. If someone wanted to fix up a business meeting, however well I knew them, they would go through my management team, making arrangements with either Seth or Hillary.

'I've got a gut feeling this is gonna be about him telling me that American *X Factor* is over. Will you come with me?'

Lily agreed because she felt the same bad vibes herself and she didn't want me to be on my own.

As we drove to the hotel I told her, 'I promise you – watch how this goes down. I can feel it.'

Richard looked all awkward and weird when we walked in, and he launched into his spiel straight away.

'Right, there's no easy way of saying this. You're going to be replaced on *X Factor* America … but your chair's still here for you in *X Factor* UK.'

I could feel the shock coming from Lily even though she was sat across the room from us, but I felt nothing, again. I had that numbness I'd had when I first took the job.

'No, I don't want it, thank you,' I told Richard.

'What do you mean?'

'I mean I don't want the *X Factor* UK chair back, but thank you.'

'You need to seriously consider what you are doing for your career,' he said.

I looked at Lily in complete disbelief now. How much front did this man have?

'Thank you, Richard, but I don't want the job, but thank you for the offer. By the way, who am I being replaced by?'

He paused for a moment and then said, 'Nicole.'

Lily was shaking her head now. She'd been right this whole time.

'They don't appreciate you as much in America, Cheryl, but they love you here. Nobody wanted you to leave *X Factor* UK. Think about it. It'll be a massive homecoming. It'll be amazing. The British audience thought they'd lost you and you're back. You'll be head judge. Can you imagine the reception you'll get when you go out on that stage?'

I let him say his piece, and the whole time I was thinking, 'This is crazy. I didn't even ask for the American job in the first place. This is all Simon's fault.'

When Richard stopped talking I looked him straight in the eye and asked, 'You're basically telling me you're doing Simon's dirty work?'

He nodded, then said again, 'You have to consider the offer.'

I was getting extremely irritated now, and I told Richard exactly what I thought.

'Absolutely not. It wouldn't be amazing at all. You've already told Gary Barlow he's head judge and suddenly you're telling me to be head judge? What would happen about stupid things like who would get Simon's dressing room? I've got a lot of respect for Gary Barlow. He's older than me and has way more experience and I look up to him in this industry. I've been brought up to respect me elders. NO WAY!'

There was also the question of somebody else losing out on a job because of me. They had Tulisa and Kelly Rowland lined up, and Richard told me it would be up to me who I wanted to work with, alongside Gary and Louis. This felt wrong on so many levels. Other people's lives were being played with, not just mine.

'Can you tell me why I'm being replaced?' I asked. 'Is that possible, because I really don't know what I've done wrong.'

Richard made reference to my Geordie accent, which I really took exception to.

'Me accent? Now you're making Fox look foolish. They're a massive worldwide company and they are not gonna employ somebody that cannot be understood. I am the same person they saw at Christmas. They sat in the audience in London. They knew exactly what they were employing.'

'Look, just consider the offer,' Richard said yet again. 'I'll give you a call later in the week.'

The UK auditions were due to start in a week's time. I knew it was going to be horrible for me now in the media whatever happened next, and so I asked Richard not to tell Simon my decision until I'd spoken to him myself. I could already imagine the headline. 'Cheryl wants to come home!' That's what Simon would tell the press so he didn't look bad, and I didn't want him to be able to put anything out there until I'd talked to him directly.

When Lily and I left the hotel she was whiter than me, and we were both laughing nervously.

'I cannot believe they'd have let you turn up to that on your own,' she said.

'*I* can't get over the fact that "big man" Simon, the same guy that told me I had the job and told me "don't wear that hair" couldn't tell me I didn't have the job! The coward didn't even have the guts to phone us or send us a message warning me what was coming.'

I was still giggling with nerves when I got back home, knowing I would have to face my mam and Garry with the news.

'I've been sacked from American *X Factor*,' I told them bluntly as soon as I walked in the door, and then I burst out laughing.

'Shut up, yer daft sod!' my mam said. 'No way! For what?'

Garry was open-mouthed. 'No way, man. Shut up! Never!'

'I promise you, I know I'm laughing but I'm not joking with you. Richard said it was because of me Geordie accent but I'm not buying that. No way.'

Then it was a question of who to phone first. Simon wouldn't have been up at this time, so I called Sundraj. He also represents Nicole, so this was going to cause him all kinds of hell.

'Hi Sundraj, I'm home.'

'Hey! How are you? How was it?'

'Funny you should ask that, actually. I've got news for you: I've been sacked.'

I started to laugh nervously again.

'You're joking, aren't you?'

'I swear I'm not joking.'

Sundraj couldn't believe that neither he, Seth nor Will had received a call.

'Cheryl, I know you're laughing but this is really bad,' he said.

'You're telling *me*.'

Seth's reaction was to say indignantly, 'How *dare* Simon do this to you!'

The terms and conditions of my contract had not been the best, but I'd settled on them so as not to hold the deal up, and because I trusted Simon completely.

'What breaks my heart is that I can see your little face looking at me and saying, "I know the contract isn't great but I trust Simon wholeheartedly",' Seth said. 'Now he's fed you to the lions! That hurts so much.'

Will went absolutely bananas. 'F*** the English *X Factor*' were his exact words. 'You're not touching that show, no way!'

The very next day it was all over the press: 'Cheryl sacked from the *X Factor* USA because of her Geordie accent'. There were spiteful remarks about my orange and purple outfit and big hair too, which was an absolute joke. That same week, *Vogue* had named me as 'Best Dressed of the Week' because, although Simon didn't know it, of course, colour blocking was about to be the next big thing, and on top of that Sarah Jessica Parker had worn the same hair as I'd had and got loads of praise for it in the American press.

I was furious with Simon for letting it happen like this. I believed we had a good friendship and I couldn't understand why he just hadn't been straight with me. It was so frustrating not knowing the truth, too. Was it that he actually *needed* me back on the UK *X Factor*, or had it *really* just not worked out for me in the US? I'd have taken it on the chin if he'd had the guts to come out and say either of those things to my face.

Despite the frustration and anger I felt, once I caught my breath and sat down and thought about it on my own, I realised I was actually feeling relieved it was all over. I knew it would be hell in the media for a while, but at least I didn't have to get back on a plane to America, or start auditions in the UK in a weeks' time. It was over, and I felt like I had my life back.

Simon got booed on *Britain's Got Talent* every night that week and was really being shown the public's wrath. I still hadn't spoken to him, so after a few days I decided it was time to get in touch.

I wrote the longest text ever. I apologise about the bad language, but this is how he made me feel, and this is what I sent to him:

'F*** you. F*** Fox. F*** *Britain's Got Talent*. F*** the orange and purple outfit. F*** big hair. F*** the UK *X Factor*. F*** you all.

I hate you. I understand you're a businessman, and what I've learned from this is that business means more to you than friend-ship. I'm sad it's got like this and I wish you the best of luck, but count me out.'

Simon texted back: 'Can I talk to you?', which I ignored. Then I switched the phone off and didn't speak to anyone, unless it went through Lily.

Then things got even messier. Seth had rung Fox and was told by Pete Rice, their Chairman of Entertainment: 'This is Simon's call. It's his show and he has control over who sits on the panel. We *love* Cheryl over here. We chose her because she's a star and this has nothing whatsoever to do with Fox. We're sad it's gone like this.'

Next, we got a call from a girl asking who I wanted to fly with and which hotel I wanted to stay in when I returned to the States for the next set of auditions in New York on the following Wednesday.

Will went bananas, all over again. 'Excuse me? This is highly disrespectful. It's all over the press what's happened. Are you taking the *piss*?'

'No,' the girl said. 'I'm just doing my job and I've been told Cheryl is expected on Wednesday, to render her duties as a judge.'

Seth got involved again, and it soon became obvious what game they were playing. When Richard had delivered the news, he had chosen his words very carefully and had not actually told me I was fired. He had said I was being *replaced*, which meant I was still employed by Fox. This meant that, legally, I was contracted to be back on the show in a few days' time.

Will phoned Simon and they had a blazing row.

'As if she's gonna rock up after all that's happened. What are you doing? She trusted you.'

'Is she coming back on Wednesday or not?' Simon asked.

'Are you *joking*? Is this all about contracts? Is it that you don't wanna *pay* her?'

There was no answer to that, and so Will ended the call by saying, 'She's a professional person. She doesn't break contracts. She'll be there on Wednesday.'

In the meantime Mike Darnell, one of the top bosses at Fox, and Cecile Frot-Coutaz, the producer, had been on the phone, making it crystal clear this had nothing to do with them either. 'Sweetheart, darling,' Cecile said. 'We all want you back. We're so sorry this is happening. We'll see you on Wednesday.'

The last thing I wanted to do was fly to New York under these circumstances, and so Will issued an ultimatum to Fox, asking for written confirmation I'd been sacked. 'If we don't get an email in twenty-four hours, she'll be there, because she doesn't break contracts,' Will said.

'We can't do it. It's a Sunday,' was the response we got back.

I was all over the place by this time. I had to get ready to return to the States just in case, not knowing what I would be going back to, and hoping I didn't have to.

Will phoned me from the gym. He was on the treadmill and I could hear him breathing heavily. 'You're not fighting this alone, I'm fighting with you,' he said. 'I know it's hard, but the good guys always win. I'm standing next to you the whole way and I'm not watching anyone trample all over you.'

It was such a comfort to have Will's support, and I believed what he said. The good guys do win in the end, but I just wondered how long it would take for the end of this particular drama to get here.

I decided it was time to text Richard Holloway. Not only had he done Simon's dirty work, but *he'd* been the one who had chosen his words carefully when it came to delivering the bad news, which was now causing me no end of trouble.

'What did I ever do to you to deserve this treatment?' I asked.

We'd worked together for three years, and now it had started to sink in that I actually felt more hurt than angry about what he'd done.

'This is the saddest day of my working life,' was his reply.

This was so not funny any more. The nervous laughter had stopped, and everything felt deadly serious. We received no email confirming my sacking, but in the event I didn't have to fly back to America because Simon issued a formal statement to the media, announcing my departure from the American *X Factor*. Thank God!

I was just so relieved I wasn't going back. It was like a massive weight had been lifted from my shoulders as soon as I heard that news.

I decided, almost immediately, that I wanted to move house. Too much misery had gone on in the house I was renting in Hadley Wood. Every time I looked at the staircases I was reminded how I'd broken down on them during the end of the last series of *The X Factor*, and over Christmas. I'd expected to be spending most of my time in my new place in LA, but instead I was here, with bad memories all around me. I would always remember this as the house I was living in when I got sacked, as well as when I moved out of our marital home, and I had to get out.

It felt exactly the right time for a fresh start, and I started to look for another place to rent. It took a little while, but the house I eventually found was absolutely perfect. It was in the Hertfordshire countryside and Rupert Grint, the actor who played Ron in the Harry Potter films, used to live there. It was old and rambling, and I just loved it the minute I set eyes on it.

The best thing of all was that it was set in acres and acres of land and had a massive space in the back. Not long before I moved in I was finally granted the injunction against the paparazzi I'd applied for. It was July now, and I'd gone through months and months of legal proceedings, with me having to prove to the courts that my privacy was being invaded by the press.

It's a very tough thing for a celebrity to do, and only a handful of people have successfully applied for it, Sienna Miller and Hugh Grant being two of them.

I had to show that I was not one of those people who played with the media by having people tip them off about when I was on a beach in a bikini, for instance. I also had to produce evidence of how I was hounded, and how the press camped outside my house twenty-four hours a day. This meant turning the tables on the paps for a while, and Lily would step out of the car and take photographs of *them*, to show the courts how many of them followed me, and how aggressive they could be.

I can't explain the relief I felt when the injunction was finally granted. It meant the paps were allowed to photograph me on a red carpet, for instance, or coming out of a restaurant, but they were not permitted to follow me or pursue me in a car or on foot, and they were not allowed to stay outside my house and keep me under surveillance.

When I got the news it was the best thing I'd heard in years and I actually jumped for joy. It meant I could now run down the fields at the back of this new house with the dogs, knowing *nobody* could take a picture.

The first time I did that I was barefoot and the sun was shining. The feeling of freedom was so amazing I literally felt like singing: 'The hills are alive with the sound of music'. It was *that* idyllic, *that* liberating. It was like being let out of jail.

My sister and some of my nieces and nephews came down to stay with me and the feeling of normality overwhelmed me. I called my new home the 'happy house'. It was amazing, and I felt like myself again for the first time in years and years.

I sat in the garden one day talking to Gillian, and it was honestly like being a kid again in Newcastle, I felt that free.

'Remember that time Dolly fell out of the wheelchair?' I said, and we both had tears running down our cheeks as we remembered the story together.

The more I had got to know Dolly when I was a teenager, the more she had started to rely on me. She got quite clingy, actually, and didn't like it if I wasn't at her beck and call.

'Eee, Cheryl, take me down to our Kenneth's,' she said one day.

'But Dolly, I've got a hair appointment in 20 minutes and I'll be late if I have to push you down there ...'

'Come on, Cheryl, it won't take long. Fly like the wind! I know you can do it!'

There was no arguing with her, and so I gritted my teeth and pegged it down the road, pushing Dolly in her wheelchair as fast as I could.

'That's it! Run like you've never run before!' she called out as I navigated the winding pavement. 'Go, Cheryl! Go!'

'I'm gonna kill you for this, Dolly, I swear!' I said, as I got faster and faster. As I spoke there was suddenly a bump and a crash. The wheelchair had hit an uneven paving stone, and Dolly was catapulted out. I was running that fast though, still clinging to the wheelchair, that I couldn't stop.

I eventually skidded to a halt about two minutes later, falling over and ripping my jacket and trousers down the whole of one side of my body. I was bleeding and aching, and this gorgeous lad pulled over in a car and helped me up while his girlfriend looked down her nose at me.

I was absolutely mortified, but when I hobbled back down the road to find Dolly it got even worse. She was sprawled out face down on the pavement, in a *Superman* position.

'Me knees have gone to mush! Me knees, Cheryl! Arghhh!'

It wasn't until I'd hauled her back into the buckled chair, deposited her at Kenneth's and run to the hairdresser's looking like I'd been dragged though a hedge backwards that I saw the funny side, and now me and Gillian were roaring our heads off all over again.

It was a real tonic to spend time like that with my family, and I was enjoying myself so much.

My name was still appearing in the media, especially when Nicole's job was officially announced on American *X Factor*, and again when the UK line-up was revealed, but with no new pictures of me the coverage got less and less.

I had no real feelings towards Nicole, by the way. I was pretty sure she had pitched for my job because she is very, very ambitious, but I didn't know the full facts back then. If anything, I felt sorry for her because she was the one who was going to be under scrutiny in the press, and I wouldn't wish that on anybody. I didn't know the whole truth until earlier this year, 2012, when Simon confirmed in his biography that Nicole actually did go after my job. I couldn't have cared less by that time. It was almost a year later, I'd moved on and in fact she probably did me a favour.

One day, in the summer of 2011, I sat in the garden of my happy house with Buster and Coco and a realisation hit me, like a bolt of lightning: 'I've not been happy like this since before the first allegations about Ashley.'

That was so true. I only knew it now because I felt so different to how I'd been for years. The first stories about Ashley's cheating had come out in January 2008, three and a half years earlier. Three and a half years! Even when we were together, before the second lot of allegations in 2010, I'd not been right. I could see that now, for the first time. I had tried so hard to move on, but I was aching inside the whole time because I was not fully healed. Now, at last, I could feel myself starting to heal, completely, as a person.

It was my twenty-eighth birthday on 30 June and I decided to have a big birthday party. I wanted to celebrate life, basically, and I wanted all the people who were special to me to be there. Everyone I invited was either family or like family to me – the girls, Lily, Will, all the people close to me.

Not long before the party I heard that Ashley went on holiday to LA, and there were more stories in the press about him being with other women. I can't even remember how I was told about them, but it was my reaction that sticks in my mind.

'So what?' I thought. 'He's a single man. We're divorced now. He can do what he wants. I'm over him, it doesn't matter to me any more.'

I wanted to invite Ashley's mam, brother and sister-in-law to the party because they are people I care about, and I still considered them part of my family, despite the divorce. It was tricky, though, because I wasn't sure how they would feel coming along without Ashley.

As soon as those latest stories came out, I realised there was nothing to stop me inviting Ashley to the party too, just as a friend. It was another hugely liberating moment in my life. I'd got shut of the paps, and I felt I had finally, finally accepted my marriage was over.

I texted Ashley and said, 'Come to the party. Come and show your face. I don't care what people think.'

Ashley agreed and I was so pleased. We'd been to a lot of really good parties together over the years. There was one time when I dressed as Catwoman and he was Batman at a Chelsea Christmas party, which was a laugh, but the times when we got together with close friends and family were always the best. We'd always had a great time partying together, and when he arrived at my birthday party it didn't feel awkward at all. I could see a few people looking at him, thinking, 'Oooh! Ashley's here. *OK* then ...' but it didn't bother me. I introduced him to Will for the first time, who told me afterwards, 'Ashley's so cool. It's cute you're willing to do this.'

I got *so* drunk on vodka cocktails and shots I really let my hair down, literally. At one point I walked up the staircase of the hotel trying to do a Beyoncé, dancing and swirling my hair in big circles as I climbed each stair, clinging to the balustrades. Ashley was looking at me as if I was a totally crazy person and laughing, so I heard afterwards. Will DJ-ed and I was rapping, apparently, too. Fergie sang 'Happy Birthday' to me, and beforehand she tried to hide the pair of us behind a curtain so it came as a surprise to the guests, but you could see two big lumps sticking through from the other side, which gave the game away. It was hilarious.

* * *

A lot of the evening is a huge blur to me, but I do remember that Ashley gave me a piggyback down the corridor and put me to bed in my apartment at the Sanderson Hotel in London, where the party was held. He even took my shoes off for me and tucked me in like a little girl, which he'd done a few times in the past.

Garry was staying in the same apartment as me, and we both woke up the next day with hangovers from hell. Mam appeared and chucked a parcel at me. 'Here, underwear,' she said, which set me and Garry off laughing. That was so typical of Mam, to deliver my birthday present without a trace of sentimentality.

'I'm starving,' I said to Garry. 'I'm ordering room service.'

I must have still been drunk because I ordered practically the whole menu. We had everything from steak and chips to pizzas and sausage and mash brought up to us. Garry ate one slice of pizza and felt sick, and I fell back to sleep without eating any of it.

The next thing I remember is talking to Lily, who came to see how we were.

'It was a fun night,' Lily said.

'I can't remember half of it. What happened?'

'Do you remember Fergie singing "Happy Birthday" to you, after you cut the cake?'

'I had a *cake*?'

Lily looked at me in astonishment. I'd had a spectacular cake the size of a coffee table, but I had absolutely no recollection of it. Lily had to show me a photograph, but it still didn't jog my memory.

'My God, it must have been a good night,' I giggled.

I didn't feel embarrassed; I was glad I'd had such a good time. I felt like I'd taken another step forward in my healing process, because there was no way I could have enjoyed myself like that if I wasn't well on the mend.

Part of me would always love Ashley, I realised. I had loved him so much I couldn't imagine a day when I would feel *nothing* for him. The difference now was that I also knew that there was so much water under the bridge I would drown if I ever went back to him.

A whole year had passed since the divorce, but I had spiralled so deep into the darkness afterwards that it had taken me this long to come up into the light, to see things this clearly.

19

'Get me into my music again!'

'Sorry to bother you with this, and I've already warned them you won't do it, but there's this new Cameron Diaz movie, and they want you to play a talent show judge ...'

It was Seth on the phone, sounding apologetic.

'Let's do it!' I said, as soon as I'd heard a few more details. It was the movie of the bestselling book *What to Expect When You're Expecting*, and they wanted me to make a tiny cameo appearance as a talent show judge. I'd be sending myself up, basically, and it would mean going to Atlanta, Georgia, for three days of filming in August 2011.

I'd done a cameo role before, with Girls Aloud in a St Trinian's movie in 2007. That had been good fun to do, even though we only made a 'blink and you'll miss it' appearance right at the end.

'Honestly, Seth, I don't take myself that seriously. I don't care if I'm sending myself up. I can easily move a few recording sessions. Let's go!'

I'd had a similar reaction a month or so earlier when Will had asked me if I felt ready to make some music again.

'Yes! Get me into the studio!' I'd said. 'Get me into my music again!' It felt like exactly the right move, and I was actually properly excited. I hadn't felt that way about work for a long, long time but I was almost tingling when I thought about working on another album.

I had no husband to think about, no *X Factor*, no malaria, and not even any paparazzi to distract me. All I had was a big back garden and time on my hands. It felt so good, and I started making plans to work on my third solo album with Will.

Now, because of Seth's call, I was about to find myself in another one of those 'you couldn't make it up' situations, and that was before we even got onto the movie set.

Me, Seth and Lily all went out to Atlanta together. I'd never been there before and I went straight out for a look around, wearing no make-up, trackie bottoms and a pair of new trainers that rubbed my feet really badly. As soon as we got back to the hotel I had to get the trainers off, and I sat down in a hallway to give my feet a rub.

'Look at the state of them,' I frowned. My feet were dirty, covered in blisters and the skin was hanging off in lumps. 'It's disgusting,' I said, as I began pulling off a layer of red skin.

'Cheryl, hi! It's so nice to meet you!'

I looked up, horrified, to see Cameron Diaz standing before me, looking amazing, and stretching out her hand to me.

'Hi!' I said, standing up on my bare feet and wishing the ground would swallow me up.

'Hey, I've got some southern fried chicken, d'you want some?'

I knew it's one of the things they're famous for in that part of America and it would have been rude to say no, so there I was, like a little street urchin, eating chicken with my grubby hands and chatting to Cameron Diaz about her latest movie.

She had no make-up on either and was not dressed up at all, but as I said to Lily and Seth later, she *is* Cameron Diaz.

The filming itself ran smoothly. I had to play a 'Celebrity Dance Factor' judge who thinks she's the real star of the show and dances on the table. It was great fun, and Cameron and her co-star Matthew Morrison were really lovely, encouraging me and praising me, as they knew this wasn't my normal day job.

'I could do this again,' I said to Lily. 'I didn't realise I'd enjoy it so much.'

I really *was* enjoying myself, and everybody could see a change in me. I sent my first ever Tweet from Atlanta, on 29 August 2011, which also made me feel good. I'd always been wary of Twitter, yet I'd spent all these years wishing I could tell the truth about what was going on without having my words twisted in the press, and now I realised I could.

'Why have I not done this sooner?' I giggled to Lily. 'It's fun. I can't believe I can actually put my own words out there, just like that.'

She was grinning from ear to ear. 'It's great to see you like this,' she said. 'Welcome back, Cheryl!'

I thoroughly enjoyed being able to interact with fans online. One thing I've always loved about touring or doing signings or anything like that is being able to talk to the fans. I've always been fascinated by their stories, and it was incredibly gratifying and humbling whenever a young girl told me I'd inspired her.

I'd started calling the fans 'soldiers' after I did 'Fight For This Love' and had that whole military theme going on, and before I knew it I had tens of thousands of 'Cheryl soldiers' following me on Twitter. That was so inspirational for *me*. My faith in the sister-hood was being well and truly restored, because I felt such a sense of camaraderie from my female followers. Some set themselves up as my protectors, defending me when I was criticised, and others offered support, telling me: 'I get why you went back to Ashley. It happened to me.'

I had a strong sense that I was turning a corner, and a couple of other big events at the end of 2011 really reinforced that feeling.

Going to Afghanistan to present a *Daily Mirror* Pride of Britain award to the British troops in September was one of them. This was an award I'd supported for several years, and it was an honour to be invited to see first-hand what our soldiers were doing at Camp Bastion in Helmand province.

I told the soldiers I didn't mind what I did out there, and they took me at my word and led me out on a very scary night-time mission. It wasn't until I'd scaled a wall and had a Taliban member actually pointing a gun at me that I realised it was all a fake prac-tice run. I had honestly never been so terrified in my life, and it was a huge eye opener about what our soldiers go through. It put a few things in perspective for me. *My* job was not a matter of life and death, and life is too short to worry about some of the celebrity rubbish that had got to me in the past.

For a laugh, the soldiers dressed up a dummy to look like Simon, and invited me to press a detonator and blow it up. I thought it was hilarious and really enjoyed the joke, and when I got home I received a text from Simon.

'Now you've blown me up in Afghanistan, can we talk?'

I had not spoken to him for six months, and I replied, 'I've just flown home and am feeling really emotional. I'll let you know when I can talk to you.'

It was his fifty-second birthday in a couple of weeks' time, and I'd heard he was trying to keep quiet about it. I saw an opportunity to have some fun at his expense and arranged for a little plane to fly around his house in Miami exactly 52 times, trailing a banner that said: 'Simon Cowell is 52 today! Ha ha ha! Love Cheryl xoxo'.

Another text arrived shortly afterwards, this time saying: 'I.am. going.to.kill.you', and then my phone rang.

'It's good to talk to you,' Simon said. 'I wasn't in the right frame of mind in LA, because of all the pressure and expectation on the American show.'

He told me that my comment to Richard Holloway, when I said 'I'm getting there' on the first day of auditions, caused alarm bells to ring.

'Wow. I see.' I said.

'Taking you off it was the worst mistake I ever made and if I could have my time back, I wouldn't do it again,' he said. 'I'm sorry.'

'Thank you for saying that.'

'And by the way, you're looking good. I'm happy to see you smiling again, and I hope we can work together in the future.'

It was October 2011 now, and I felt like I was healing more and more, all the time. Breaking the ice with Simon was part of the process. I didn't want to work with him any time soon, but to be in touch again felt like a cloud had been blown away from my life.

Work on the next album was going well, and I'd been lucky enough to get a brilliant track with a heavy urban beat called 'Ghetto Baby'. It was sent to me with no fanfare whatsoever, but as soon as I heard it, I loved it and desperately wanted it for the album.

'Who's it by?' I asked Ferdy, one of the top guys at Polydor, who sent it to me. 'It's incredible.'

'An up-and-coming artist called Lana Del Rey. You've got good taste in music – she'll be big.'

Another of my favourite tracks on the new album was written for me the day after I went to a party at the Roundhouse in Camden. Will was DJ-ing and I was letting my hair down and drinking too much champagne. 'Are you sure you want to drink all that?' Lily asked, to which I gave her a cheeky look and put my middle finger up.

Just for fun, she took a picture of me and posted it on Twitter with the caption: 'Really??? ... step away from the Dom Perignon!!'

The next day I was meant to be recording a track called 'Deny Me', but I was so hung-over I couldn't get the words out of my mouth. The producer and writer sent me home and used the studio time to work on new material instead, and the picture of me on Twitter inspired them to write 'Screw You', which eventually ended up on the album. I loved the power and attitude of the song straight away, and I knew people would relate to it because we all have that someone we want to stick the middle finger up to. I'm not surprised there were stories that I wrote it about Ashley, but the truth is I wasn't even capable of writing my own name that day, let alone a song.

The Cheryl Cole Foundation was well off the ground by now. One of the first things I'd done for charity was to auction off 20 of my old dresses several months earlier, which raised more than

£50,000. It had been bothering me for a long time that I had so many gorgeous dresses just hanging there in wardrobes, but I'd underestimated just how good it would make me feel to make use of them. It was really liberating to see them go, and looking back, it was another important part of my healing process.

When we started to discuss how to spend the money raised, I met two amazing people: an ex-cocaine dealer who's now a charity worker; and a girl who runs a flower shop who used to be a drug dealer. They were so inspirational, and my need to help others like them felt so powerful, it took my breath away. They were people who had wanted to help themselves and just needed that bit of help.

I thought of Lee Dac and John Courtney and the other friends I'd lost to drugs, and felt so sorry that they hadn't had help available to them when they needed it. I cried for them both, all over again. It was such a waste. It was too late for them, but it wasn't too late for so many others. I still dared to hope that my brother Andrew might want to reform one day. I was getting some meaning and inspiration back into my life, and I was feeling more optimistic about the whole future than I had done in a long, long time.

'It's arrived,' Lily said to me one morning, handing me a large envelope.

It was November 2011. Inside was a copy of my official 2012 calendar, which I'd shot in the South of France several months earlier. I flicked through the pages, looking at each month in turn, and felt butterflies in my stomach.

'What's the matter?' Lily asked.

'Nothing,' I said. 'I'm pleased with it, really pleased.'

I loved the pictures, but what I was really thinking was that I had all these blank pages in front of me in 2012, and I wasn't quite sure where my life was going.

There were events in the diary, of course. It was Girls Aloud's tenth anniversary, which we all wanted to mark in some way. We'd promised to talk about it at the beginning of 2012, to make

sure we came up with something really special by our big day in
November.

I'd created a range of shoes for Stylistpick, which had been pure
pleasure. I'd chosen the materials and helped with the designs, and
I'd be doing a signing to launch them in London in February. I've
always loved shoes and that was real girly fun for me, not work.

I also knew there would be a couple of red carpet events to look
forward to. I was attending the Cannes Film Festival for L'Oréal
in May, and the premiere of *What to Expect When You're Expecting*
was taking place at Leicester Square the same month.

Kimberley was finishing her run as Princess Fiona in *Shrek* in
the spring too, and I was definitely going to her last performance,
and Gary Barlow had been in touch about doing something at the
Queen's Diamond Jubilee in June.

Before I knew it my next single would be out, then the new
album … and I would be turning 29 on 30 June.

I stared at that date on the calendar. I could barely believe that
I was going to be 29, and it brought mixed feelings.

I had all these exciting events to look forward to, but nobody to
share them with. I should have been looking forward to celebrating my sixth wedding anniversary with Ashley, but now he wasn't
even in my life. I hadn't seen him since my *last* birthday.
Occasionally I'd seen him on an advert on TV or his face would
pop up on Twitter, but I had not physically seen him for half a
year. I'd moved on in many ways, though. I was happy again, and
I was finding myself as a person.

I had a heart to heart with my sister Gillian not long after this.
We spent a fantastic family Christmas together and I looked at her
and the kids and wished for so much more normality in my life.

'I want some balance in my life,' I told my sister. 'I don't want
any extreme highs any more.'

'Are you sure you mean that?'

'Yes, because whenever things are going right, something goes
wrong. It's like the happier I am, the worse the crash.'

Perhaps I had tempted fate in saying that, who knows?

*   *   *

Literally a few weeks later I received one of Sundraj's dreaded phone calls, the kind that starts with: 'I'm sorry, Cheryl, but …'

'Go on, what now?'

'MC Harvey is claiming you had a secret relationship with him in 2010. Is it true?'

'You're joking? MC Harvey? Are you crazy? I don't even know him, and I haven't even set eyes on the guy for years.'

'He's saying you got close after your divorce.'

'You *are* joking! I think I met him once, when I'd just got in Girls Aloud.'

I'd seen him with So Solid Crew at a party God knows how many years ago, but we never even had what you could call a conversation.

'He's given an interview to *Now* magazine, and he's alleging it started in 2010, after your divorce, and ended when you went off to do American *X Factor*.'

'You mean when I was having my nervous breakdown? This is sick.'

I started thinking about how Harvey cheated on Alesha Dixon and how she had texted me a message of support when Ashley first cheated on me.

'Sundraj, nobody in their right mind is going to believe I left my cheating husband to go with somebody else's cheating husband and, just for good measure, picked someone whose ex-wife I actually know personally, and have bonded with over how we've both been hurt.'

'He has emails.'

'Right, I'm not having this. I am just not having it!'

I went on Twitter and tweeted to Harvey: 'Was this "relationship" happening in your head?'

I didn't know if he'd made the whole thing up for publicity as I'd heard he had a single coming out soon, or if he'd been had, and had been duped into swapping emails with somebody posing as me. That was the only other possible explanation I could come up with, but to my surprise he responded on Twitter and stuck by his story.

I was so furious that somebody could make up something like this out of absolutely nothing, *and* think they could get away with it. It was a complete and utter fabrication and I decided to sue the magazine's publishers for libel. I was absolutely stunned when they published a second story a week later, making things worse by saying their lawyer had seen the emails, proving Harvey's claims were true.

'Are you sure about suing?' my brother Garry asked. He knew first-hand what a draining and long-winded process it is to sue for libel, because he'd done it himself, successfully, the previous year after a magazine and a newspaper had printed a story saying he was a convicted criminal.

'The thing is, *I* had no choice,' he said. 'I mean, when I apply for another job in the future I'll need proof of the truth. But there are thousands of stories out there about you that aren't true. Is it worth the hassle?'

We had a bit of fun listing some of the silliest and most annoying stories: the supposed boob job I'd had that upset my dad; the weight-reducing wind tunnel I'd apparently installed in the gym at my old house; the raw salmon and peppermint tea diets I'd somehow survived on and the 'extensive' dental surgery I'd vainly undergone.

'None of those things are worth losing sleep over,' I said to Garry. 'What does it really matter that I've actually never had plastic surgery and I've only ever had two teeth capped? I understand that journalists have papers to fill and are under an immense amount of pressure to make headlines, and I get that people don't want to read that I'm just a normal girl who plucks her own eyebrows and has her nails done once a fortnight.'

The Harvey libel case was very different to anything I'd experienced before, though. Other stories linking me to different men were simply journalists adding two and two together and coming up with five. This was not like that at all. This was one person in the limelight saying things about another human being on a very personal level.

I thought about Ashley now too, and how I'd seen him tormented by the stories about his cheating. I'd believed enough of the stories to end my marriage, but I had never believed every single claim. For one thing, I had been on a Virgin flight once and heard an air stewardess actually admit that she'd sold a kiss-and-tell on another footballer, just to make money. 'Who cares if it's true?' she bragged to her mate. 'It's worth a lot of money to me.'

I'd also had a text from Tulisa recently. I'd offered her support when she first joined *The X Factor* the previous year, because I knew how young she was and what she was letting herself in for. I'd invited her to my birthday party at the Sanderson Hotel too, even though it was only for very close family and friends, because I wanted her to know I was there for her.

'I don't want to stick my nose into your business, but I think you should know this,' Tulisa had texted. 'I have just met one of the girls who claimed she slept with Ashley, and she's admitted to me it wasn't true, but the newspapers just printed it anyway.'

I'd gone beyond looking for evidence that Ashley *hadn't* cheated on me as I had done to begin with. I knew he had, and so this news didn't comfort me in that respect. What it did do, though, was make me understand Ashley's fury and frustration at some of the claims that weren't true. His words 'They're out to get me' took on a new meaning because now I was experiencing first-hand how infuriating it is to be wrongly accused. I was the victim of a false allegation about an affair now, and I was learning exactly how hideous that is.

I was very glad I'd decided to sue, because Harvey then took things to another level. Next he claimed that not only did he have emails from *me* that proved we'd had a relationship, but from my *mother* too. Garry phoned Mam up.

'Mother, you're not gonna believe this, but this guy Harvey is saying *you* sent him a email as well.'

'Eee, that's the first I've heard,' she replied.

Garry and I laughed, because we both know you're lucky to get a text out of Mam, let alone an email, but it really wasn't funny.

She was at Langhorn Close, my old family home, and the thought of this poison spreading up to Newcastle really annoyed me. To get my mother mixed up in this was unforgivable.

One of the stories that had most upset me when Ashley and I got divorced was the one about my mam being part of our marriage problems, because she lived with us. I was so upset about that because my mam only ever came to stay to help us out and to look after us and the dogs when we needed her. She spent most of her time in Newcastle, because she's a grandmother of 10 and they all want her up there. When she was down south she didn't even live with us properly either, because she always stayed in the flat on the side of the house.

I hated that she'd been wrongly accused in the past, and I hated that she'd been dragged into this latest drama too. I lodged my libel case at the High Court, suing IPC Media, the publishers of *Now* magazine. The magazine responded by standing by Harvey and their story, and saying: 'The article is not defamatory and was published in good faith – we will strongly defend it.'

My mother was sent an email from my lawyers, with an attached letter that she had to print off and sign, to say she had never had any email contact with Harvey. She went straight to the post office and paid £6 to have it delivered the next day, but when she got home she realised she'd made a mistake.

'Eee, I'm sorry Cheryl, you'll never guess what I've done. I've printed off the email and signed that, instead of the attachment.'

That said it all. It was perfect, really, because it showed what an utter load of nonsense this all was. My mother wasn't even technically minded enough to print off an attached letter, let alone get involved in sending emails about some secret affair I was meant to be having.

'You know what,' I said to Garry, when I put the phone down to my mam. 'That's it. I'm sick of people writing lies about me. I'm not only suing, I'm going to do my book. Bring it on!'

I had offers from publishers on the table to write my autobiography, and now I knew for certain it was the right time for me to do it. The lies and the speculation had to stop. All that media scrutiny had nearly turned me crazy, and there was no way in the world I was going back there again. I was in a happy place now, and I was not going back into the darkness.

I opened my laptop and started work on this book, right there and then. I was ready to tell my story exactly how it is, straight from my heart.

I hope you have enjoyed reading it.

Epilogue

'It's being broadcast to two billion people,' I heard someone say.

I was due to perform a duet with Gary Barlow at the Queen's Diamond Jubilee concert, and I had been quite calm until this moment.

'Did I hear that right? Two billion people?'

It was true, and suddenly I went from enjoying the vibe back-stage to buzzing with nervous energy.

When Gary and I actually stepped out on the stage in front of Buckingham Palace I felt completely overwhelmed. The royal family was sitting over to my left and the Mall was swaying with hundreds of thousands of people. I'd literally never seen anything like it, and I tried to just take it in for a moment.

'Wow,' I thought. 'It doesn't get any bigger than this.' If ever I needed proof that dreams can come true, here it was, stretched out for miles in front of me.

Gary and I sang Lady Antebellum's 'Need You Now', which was a song we had originally planned to perform as a surprise for Children in Need in November 2011, but I'd had to pull out because I was poorly and lost my voice.

'We should do it for the Jubilee instead,' Gary had said.

'That's a good idea.' It was that casual and easy to arrange that I don't think the magnitude of the occasion really hit me, until I was there, being watched by the biggest audience of my life.

At the end of the concert all the performers were lined up on stage before the Queen and Prince Charles were brought out, and

it was pure chance that I happened to be standing right behind
Her Majesty as Prince Charles made his speech. It was a moment
I will never, ever forget. I knew my family would all be watching,
filled with pride, and that meant everything to me.

The party in Buckingham Palace afterwards was *incredible*. Just
being inside the palace on such an occasion was an honour, and
everywhere I turned I saw amazing artists, people I'd admired for
years. I looked at Tom Jones, Stevie Wonder, Sir Paul McCartney
and Elton John and thought: 'What is my life all about? Music!'

Just when I was thinking the day couldn't get any more incredible, Prince William and Kate came over to me for a chat.

'Did you know you've got a bit of competition?' Wills said with
a cheeky look in his eye.

'From who?'

Wills looked at Kate and they both started laughing before
Kate confessed that she dressed up as *me* on her hen night,
in a body suit and split trousers, and sang 'Fight For This Love'.
She even learned the dance routine and was step perfect by all
accounts, as her sister Pippa and brother James also came over and
told me all about it.

'Well, I'm very flattered' I said. I could just imagine her, and it
was so surreal.

Prince Harry came over to say hello, and we had a laugh about
the daft stories that had appeared about us recently. It was my
fault. I'd made a joke in a magazine that I'd had a dream about
marrying him, which had been blown up out of all proportion.

'I *was* only joking,' I reassured Harry.

'I found it all very funny,' he replied. 'At least you can now put
the record straight. I hear you're writing a book. Whose should I
buy – yours or Simon's?'

I smiled. 'If you want the truth – mine, of course.'

As I come to the end of my book I can't describe how therapeutic
and liberating it has been to tell my story. I got lost in darkness for
a long time, but now I feel strong and happy again.

I turn 30 next year and I'm really looking forward to it, because I know who I am again, and what I want out of my life.

I've rediscovered my first love and passion – music – and I feel excited and inspired by it. Having my single, 'Call My Name', go to number one in June, becoming the fastest-selling single of the year, was a massive moment for me. With my first two solo albums I always had critics claiming they only did well because of Simon or *The X Factor*, but now I've done it all by myself, and that makes me feel very proud.

I have never claimed to be the best vocalist in the world. I'm a performer, and putting on a show is what I enjoy most of all. That is why I started to plan my first solo tour as soon as my album, *A Million Lights*, came out after the single. It's all I ever wanted, from when I was a child. I dreamed of making number one records and being up on stage, singing and dancing and entertaining the audience, and I'm so happy to back doing what I love.

I got together with Girls Aloud several months ago, which was another high point of this year. We've put up with so much specu-lation about our three years apart, but now we're proving that we haven't had the fall-outs the press would like to think we have. We've simply grown into women, and have different lives to the ones we had as young girls. I hadn't seen Nadine for two whole years and had only seen Sarah a few times, but when the five of us were together again it was like we'd never been apart.

By the time this book is published Girls Aloud will have recorded this year's Children in Need single, which is also a cele-bration of our tenth anniversary as a group, and we'll hopefully be working on a tour and greatest hits album. Then I think that's it for Girls Aloud. We've achieved far more than any of us ever dared to dream of and, whatever happens next, I know we'll always be in each other's lives.

*   *   *

I feel incredibly lucky to have had 10 successful years in the music industry, with the girls and as a solo artist. Every day I wake up and I want to go to work and do the job I love, and I know that in this economic climate that is an absolute gift and a privilege.

I hope I'm lucky enough to have children one day, and I want a stable, happy home. That, and keeping going with my music and making my family proud, are my priorities now. My family are my real world; they're not in the dream that my life becomes sometimes, and when I need a leveller I turn to them. They've watched me have a dream, pursue it and live it, and now having a family of my own is my next big dream.

Simon actually phoned me up in April this year and asked me if I wanted to do the American *X Factor* again, and I think you can guess what my answer was. It would take me away from my family and my reality, and throw me back into the craziness again. That's not what I want right now, not at all.

My twenties have been full of the highest highs and the lowest lows, but now it's time for me to find some balance, and my happy place.

Picture credits

Section one: all images © Cheryl Cole except p.5 bottom left © North News and Pictures. Section two: p.1 top © Ken McKay/Rex Features, bottom © Mirrorpix; p.2 top © Huw John/Rex Features, middle left © Cruise Pictures/Press Association Images, middle right © Sipa Press/Rex Features, bottom © *OK! Magazine*/Express Syndication; p.3 top left © Talkback Thames/FremantleMedia, middle © Dave Hogan/Getty Images, bottom © Chris Jackson/Comic Relief; p.4 top left © Talkback Thames/FremantleMedia, top right © Talkback Thames/FremantleMedia, bottom © ITV/Rex Features; p.5 top left © Xposurephotos.com, top right © bigpicturesphoto.com, bottom © bigpicturesphoto.com; p.6 top © Talkback Thames/FremantleMedia, bottom © Rex Features; p.7 top © Rex Features, bottom © Talkback Thames/FremantleMedia; p.8 top © David Hillhouse/Rex Features, bottom © Rex Features.